Troutmouth

Hugh Clegg announces death of Baby Face Nelson, 1934. (© Bettmann/CORBIS)

Troutmouth

The Two Careers of Hugh Clegg

Ron Borne

Ronald F. Borne

To Logan: Hope you enjoy this bio and hope you are doing well — Thanks for your friendship!

All the Best,
Ron

UNIVERSITY PRESS OF MISSISSIPPI   JACKSON

www.upress.state.ms.us

The University Press of Mississippi is a member
of the Association of American University Presses.

First printing 2015

∞

Library of Congress Cataloging-in-Publication Data

Borne, Ronald F.
  Troutmouth : the two careers of Hugh Clegg / Ronald F. Borne.
    pages cm
  Includes bibliographical references and index.
  ISBN 978-1-62846-208-1 (hardback) — ISBN 978-1-62674-545-2 (e-book) 1. Clegg, Hugh H.,
1898– 2. United States. Federal Bureau of Investigation—Officials and employees—Biography.
3. Criminal investigation—United States—History—20th century. 4. Gangsters—United
States—History—20th century. 5. University of Mississippi. Office of the Chancellor—Of-
ficials and employees—Biography. 6. College integration—Mississippi—Oxford—History. 7.
University of Mississippi—History—20th century. I. Title.
  HV7911.C578B67 2015
  363.25092—dc23

  [B]

                          2014036404

British Library Cataloging-in-Publication Data available

To Jere R. Hoar and David G. Sansing

Great Teachers, Great Writers, and Great Friends

Contents

Prologue

When I moved to Oxford, Mississippi, in 1968 to assume a faculty position at the University of Mississippi, I began a housing search and eventually purchased a home I could afford located near the University Oxford Airport. Almost every day I passed the sign at the airport that designated it University Oxford Airport–Clegg Field. After serving Ole Miss teaching medicinal chemistry and living in Oxford for forty years, I had never heard the name Clegg mentioned, and my curiosity to learn more about this person Clegg began. When I retired, my curiosity grew even more, and I began to explore. I learned that this Clegg was, in fact, Hugh H. Clegg, a Mississippian with two outstanding careers of service: one in the FBI and the other at Ole Miss in an administrative leadership position. During those careers, Hugh Clegg was involved in many events at the federal, state, and international levels that helped define our country, and this accounting of his career is the result of my search.

Few individuals have had the opportunity to experience two different and successful careers in their lifetimes. Hugh H. Clegg combined a twenty-eight-year career in the Federal Bureau of Investigation—rising to the number three administrative position as assistant director—with a fourteen-year career as executive assistant to the chancellor and director of development with the University of Mississippi, also affectionately known as Ole Miss.

The book *Public Enemies* (2004), by Bryan Burrough, and the subsequent movie by the same name invigorated my interest. In the introduction to this book, Burrough listed a "Cast of Characters," and among those characters depicted in the Federal Bureau of Investigation section was Hugh Clegg. His position was listed as an assistant director of the Bureau. Near the beginning of the first chapter, Burrough referred to the Kappa Alpha (KA) chapter at George Washington University (GWU), at whose house visiting agents often stayed. "It was there [at the KA house]," Burrough writes, that "Hugh Clegg, a courtly young Mississippi attorney who would rise to become an FBI assistant director, was hired."[1]

The two careers of Hugh Clegg were characterized by his strongest quality—loyalty. He was loyal to his work and to the people he worked with and for. He was loyal to his hometown of Mathiston, Mississippi, returning there often during his life after moving to Washington and Oxford. A longtime resident of Mathiston, Dempsey Blanton, recalls that Clegg returned to present the high school commencement address at Mathiston High School on several occasions.[2] Since he had also served as president of the Wood Junior College Alumni Association in Mathiston, he would also return there to attend numerous functions.

His days in the FBI were defined, according to one source, by his being "one of Hoover's favorite agents, much valued for his loyalty and his indiscriminately high opinion of Hoover's leadership. That loyalty, coupled with his unquestionable bravery, led to his promotion to assistant director in 1932, after only six years in the Bureau."[3] And his loyalty to his fellow agents, in particular to the controversial Melvin Purvis, was well-known and serves as a good illustration of the way he functioned at the FBI. Referring to Purvis, Clegg said,

> His loyalty is intense. . . . He has a feeling that as part of the
> Bureau it is his organization and he is willing to go to the limit
> for the organization and for anyone connected with it, from
> administrative officials down to the lowest salaried clerical employee; yet, if an employee gets off the reservation he is equally
> alert to protect the Bureau's interests.[4]

When Purvis came under intense criticism by Hoover for the way he publicly responded to the death in a shootout with Baby Face Nelson of fellow agent Sam Cowley, Clegg once again came to Purvis's defense. When Clegg was charged with evaluating Purvis at a conference of agents in charge after Purvis had been on restricted duty, Clegg noted that Purvis's major problem was being too protective of the agents under his supervision. Clegg said, "He has participated in a considerable number of raids and I believe is somewhat too much inclined to personally participate in some of the investigative activities of this character rather than to delegate the leadership to others." Despite Hoover's placing Purvis in administrative purgatory, Clegg told the conference, "I feel in all sincerity that he is intensely loyal to the Director and to the Bureau. His high personal regard for the Director continues unabated in spite of what he probably feels to be some sort of punitive administrative action which has been taken in his case." But Hoover was not impressed with Clegg's evaluation and his support for Purvis.[5]

Few people who knew Clegg during his days at the FBI are still living. One is Margaret Elizabeth "Betty" Turner, who was a secretary at the FBI when Clegg introduced FBI agent William A. Murphy to her. The two married not too long thereafter. Mrs. Turner, now Mrs. Murphy, was not able to provide many insights into the days when she worked with Clegg but her daughter, Betsy Dyke, emphasized the loyalty that Clegg, and her father, showed to Hoover.

That quality of loyalty stood him in good stead during his career at Ole Miss as well. His loyalty to Chancellor J. D. Williams and the University of Mississippi is well documented. Surviving Ole Miss colleagues had general impressions of Clegg but did not offer great insight into his personality. Common descriptions included terms and phrases such as tough but fair, efficient, effective, the Chancellor's right-hand man, good family man, good church man, excellent public speaker, an excellent representative of Ole Miss, a man who accomplishes what he sets out to do, a good sense of humor that he seldom showed, guarded, private, and loyal.

Other characteristics Clegg demonstrated became evident as I researched his life. He was a devoted Mississippian and American. He was comfortable being out of the spotlight, preferring to let it shine on his bosses. He always shared credit for his successes and took full blame for his failures. He was a capable administrator but disliked the boredom of paperwork. An affable individual, he made friends easily and maintained those friendships all of his life. He was well liked, with the exception of some jealous fellow agents at the FBI. He was neither a conniver nor a backstabber.

Two incidents that occurred during his time at Ole Miss reflect on Clegg's character. When he first came to the campus, Clegg seemed quite intimidating to many at the university. His federal experience and his contacts at both the federal and state levels earned him considerable respect. He projected an intimidating image of being in full control that, in an academic environment, was often interpreted as making him a man to be feared. Ed Meek and Larry Speakes were student workers in the Ole Miss public relations department and were also reporters working for daily newspapers and wire services. Meek recalled that almost everyone seemed wary and even scared of Clegg at first, in part because of his background, but also because they thought he looked like Nikita Khrushchev, the leader of the Soviet Union at that time.[6] The public relations department reported to Clegg during the time when Clennon King attempted to desegregate the University of Mississippi in 1958 (see Chapter 11). Meek, who would later be honored by having the journalism school named the Meek School of Journalism and New Media, and Speakes, who would later become the president's spokesman during the Reagan administration, were about to release their story relating the way in which King's attempt to be admitted had been handled by university administrators. Clegg became aware of the soon-to-be-released story and called them both to his office under the pretense of relating an "off the record" account of the way the university had handled the situation. As Meek and Speakes were leaving that meeting, Speakes told Meek that they had just been had, that everything Clegg told them "off the record" was included in their release, thus blocking the two young reporters from releasing their story. Meek said he was miffed and muttered to Speakes that Clegg was "an S.O.B." Clegg's secretary overheard the remark and immediately reported it to her boss. The next day, according to Meek, Clegg called him to his office and said, "Son, I understand that yesterday you called me a S.O.B. in front of my secretary. Is that true?" Meek, scared as he was, responded, "Yes sir." Meek says that Clegg came from behind his desk, put an arm around his shoulder and said, "Well, son, you were right. I did act like an S.O.B. yesterday." Meek and Clegg would go on to become good friends.

Clegg could also be quite charming. In 1957, when Harter Crutcher, the daughter of Chancellor J. D. Williams, gave birth to her son, Robert Pepper Crutcher Jr., Clegg wrote a welcome letter to the infant[7]:

Dear Young Robert:
Congratulations upon your arrival! The world into which you have made an entrance has many problems; but, the wisdom which you have already demonstrated in choosing your parents bespeaks the splendid contributions which will be expected of you in helping successfully solve the problems of your generation. We wish for you and your parents a long life of joy, good health, and prosperity.
   With every good wish.
    Sincerely,
    Hugh Clegg

Following his retirement to Anguilla, Mississippi, Clegg gave four extensive interviews on October 1, 2, and 23 of 1975 and July 1, 1976, that were included in the Mississippi Oral History series produced by the University of Southern Mississippi.[8] Three of the interviews were conducted by Mr. Michael Garvey and the last by Dr. Orley B. Caudill. It became apparent during these interviews that Hugh Clegg was a Mississippian of considerable influence in both the national and regional arenas.

As I began to put this biography together, there were other major sources that proved helpful, including an unpublished manuscript, "Somebody Jumped the Gun," written by Clegg after his retirement from Ole Miss. That manuscript is housed in the Archives Department of the John D. Williams Library on the Ole Miss campus.[9] An invaluable source of information on Clegg's days with the FBI was the approximately two-thousand-page personnel file the FBI maintained on Clegg, which was obtained under the Freedom of Information Act.[10]

In the FBI files, one finds that Clegg intended to write a memoir of his days in the FBI, "Inside the FBI," after his retirement from Ole Miss. But despite considerable effort, no manuscript has been located. Clegg's daughter, Ruby Kathryn Clegg Patterson, is unaware of where the manuscript is.[11] If this manuscript in fact exists, it would doubtless add considerable insight to Clegg's days with the Bureau.

Troutmouth

Introduction

The room was filled with thirty-five white, nervous accountants and lawyers aspiring to become a member of one of the world's leading law enforcement agencies: the Federal Bureau of Investigation. Ranging in age from twenty-three to thirty-five, they could have been clones. The candidates were telling jokes and making small talk when the door burst open. A large, out of breath, intimidating man stepped in, and the group immediately grew silent. Hugh H. Clegg, the number three man in the agency and the head of Training and Inspection, stepped behind the lectern, caught his breath, and began to speak. His nickname within the Bureau was "Troutmouth," but no one ever called him that to his face.[1] The nickname was given because he had an odd way of pursing his lips when he spoke. Clegg, true to his nickname, pursed his lips and bellowed "Good morning gentlemen!" He reminded the group of the role of the FBI in law enforcement and stressed the high standards of performance expected of them, not just as members of the FBI but in their private lives as well. He challenged them by saying that if any of those present could not meet those high standards, they should leave the room now. Clegg paused and looked around the room. No one moved from his seat.

Satisfied, Clegg then barked, "Please stand, raise your right hand, and repeat after me: I, state your name, do solemnly swear . . ." as he had them take the Law Enforcement Oath. When the oath was completed, some of the men appeared to tear up. Clegg then congratulated the group and said, "You are now Special Agents of the Federal Bureau of Investigation. Always remember, you are a personal representative of Mr. Hoover. Please, for your own sake, try not to embarrass the Bureau."[2] The new agents were aware of Clegg's loyalty to Director J. Edgar Hoover and were also aware of Clegg's influence and power within the agency. After further orientation and lunch, the agents were lined up for inspection wearing their hats and overcoats—the "official" uniform of the FBI. Clegg conducted the review in drill-sergeant fashion to enforce the agency's rigid dress code and would stop to straighten a tie or to order an agent to get a new hat—preferably a snap-brim type—or to tell a grown man to get a garter for his socks as he passed in review.

Hugh Clegg would become involved in several of the most significant matters in America during the twentieth century: the chase of gangsters and kidnappers; the capture of atom bomb spy Klaus Fuchs; and the pursuit of major civil rights issues, including the attempted desegregation of the University of Mississippi by Clennon King and the riots at the university that accompanied its desegregation by James Meredith. Hugh H. Clegg had come a long way from small-town Mathiston, Mississippi.

Chapter One

Growing Up in Mathiston

The 11th Commandment here is: "Thou shalt speak no ill
of Mathiston."—Lavelle McAlpin

L IKE MANY CAREERS OF SUCCESSFUL INDIVIDUALS, Hugh
Clegg's was defined by the quality of his young life and his
roots: his family, its church ties, and the environment in
which he was reared. He was born and grew up in the small town
of Mathiston, Mississippi, located in what is now named Webster
County, and was strongly influenced by the character of its people.
To this day, residents of Mathiston are proud of their heritage and
of their town that was once a bustling center of business activity and
one of the more progressive communities in Mississippi. In its day,
Webster County could boast of being an education center with a
thriving Wood College, a religious center anchored by the Methodist Church, and a railway transportation hub. Local historian Lavelle
McAlpin is proud to boast that during the first quarter of the twentieth century, Mathiston could claim three famous citizens in the same
period of time who knew each other well: a future assistant director
of the FBI (Hugh Clegg), a future governor of Mississippi (Thomas L.
Bailey), and a future editor of the *New York Times* (Turner Catledge,
who lived in Choctaw County to the south but spent much time in
Mathiston). According to McAlpin, Clegg was proud of Mathiston
and described anyone and everyone in the local area as being from
Mathiston. For example, although Tom Bailey was actually born and
raised outside Maben before living in Mathiston for a time, McAlpin
claims Clegg would never have described him as being from Maben.

Residents of Mathiston remain proud of their town's history and share with residents of nearby Maben pride regarding the time a young Charles Lindbergh, on a barnstorming trip in May 1923, was forced to land his Curtis JN4-D biplane, known as the Jenny, to avoid an approaching storm. He found an open field, but when he landed he hit a ditch and broke the propeller. A crowd began to assemble in the rain around the crippled plane and when Lindbergh asked where he was, they told him where he had landed—about midway between Mathiston and nearby Maben. Lindbergh spent several days in the area awaiting shipment of a new propeller. He rented a room at the old Southern Hotel in Maben and often dined at the home of John Milton McCain in Mathiston.[1] When Lindbergh installed the new propeller, he offered many of those who gathered a ride in his plane. Several bystanders took him up on his offer and paid him enough to cover the cost of the new propeller.[2]

Local pride continues to this day as residents of Mathiston like to brag about producing notable personalities, such as the distinguished artist William Dunlap; the noted journalist and author Mary Lynn Kotz; and the former general manager of the Tennessee Valley Authority, Bill Willis. Not bad for a town with a population of 647 people, according to the 2010 census. Over the years, members of the Clegg family were major contributors to the creation of this nurturing environment.

Webster County was formed in 1874 as Sumner County, created from various parts of Chickasaw, Montgomery, Choctaw, and Oktibbeha counties. The county name was changed in 1882 to Webster County in honor of Daniel Webster, American leader, statesman, and Massachusetts senator. The town of Mathiston was settled in 1888 on eighty acres of land sold by Hugh's grandfather, George Polk Clegg, to W. G. "Bill" Mathis for four hundred dollars. The tract of land that would become the town of Mathiston was situated on the old Natchez Trace on mounds that originally comprised a Choctaw Indian settlement. In 1889 Mathis conveyed a twenty-acre tract through this land to the Georgia Pacific Railroad Company for the purpose of establishing a depot. George Polk Clegg had also acquired considerable land in the area. The Mathis family owned the north side of rail track, and the Clegg family owned the south side. The town was incorporated in 1890 and was named Mathis Town in honor of Bill Mathis's donation. But if the decision had been made to build a depot on the north side of the track rather than the south side, Mathiston would perhaps be known as Cleggsville or Cleggstown. The new settlement had only three resident families: those of George Polk Clegg, H. M. Hardin, and Luke DeVore.[3]

Mathiston, despite its small population, became a major railroad town as the tracks afforded travel in all four directions. Storekeepers and farmers had routes of communication and the ability to attract customers from a large surrounding area. The railroad also allowed the small town to link with major population areas, since it ran from Greenville to Columbus and from Columbus to Birmingham, Atlanta, Washington, DC, and on northward. Trains from these cities ran through Mathiston. Because of the railroad connection, a variety of stores, including Clegg Brothers, began to prosper.

Hugh Clegg was born on July 17, 1898,[4] the first of five children born to James (Jim) Monroe Clegg and the former Sallie Delma Conley. His great-grandfather, George Washington Clegg, and his family were from Rochdale in Lancashire, England. There is a stone manor, which some believe to be haunted, built in the seventeenth century and named Clegg Hall, located two miles northeast of Rochdale in the town of Littleborough in the Greater Manchester area. The Hall was named not after the Clegg family but after the location on which it still stands, where an earlier Clegg Hall was located. While there is no evidence that the Clegg clan in actual fact lived in the current manor, they apparently did inhabit the older Clegg Hall. The Cleggs date their ancestry in that area to the early twelfth century.

The Clegg family migrated to America and settled in South Carolina before deciding to move to Mississippi, hoping the land would be more fertile. George Polk Clegg followed the family wagon, walking the entire way from the Edgefield district of South Carolina through Augusta, Georgia, and on to Mississippi. The family settled in the area now known as Webster County but was disappointed to find the soil less fertile than had been hoped and soon decided to return to South Carolina. Clegg claimed that George Polk walked the whole way back home. After another year in South Carolina, the family members once again changed their minds and then decided to establish a home back in Webster County.

Hugh's grandmother on his father's side was Rosa Caroline Shaffer, the youngest of nine children born to John M. and Mary Dolly Shaffer. She and George Polk Clegg married in Choctaw County in 1868 and had five sons (John Elisha, James Monroe, William Henry, Samuel Levi, and George Webster) and one daughter, Sallie, who died at a relatively early age. George Polk Clegg, the son of George Washington and Hannah Hill Clegg, joined a company of old men and young boys and fought in the Civil War before returning home to assume a life of farming. George Polk and Rose Shaffer Clegg had six children.

Hugh's father, James Monroe Clegg, was born on April 8, 1874. He was well educated and excelled in mathematics and English while also gaining the reputation of being a peacemaker; people in trouble or who were quarrelsome would come to him for arbitration. James Monroe worked his father's farm and then became a clerk, bookkeeper, and manager of a store owned by a Mr. Yates. Sallie Delma Conley, who was born just outside of Mathiston on September 12, 1878, met James in Mathiston, and they were married on October 17, 1897. Sallie Delma was religious, a devotee of the Bible, and a strong believer in education. Hugh was born nine months to the day following their marriage. He was born at home on a little hill about a quarter of a mile west of downtown Mathiston on the current US Highway 82. His birth was difficult and attendants worked on his mother so intently that "the baby was almost forgotten put away somewhere on a table, and they continued working with mother until she revived, regained her strength and then somebody remembered the baby."[5] Sallie's father, William Conley, was a farmer and preacher from North Carolina and later eastern Tennessee. Since he did not believe in slavery, he joined the Union Army and was with Union forces at the Battle of Shiloh. William had been married previously and had four children when his first wife died. He then married Mary Starnes, the daughter of Joe Starnes, who owned a large tract of land north of Mathiston. They had several children, among whom were Joe Turner, Sallie Delma (Hugh's mother), A. Onessimus, and John.

James Monroe Clegg and Sallie had five children: Hugh, Irene, James Ellis, Berniece, and Kate Hardison. Hugh Clegg said his parents "couldn't find any other name they thought was good enough for their little baby, so they gave me the privilege of adding an initial or a name when I grew up so I added the initial which has no significance other than an initial."[6] He thus became Hugh H. Clegg.

Irene graduated from Grenada College (later part of the Millsaps College system) and taught English, mathematics, languages, and finance in several school systems. She married Charles Russell Smith, half owner and manager of the Service Lumber Company, and became quite wealthy by investing in railroad and oil stocks the five hundred dollars she received upon her husband's death from a cerebral hemorrhage in 1949. Irene passed away in 1998.

Hugh's brother, James Ellis, or J. E. Clegg, graduated from Mississippi A&M where he played baseball. J. E. later joined Hugh in Washington and graduated from the National Law School. Like his older brother, he joined the FBI and was in charge of field offices in Albany, New York; Springfield, Illinois; and New Orleans, Louisiana. He left the FBI during World War II to join the Humble Oil and Refining Company in Baytown, Texas, as head of security operations. J. E. married native Minnesotan Hildur Virginia Lehn, and they had one son. J. E. passed away in 1968. Despite the fact that Hugh and J. E. were close throughout their lives, Hugh makes little mention of his brother in his oral history.

Hugh's sister Berniece attended Mississippi State College for Women (MSCW) and transferred to Peabody College in Nashville when MSCW almost lost accreditation during Governor Theodore Bilbo's administration. She graduated, taught school in Grenada, Mississippi, and married Henry Gaston Gary. Gary was a graduate of Mississippi State College and became a teller at the Bank of Louisville.[7] Gary served with General George Patton in World War II and received several citations. He was later employed at the Mississippi State Tax Commission.[8] Berniece died in 1998 and Gary passed away two years later.

Hugh's youngest sister, Kate Hardison, graduated from Wood Junior College and married James D. Dudley Gardner.[9] Kate and James worked for the US Postal Service and had three children: James Hugh Gardner, Sallie McComb, and Gary. Both Sallie and Gary are still living at the time of this writing, Gary in Mathiston and Sallie in Aberdeen, Mississippi. Gary recalls that when he was somewhere between eight and ten years old, his Uncle Hugh brought him an Ole Miss baseball uniform. Hugh made little mention of Kate in his oral history.

One year after he married, James Monroe Clegg and his brother, Henry, formed a mercantile business and named it Clegg Brothers. James Monroe was elected as town clerk and served as community lawyer drawing up deeds and mortgages at no charge. He also taught Sunday school until the age of eighty-one. Hugh recalled that

> Sunday School members were local Methodists, plus Wood Junior College faculty members who would come down and join the class. Dad would tell them what the literature of the church said about the issue of social problems. Then he would lay the book down and say, "Now, here's what I think." And they were not exactly identical![10]

Although the business prospered, James Monroe suffered a heavy financial loss in a rather bizarre case. Three brothers from Barnesville, Georgia, carried out a bank embezzlement scheme worthy of a book or movie. Newspaper accounts of the incident's details are confusing and somewhat inconsistent. According to the *Atlanta Constitution*, in 1914 James Edwards Dunn was president of the Merchants and Farmers Bank of Mathiston as well as the president of the Bank of Heidelberg.[11] His brother, C. Marik Dunn, was a cashier at the Bank of Weir, where his wife also worked as a cashier. A third brother, G. Dunn, was a cashier at the bank in Mathiston.

In January of that year the brothers were accused of embezzling either thirty thousand or sixty thousand dollars (both figures are cited in the *Atlanta Constitution*) from the three banks and left their respective towns at about the same time with their whereabouts unknown. C. Marik Dunn's wife was arrested, held on a $3,500 bond, and charged with receiving deposits, despite the fact that the bank had been declared insolvent. She was, however, thought by most of the townsfolk to be innocent of any involvement, since just prior to the disappearance of her husband, he had instructed her to assume the responsibility of managing bank activities.[12] Clegg's father was one of the heaviest losers in the embezzlement. According to a subsequent report in the *Atlanta Constitution*,[13] on May 31, C. Marik Dunn was arrested in Seattle, Washington, and jailed in Ackerman, Mississippi.

Fifty years later, the case somehow came to the attention of the FBI. C. Marik Dunn filed an affidavit in Georgia to the effect that his brother, James Edwards Dunn, had died and left an estate in Arizona. Clegg's father was still alive at the time the case was reopened in 1957 (he died in 1958) and was interviewed by the FBI. In a memorandum dated October 30, 1957, the special agent in charge of the New Orleans FBI office brought to the attention of Director Hoover that in a letter dated five days earlier, Hugh had indicated that he hired W. D. Gary, an attorney from Eupora, Mississippi, to look into the matter. Hugh also indicated that he hired an attorney in Arizona to handle the family interests "in attempting to recover some of the money stolen for the benefit of his father and other depositors."[14] James Monroe Clegg, who was on the board of directors of the bank at the time of the defalcation, made every effort to make sure none of the customers of the bank lost any money. That included even paying them back using his own funds despite having lost a considerable sum himself. His generosity and concern are characteristics of the Clegg family. Hugh Clegg makes no mention of this incident in his oral history.

Since he was the oldest child, Hugh did most of the household chores of scrubbing floors, drying dishes, and helping his mother wash the clothes—doing everything except milking. When Hugh was growing up, one of his family's nearest neighbors was a black family that lived about a quarter-mile away. The neighbors, Ben and Betty Walker, had a son, Jesse, who was Hugh's first remembered friend. Hugh and Jesse were playmates. Jesse was Clegg's closest friend as a three-year-old. The boys played together and explored together.

Hugh told the story of the time when he and Jesse went down to one of the fence corners and saw some attractive looking berries, which they thought were edible, and could not resist the urge to gorge themselves. "We came home all covered with red stains. We had eaten a whole lot of pokeberries. I can remember my mother going to the back porch and calling Betty on the next hill and saying she'd just given me a dose of castor oil and 'you'd better give Jesse one.'" Jesse died a few years later, breaking Hugh's heart.[15] Clegg's attitude regarding racial issues later in life was forged in part by this experience as well as by his upbringing and his grandfather Conley's attitude towards slavery.[16]

Another event in Mathiston during Clegg's childhood was forever etched his memory. When he was eight years old, a major tornado came through central Mississippi, striking Winona and then Mathiston on November 17, 1906. The tornado destroyed at least twenty-five homes, an entire city block, consisting of seven wooden stores, and cotton crops. It blew away the old wooden two-room schoolhouse—the schoolhouse at which Clegg had started school. One black woman was killed in her home.[17] Clegg would later recall,

I remember I was sleeping in a room where they still had a fire burning. As the neighbors would come in, their homes having been blown away, or destroyed, or otherwise was uninhabitable, during the terrific downpour, I would hear them talking. I remember very vividly how frightened I was. Many were left homeless and numerous people gathered at our home which was moved slightly away from the chimney on the west side, probably as much as an inch or an inch and a half, but it was still waterproof and still standing. The noise in the room and the reciting of the experiences frightened me very much.[18]

With the schoolhouse destroyed, the centerpiece that brought the town close together was the Methodist Church, which offered its sanctuary as a school. The town of Mathiston recovered and without delay approved funding to construct a new, brick, two-story, eight-room schoolhouse with a large auditorium.[19]

Hugh's mother and father gave their children's education a high priority. Of their five children, all completed college except for Kate, who married before she was eighteen years old. Hugh spent his early years in rural Mississippi and went to Mathiston public schools. As a precocious youngster, he was designated to call Henry L. Whitfield, the president of the Industrial Institute and College (IIC)—which would later become Mississippi University for Women—to invite him to be a speaker at the Mathiston Trade Days festival. Whitfield accepted without hesitation and Hugh was given the honor of introducing him. Despite his young age, Clegg made a bold prediction by introducing Whitfield as the next governor of the state of Mississippi. Clegg figured that all of the women who had gone to IIC and their children would support Whitfield, thus assuring his victory. The prophecy was born out in 1923, when Whitfield defeated Theodore Bilbo and was elected governor in the first election in which women were allowed to vote for that office in Mississippi.

Hugh had a strong interest in languages, taking Latin for eight or nine years and French for two years. He said he even taught Latin for two years (presumably at Millsaps, where he also served as an assistant in a chemistry laboratory). His favorite teacher, although she was disliked by many in his class, was his Latin instructor, Mrs. Ruth Spraggins, a graduate of IIC. Hugh likened translating Latin to solving a crossword puzzle. But the teacher he remembered most was Miss Woodward, not so much for her teaching ability but "because she had the cleanest, shiniest hands and my hands were always a mess and chapped, and then a mess on top of that."[20]

Another influential teacher, Boyd Campbell, urged four or five eighth graders, including Hugh, to go to Walthall, the county seat, and take an eighth grade examination that was offered for those who volunteered to take it. Everyone passed. Hugh could not forget that one of the questions was to name and locate all the bones of the body. Campbell played football at Millsaps College and organized a football team at Mathiston, despite the fact that there were barely enough students big enough and old enough to play. In their first game, Maben was beating Mathiston so badly that Campbell asked permission to put on a uniform and play. To the surprise of those in attendance, his request was granted. One of the Maben boys broke loose and was about to score when Campbell caught him and threw him back over his shoulder, breaking the runner's leg and arousing the anger of fans of both Maben and Mathiston. Campbell would later establish the Mississippi School Supply Company and become president of the US Chamber of Commerce. Hugh would maintain a long friendship with Campbell until Campbell's death.[21]

Hugh excelled at declamation and took an active role in the Friday Night Debating Club, or the Lamar Literary Society, as it was called. Hugh's interests were diverse: playing a role in a musical show, playing basketball, and taking piano lessons for a while. Mathiston had no movie house, but once a year a tent show would pass through town. Hugh and his family went to the shows in spite of the outrageous prices of admission—ten cents for kids, fifteen cents for adults. The earliest job he could recall was sweeping out the Southern Methodist Church on Saturdays for fifteen cents. He also sold and delivered the newspaper, the *Commercial Appeal*, and worked in his father's store.

His father wanted him to learn farming on the four-acre tract of land on which he grew oats and cotton and an abundant amount of other crops. But attacks by boll weevils ate up the profits. His parents and his uncle never made much money running their business. They allowed people to build up debts at the store and customers often moved away, leaving their debts behind. Yet Hugh's father, a good humanitarian, could not turn them down, saying, "Everything we earn, our livelihood, comes from these people."[22] Clegg Brothers consisted of two stores that bought and sold all types of commodities, including chickens and cross ties for the New York Central Railroad that employed blacks to haul the cross ties. Hugh grew up watching the employees haul the cross ties while singing the whole time, gaining a great deal of respect for them.

Clegg recalled a humorous incident that occurred when several Cleggs gathered in the local drugstore, an incident indicative of how strongly bound the family was. Several people sat around drinking their midmorning Cokes; coffee was not such a popular morning beverage as it is now, but Cokes, other soda pops, and chocolate milk were. On that day, there was quite a crowd gathered around the soda fountain and someone remarked, "'Well, it looked like the Clegg's [sic] and the pissant's [sic] are taking the place over.' One of the Cleggs said, 'Yes, one, two, three, four, five Cleggs and one, two, three pissants.' So that ended that type of conversation."[23]

Hugh suffered from tonsillitis from the time he was eleven until he reached the age of fourteen and missed a lot of school as a result. His family doctor knew a man in nearby Eupora who claimed he could remove tonsils. He came with a gadget that sliced the tonsil in half, but to Hugh's regret, the tonsil would grow back. His procedure didn't work on Hugh and the next year Hugh again had tonsillitis and went through the same procedure. Once again the tonsil was split but again it grew back. Hugh had difficulty eating and grew quite skinny. Frustrated by the failed efforts of the tonsillitis "expert," Hugh's father took him to Memphis, where the tonsil was successfully removed one piece at a time. Hugh would spend time in the hospital library overnight, fascinated with all the books waiting to be read.

In 1914, a school in Clarkson—located nine miles north of Mathiston—burned down. It had been established in 1865 as a missionary school named Bennett Academy. Rather than rebuild a new school at the same site, Bennett Academy (years later Wood Junior College) was built in Mathiston. Bennett opened its doors in 1914 and offered one grade higher than the high school in Mathiston. Hugh finished the local high school and then went to Bennett. He gave the valedictory address when he graduated in 1915 and was later invited to give two commencement addresses at Wood Junior College. Hugh's excellence in public speaking would prove to be a valuable asset for the rest of his life. He later became president of the Wood Junior College Alumni Association.

Clegg's father felt that Hugh would encounter a lot of theoretical material in college and would therefore benefit from a practical background. So Hugh gained valuable practical experience in the general mercantile store for one year following graduation from high school by working as assistant general manager, merchandise buyer, cotton buyer, crosstie buyer, bookkeeper, and seller of whatever the customers wanted. He would later use these talents to sell higher education in Mississippi.

Hugh entered Millsaps College in September 1917, choosing Millsaps because many people he respected, including Boyd Campbell, Tom Bailey (a future governor of Mississippi), and a cousin, Millard Fillmore Clegg, all went there. To Hugh, it seemed natural to follow in their footsteps.

At Millsaps he took Latin and social science subjects in addition to the required courses. He later joked that he thought his knowledge of Latin would come in handy in his career when he went to England for the FBI. Since England was involved in World War II, the safest way to travel there was through Portugal. Hugh thought Portuguese was close to Latin but quickly learned that this was not true. While in Portugal, he took a taxi to go to the British Overseas Airways Ticket Office. He tried out his best Portuguese, based on his knowledge of Latin with the additional help of a Portuguese-English dictionary. Speaking with a heavy accent, he gave the driver an address, and forty minutes later the cab arrived at a cafeteria.[24]

He encountered several great teachers at Millsaps, among them English professor Dr. Alfred Allen Kern, who would become one of his great heroes. Others were social science teacher Prep Noble, history professor J. Reese "Ducky" Lynn, Latin professor Dr. D. M. Key, physics and astronomy professor Dr. G. L. Harrell, and mathematics teacher Dr. Benjamin Mitchell, who would later teach at Ole Miss when he retired from Millsaps. (Hugh met up with Dr. Mitchell again when he went to Ole Miss after retiring from the FBI.) He thrived at Millsaps and continued his interest in public speaking. He and an unnamed partner in the Lamar Literary Society won a debate against the Galloway Literary Society, and Hugh won the freshman declamation medal and the sophomore oratorical contest. As a sophomore, he also won the Durant Debate against Mississippi A&M and the Triangular Debate between Millsaps, Mississippi A&M, and Mississippi College. Clegg bragged about having good partners in these debates but failed to name any of them.

Clegg was elected to membership in the Kit Kat Club of the Sigma Upsilon literary fraternity and became president of the Lamar Literary Society, Kappa Alpha, and the senior class. He was also selected for membership in the All One Club started by physics professor Dr. George Lott Harrell for students who made all "ones" in their grades the previous month. Clegg never bragged about his athletic skills, or lack thereof, but he and an unnamed partner won the Millsaps junior-senior doubles tennis championship as a junior.

During his career at Millsaps, male students were concerned with the events taking place in Europe during World War I and the possibility of impending military service. Hugh was a member of the student army training corps, but only from October 3, 1918, until December 10, 1918, since the Armistice occurred on November 11, 1918. Nevertheless, he would recall his serial number, 3003136, and having a Russian rifle number, 4742.[25]

A key to Clegg's success was his lifelong ability to establish contacts with important individuals, and he did not mind mentioning their names. Among his acquaintances at that time were Thomas L. Bailey and Henry L. Whitfield—both of whom would later serve as governors of Mississippi. Other important contacts included Fred Lotterhos, who would later become a member of the Mississippi Supreme Court; Mike Conner, who was speaker of the Mississippi House of Representatives when Hugh first met him and who would later become governor; A. Y. Harper, a counsel for Standard Life; Leonard Calhoun, counsel for the Social Security Administration; Lawrence Long and Carter O'Farrell, both distinguished Jackson surgeons; Fred Sullens, editor of the *Jackson Daily News*; and George Lemmon Sugg, who would run the Mississippi Power Association. Hugh found himself immersed in the Mississippi political and fiscal power structure.

Clegg was first introduced to politics during his time at Millsaps. One of the more controversial figures Clegg knew there was Julian B. Feibelman, who would later become a key figure in civil rights controversies. Feibelman, a native of Jackson, Mississippi, graduated from Millsaps in 1918. Following his graduation, he enlisted in the army during World War I. He started law school at Ole Miss but decided to enter the rabbinate and was ordained in 1926. He earned an MA and PhD from the University of Pennsylvania and moved to New Orleans in 1936 to become rabbi at Temple Sinai. He became involved in efforts to achieve integration in New Orleans public schools. He was responsible for one of the first integrated meetings in New Orleans when he invited Nobel Peace Prize laureate Dr. Ralph Bunche to speak at Temple Sinai after Bunche had been denied use of facilities at Tulane University. Feibelman ignored death threats and opened the doors of Temple Sinai.[26] There were allegations of animosity toward Feibelman at Millsaps because of his alleged liberalism, but there were also strong indications that this animosity may have been sparked by his Jewish ancestry. Clegg, however, claimed he was unaware of any criticism of Feibelman at Millsaps.

Clegg was a freshman when Feibelman was a senior and the freshman considered him to be a great man. Feibelman encouraged younger students to try out for the literary teams. He represented Millsaps in the Mississippi Intercollegiate Oratorical Association. Hugh knew him, and although they were not close friends because of their age difference, thought him to be popular among all types and classes of Millsaps students. Clegg remembered that Feibelman was very emotional, oftentimes crying after an oratorical victory. The political atmosphere of Millsaps at the time was staid. There was no obvious expression of liberalism. Rather, everyone appeared to be conservative. Clegg considered himself to be a liberal in matters of civil liberties but a conservative in matters involving government expenditures.[27]

The biggest controversy during Hugh's stay at Millsaps was the adoption of a constitution for the honor system. Hugh felt that a constitution should be positive—eliminating ignorance, encouraging honesty and integrity—but a large group of students urged a more limited approach, the elimination of cheating and fraud. That group won, but the constitution was later abolished.

Clegg's political education continued when he saw and heard Mississippi's controversial US senator, Theodore Bilbo, for the first time. Bilbo had come to Mathiston to give a speech to a crowd of a hundred people from the front porch of Dr. J. H. Stennis, an uncle of future US senator John Stennis. Bilbo was a white supremacist who twice served as governor of Mississippi and later as US senator. Bilbo used a ploy by which he sought out and attacked an unpopular member of the crowd, thereby arousing its emotions. On this occasion, Bilbo singled out a newspaper editor, Preston E. Williams, who had waged a long battle against him. Hugh was a friend of one of Williams's sons, and Williams rented a store to publish his paper from Clegg's father. The Clegg family felt Williams was doing a creditable job, so Bilbo's attack on him was not well received and Bilbo knew it. Bilbo's reputation as a bigot who attacked Jews, Italians, and blacks would hurt Mississippi's reputation in Washington and the nation. Yet he was considered a "redneck liberal" in the US Senate for his support of the New Deal.

Clegg felt Bilbo had done some notable things as governor, such as pushing for laws that protected fish, game, and wildlife while losing favor for his "Bilbo Bath"—a law requiring cattle to be dipped in insecticide to eliminate ticks and thus prevent Texas Fever—a disease that crippled the US cattle industry. Clegg claimed to have no special feeling against Bilbo since he was, after all, one of his senators. Also, he bragged that he had a penchant for being loyal to "his crowd," and Bilbo was part of "his crowd" when he was in the Senate. But in 1934 Bilbo defeated incumbent senator Hubert Stephens, whom the Clegg family supported, for a seat in the US Senate, and the family never forgave Bilbo for that.[28]

Years later Clegg recalled meeting Senator Bilbo in Washington when Clegg was a special agent with the FBI. The senator told Clegg he had a problem and wanted to meet with him. Clegg caught a taxi to the Senate Office Building and was invited into Bilbo's office. As they were shaking hands, Bilbo told him, "Well I'm glad to see one of you Cleggs. All of you were always opposed to me and never voted for me, and I'd just like to see what stuff you are made of." Clegg replied, "Well, Senator, I'm glad to see you and I've been looking all over to see where you stuffed your forked tail! And where are those horns that you're supposed to have?" After telling Clegg a dirty joke, Bilbo got to the problem he had called Clegg about. The senator wanted one of his cousins from Pearl River County in Mississippi to be appointed as a special agent in the FBI. Clegg asked Bilbo if his cousin was a lawyer. Bilbo replied, "Oh, hell no. I don't even know whether he can read or not." Clegg then asked if he was an expert accountant. Bilbo replied to that saying, "Now, that I know he's not. I don't think he could add up two figures, small ones at that." Clegg then told him his cousin had no chance of becoming an agent in the FBI because Director Hoover only accepted lawyers or accountants. Rather than getting angry, Bilbo told Clegg,

> Well, I'll be dogged. You know you and I are going to get along just fine. I was up here as what they called "the Paste Master General" for a long time in the Agriculture Department. They had me running errands and doing menial work. Then I became a senator and I'll call up and ask my former friends and people in other departments, "what about this and what about that" and they always beat around the bush and never give me an answer. You're the first damn fellow I ever saw in my life in Washington that would give me a specific answer.

Clegg said they remained friends, but at a distance.[29]

Clegg majored in education at Millsaps and earned his AB degree in 1920. He was awarded a Lifetime Teacher's Certificate along with his diploma. He would be awarded an Honorary LLD degree from Millsaps in 1941. Hugh now wanted to become a lawyer or a social science professor. Clegg had realized the dreams of his parents. Their oldest son was now a college graduate and was ready to move on.

Chapter Two

A Move to Washington:
The Early Days at the FBI

Democracy cannot survive without the guidance
of a creative minority.—Harlan F. Stone

AFTER CLEGG GRADUATED FROM MILLSAPS, he accepted a job as instructor at Bennett Academy in 1922–1923, but as much as he enjoyed teaching, he had been thinking about law school and finally decided to abandon teaching and return to school. He chose George Washington University Law School for several reasons. As much as he loved Mathiston and Mississippi, he was eager to go out and see what the rest of the country was like. Also, he thought he had a better chance of getting a job in Washington, DC, one that would enable him to pay his way through law school. Through contacts with US representative Thomas U. Sisson of Winona, Mississippi, he found a job working the late shift at the Library of Congress, where he was in charge of all the books on American history at a salary of $420 a month. By the time he resigned that position in June 1924, his salary had been raised to $600 plus bonus. He then worked thirteen months at a higher salary at the Bureau of Internal Revenue and taught chemistry, physics, Latin, and history for nine months at Emerson Institute—a preparatory school for candidates for Annapolis and West Point.[1] Clegg was no stranger to hard work. He went to classes at the law school in the morning and as soon as classes were over, he hopped on a streetcar that took him to the Capitol, where he would listen to debates in the Senate, enjoying and absorbing every word. Clegg had many lifelong heroes and held Senators Jim Reed of Missouri—whom he considered the greatest debater he ever heard—George Norris of Nebraska, Hiram Johnson of California, Claude Swanson and Carter Glass of Virginia, Royal Copeland of New York, Bob La Follette of Wisconsin, William Borah of Idaho, Joseph Robinson of Arkansas, Henry Ashurst of Arizona, and Henry Cabot Lodge Sr. of Massachusetts all in very high regard and would become close friends with many of them. In midafternoon he would report to his job at the Library of Congress, where he worked the 2:30 to 10:30 shift.

Clegg said the two senators he came to know best were Virginia senators Claude Swanson and Carter Glass. Several years later, both senators supported an elderly person from Virginia whom they wished to be appointed as a US marshal. The FBI investigated their candidate and learned that this individual had been having a clandestine affair with a waitress. FBI Director J. Edgar Hoover thought both senators should be made aware of their candidate's transgressions and sent Clegg, who was then with the FBI, to inform them. Clegg set up a joint meeting with the senators and informed them of the findings of the FBI investigation. Rather than being angry about this discovery, Glass "reached over and slapped Swanson on the knee and said 'The son-of-a-gun. This old rooster is younger than we thought? All of his opponents have said that he was too old to be marshal and this proves [we] were right!'"[2] The candidate was appointed anyway.

Clegg had a great experience at GWU and maintained a lifelong involvement with the university. He was the president of the Alpha Nu chapter of the Kappa Alpha Order, serving as homecoming chairman for three years and was a member of Gate and Key and the national leadership society, Omicron Delta Kappa. He later served as president of the GWU alumni association. His relationship with Kappa Alpha fraternity would prove to be a rewarding and meaningful experience. He was elected to the court of honor of Kappa Alpha and would later receive its alumni achievement award. Of utmost importance, however, the fraternity house of Kappa Alpha served as a conduit for Clegg's introduction to the FBI.[3] Several alums who were special agents in the Bureau would hang around the fraternity house when they were in Washington. They appeared to Clegg to be enthusiastic about their jobs, and he appreciated the hard work they put into their work. The agents built up their boss, J. Edgar Hoover, and talked about how proud they were to serve under him. Hoover was a strict disciplinarian and "the escutcheon which identified the FBI."[4] The agents said that Hoover did not just demand loyalty; he obtained it and commanded it after he acquired it. Clegg became interested in joining the organization. Once again his close contacts with important individuals paid off when the fraternity counselor, Frank Myers, who later became a judge, encouraged Clegg to consider working for the Bureau. Myers made an appointment for Clegg to meet Hoover.

Hoover liked Clegg upon their first meeting and the feeling was mutual. Clegg said he went to see Hoover at 10:30 on the morning of June 10, 1926. At 8:00 that night he received his degree in law at the GWU commencement. As soon as the commencement was over, Clegg filed an application with the Bureau, listing W. M. Bailey, the mayor of Mathiston, and Dr. D. M. Key, the president of Millsaps, as references. Following an intensive screening and physical examination, two months and two days later he received his appointment as special agent. Clegg never took the bar examination.

Clegg joined the bureau at the right time. President Warren Harding died in 1923 and his successor, Calvin Coolidge, replaced Harding's cronies in the cabinet. Hoover was appointed acting director of the Bureau to replace William J. Burns on May 10, 1924, by Attorney General Harry M. Daugherty. Shortly thereafter, President Coolidge replaced Daugherty with Harlan F. Stone. By the end of the year, Stone had named Hoover director of the Bureau. Hoover wasted no time in effecting changes in the atmosphere of the Bureau, which at the time was riddled with political appointees. Typical of the cronyism and lack of accountability existent in the Bureau, Burns had continued to run the Burns Detective Agency while serving as the Bureau director.

Daugherty had sent Burns to investigate Montana senator Thomas J. Walsh for evidence of criminal misconduct, a move in retaliation for Walsh's opposition to oil leases granted by Secretary of the Interior Albert Fall. This incident became known as the Daugherty-Burns scandal. Burns was later also involved, in an indirect way, in the 1927 Teapot Dome scandal in which naval oil reserve lands— the Teapot Dome naval oil reserve—were secretly leased to private companies. Burns used his agency to investigate jurors when Harry F. Sinclair was put on trial for conspiracy to defraud the government in leasing the Teapot Dome reserves.

Because of Burns's corrupt background, the new attorney general, Harlan F. Stone, forced him to resign and then hired Hoover to direct and reform the Bureau. Under Burns, the Bureau had shrunk from a high of over 1,100 personnel to around 600 by the time he stepped down. While Hoover had served as assistant director of the Bureau during the Burns-Daugherty era of the early 1920s, he avoided any taint of corruption or abusive conduct despite criticism of the General Intelligence Division (GID) that he headed. Stone and Hoover teamed up to reform the Bureau's operations and restore public support without generating fears of developing a federal police force. Stone abolished the GID, limited Bureau investigations to violations of federal law, and prohibited any investigation of the political beliefs of US citizens.

Given Burns's reputation of having appointed to the Bureau anyone a senator, congressman, or any higher-up wanted appointed, regardless of qualifications, Hoover was also directed to remove incompetent agents and abolish the patronage appointment system.[5] Clegg was aware that the Bureau had gained a poor reputation under Burns and the Harding administration. He recalled, "There was one fellow that I knew, he was still in when I was there, that would come into the New York office which had fifty or sixty men in it, that was a big office in those days, and he would come in every payday and get his check but he didn't do any of the work."[6] From his discussions with Bureau agents visiting the Kappa Alpha house, he was also aware that Hoover retained personnel who were competent and qualified and was getting rid of the deadwood. Hoover was not afraid to make people angry, including many politicians. He was able to eliminate the patronage system by raising the qualifications of a special agent by recruiting only law school and accounting school graduates between the ages of twenty-three and thirty-five. Hoover received criticism for being ruthless and dictatorial, but it was necessary in order to remove the worthless political hacks. Clegg was excited about joining the Bureau and working for a man like Hoover.

Once he received Clegg's application, Hoover, on June 11, 1926, ordered Agent J. M. Keith to conduct an extensive background check of Clegg. Keith went to Mathiston to investigate Clegg's background. After graduating and submitting his Bureau application, Clegg returned to Mathiston. One night while he was having dinner at home the telephone rang. "The man at the barber shop called me. He said 'Hugh, there's a federal investigator up here checking on you. Do you want us to get together and run him out of town?' He was serious. I said 'No, you be awfully good to him. He's trying to find out if I'm going to get a job with them.'"[7]

In addition to listing Bailey and Key as references, Clegg thought he would impress Hoover by also listing other influential individuals: Robert M. Heth, an attorney in Washington, DC; W. H. Randolph, principal of the Emerson Institute; W. C. Van Vleck, the dean of the GWU Law School; Mississippi senator Hubert D. Stephens; and Mississippi representative Jeff Busby. During the application process, Clegg continued to use these influential friends. On June 15, he wrote the Bureau to modify his original application to change his address effective June 16. The letter was filed on stationery of the US Senate Committee on Banking and Currency, on which committee Senator Stephens served.[8]

All of his references provided glowing evaluations and recommended Clegg to the Bureau without reservation. Agent C. J. Estopinal went to interview Clegg in Jackson and recommended him as "a high class young man" with a "pleasing personality" and a man who "would be a credit to this Bureau."[9] Typical of the problems of communication in the Bureau, Hoover sent a memorandum to Agent Harold "Pop" Nathan complaining that Clegg "has not as yet been interviewed," not knowing that Estopinal had already interviewed him on July 8.[10] Hoover wanted to wrap up the screening as soon as possible and on July 29 wrote Clegg, who was still in Mathiston, requesting a report on his present physical condition. Clegg was given a choice of consulting his own physician in Mathiston or traveling at his own expense to be examined at the US Public Health Service in Memphis.[11] Clegg chose to be examined in Memphis and sent Hoover the results of the exam on the stationery of the Peabody Hotel.[12] Hoover must have anticipated a good report on Clegg's physical exam because on July 26, 1926, three days before Clegg's physical, he sent a letter to the appointments clerk directing him to prepare a letter appointing Clegg as special agent. On that date, the appointment letter was drawn.

However, Clegg had to wait for a vacancy to open among the slim number of agents—only about 270 were serving in 1926. It was not until August 6 that Hoover wrote Clegg informing him that he had been appointed a special agent of the Bureau of Investigation at a salary of $2,700 per year. He was first assigned to the New Orleans office, where he would be sworn in. Hoover further informed Clegg that his travel expenses would be allowed and a four dollar per diem expense would be allowed in lieu of subsistence. The appointment was tendered "for a probationary period of three months" with the understanding that if Clegg performed in a satisfactory manner, the appointment would be permanent. Hoover pressured Clegg for a decision, stating that if the offer were not accepted in one week's time it would be cancelled. Once he was sworn in, he would be furnished with transportation to Atlanta, where he would report to Special Agent in Charge Lewis J. Baley. Hoover ended the letter admonishing Clegg to "consider this letter strictly confidential. No publicity."[13] On August 10 Clegg wrote Hoover, on Clegg Brothers letterhead, accepting the offer and indicating that he would depart for New Orleans the following day.[14] Clegg became one of the fewer than three hundred special agents of the Bureau.

When Clegg joined the Bureau, his intention was to work there for a short period of about thirty months so he could gain the experience necessary to practice law at government expense. But Clegg soon realized that no real law was being practiced anywhere that matched the exciting and meaningful work with the Bureau, and he ultimately stayed with the agency for twenty-seven-and-one-half years.

Clegg left Mathiston to travel to Winona to catch a train on the Illinois Central Railroad to New Orleans. He reported to Agent E. B. Sisk and learned firsthand of the poor system of communications in the Bureau. On August 11, Sisk discovered that his office did not have any Oath of Office forms on hand and wrote Hoover requesting a form to swear in Clegg and requesting additional blanks as well.[15] On August 12, Sisk wrote Agent Baley, notifying him that Clegg had not taken the oath since the New Orleans office had no forms. Sisk suggested that if Baley had such forms, Clegg could take the oath when he arrived in Atlanta and then the form could be forwarded to Hoover.

That same day, Clegg wrote Hoover from New Orleans that he was aware of all the terms of his appointment and that he accepted the appointment agreeing "to abide by each and every one of the conditions specified."[16] The next day, Sisk wrote Hoover acknowledging that Clegg had agreed to the conditions of appointment and furnished Clegg with railroad transportation to Atlanta. Sisk also reminded Hoover that his office did not have any Oath of Office blanks and suggested Hoover send a form to Agent Baley.[17] It was not until August 14 that he received a reply enclosed with four blank oaths of office. On August 13, Baley wrote Hoover to inform him that Clegg had reported to his office for assignment. Clegg told Baley that he did not take the oath in New Orleans as advised because there were no blank forms. Baley told Hoover that he did not have any forms either, but that he had made one up and Clegg "has taken the oath of office here today."[18]

Baley was concerned that since Clegg had not taken the oath before leaving New Orleans, his expenses might not be reimbursed. And then, in typical government fashion, Baley was informed on August 19 that Clegg should have taken the oath in New Orleans but that nevertheless, Clegg could charge his expenses for the trip from New Orleans to Atlanta even though he did not take the oath until he arrived in Atlanta. "It should be stated in the voucher that he entered on duty at New Orleans and an explanation should be given as to why he did not there take the oath of office."[19]

Clegg's first assignment was to be special agent in charge of letters. His first task out of the Atlanta office was to go to the Atlanta Penitentiary to obtain and copy the record of a fugitive who had been imprisoned there. The Bureau was interested in knowing the names of those individuals with whom the fugitive had communicated while in prison. Clegg's boss had contacted the warden, and when Clegg met him, the warden asked to see his credentials. But Clegg had just joined the Bureau and did not have any credentials yet. He naively told the warden, "'I am sorry, I do not have any.' The warden said, 'Well, aren't you required to have them?' I said, 'I'm a Special Agent.'"[20] The warden and his boss laughed at his naiveté and did not let Clegg forget the incident.

Clegg endured the required probationary period and awaited his first evaluation. Six weeks after joining the Bureau, he received his first Efficiency Rating Sheet, submitted by Agent Baley. Clegg's highest marks were received in dependability, health, industry, loyalty, promptness, teamwork, personal appearance, habits, and attitude toward work. His lowest marks were received in office work and executive ability—an evaluation that would later prove to be, for the most part, accurate. High, but not among the highest, marks were also received in accuracy, aggressiveness, initiative, judgment, speed, knowledge, leadership, resourcefulness, and tact. His total rating was 87 out of a possible score of 100. Baley remarked, "This agent is a lawyer and is a clean upright young man. Has been in the service only a short time but is taking hold on the work in good shape and impresses me as having the qualifications and with experience should make a splendid agent."[21] Clegg was off to a good start.

A couple of weeks later, Clegg was assigned to Asheville, North Carolina, to work on a bankruptcy fraud case. The complex case took a long time to finish, and Clegg did not arrive back in his Atlanta office until Christmas Eve. But the perpetrators were all convicted and Clegg earned the title of Bankruptcy Expert.

Agent Baley again evaluated Clegg in March 1927. This time his total rankings improved from the previous score of 87 to 92, and Baley remarked that with a "little more general experience he should make one of the best agents in the service."[22] Soon thereafter, his salary was raised to $2,900 per annum. Clegg was pleased that he had earned a raise, no matter how small.

Agent Frank Cole of the Kansas City office was informed that Clegg was one of the agents selected to be given experience in antitrust matters and become qualified to pursue antitrust investigations without assistance. While he gained experience in this area, there was to be no interference with his regular work. The Atlanta office was informed of this selection on February 12, but Clegg had already been transferred to Kansas City.[23] His next assignment was another bankruptcy case there. When the investigation resulted in a trial, Clegg thought afterward that the US attorney had presented an open and shut case. However, the jury returned a verdict of not guilty, surprising almost everyone, including the judge. When the courtroom emptied, the judge sent word for Clegg to meet with him in his chambers. The judge told him, "Now, Mr. Clegg, don't worry about that. The truth is the jury didn't know the difference between assets and chair cushions."[24]

Like most new agents, Clegg was shifted from field office to field office. After his experience in Kansas City, he was transferred to New York; did some work in Newark; and then was assigned to the Washington, DC, field office. In New York, he worked with James E. Amos, the first black agent hired by the Bureau. He was one of the few minority agents in the FBI during this period. Amos had served Theodore Roosevelt in several capacities, including personal attendant, confidant, and bodyguard. He was an expert marksman whom Roosevelt had called "the best shot he had ever seen."[25] He had also served as a special investigator for the Burns Detective Agency, and when William J. Burns became the fourth director of the Bureau in 1921, Amos applied to the Bureau as an agent using former president

Roosevelt as a reference. He was considered to be a superb agent and served the Bureau for thirty-two years, bringing several notable criminals to justice.

In the DC field office, Clegg met Lenore Houston, the first female special agent he would encounter. In November 1924, Houston became the first and only female special agent hired by Director Hoover. She was hired as a special employee but, under some political pressure, her title was changed to special agent. While serving in the Philadelphia office, agent Houston received excellent performance ratings and was earning $3,100 a year by April 1927. She was then transferred to the Washington field office.[26] In his forty-eight years as head of the FBI, J. Edgar Hoover refused to allow additional women as special agents.[27] In fact, the Bureau's and Hoover's record in hiring minorities and women was deplorable, even for the times.

The first woman special agent of the Bureau was Emma R. Hotchkiss, who served from 1911 until 1919. During the 1920s, a trio of women known to serve as special agents in the Bureau included Alaska Davidson, Jessie Duckstein, and Lenore Houston. Although they performed up to standards in training, Davidson and Duckstein were dismissed when Hoover was appointed director of the Bureau in 1924, due in part to the dramatic cuts in the Bureau budget as a result of the Teapot Dome scandals. Houston was hired following these cuts and was the longest-serving agent of the trio, but she was asked to resign in 1928.[28] Women suffered a worse employment fate than not only males but also than minorities during this period.[29] Some African American male agents were conducting important investigations during this period.[30]

The policy established by Hoover of not hiring women remained in effect for almost fifty years until FBI acting director L. Patrick Gray, who was appointed following Hoover's death in 1972, decided to end the men-only policy. Gray accepted two women into the Bureau, Susan Lynn Roley and Joanne E. Pearce. He was nominated as permanent director by President Nixon in February 1973, but Gray was not confirmed by the Senate because of his involvement in mishandling the 1972 Watergate crisis.

During the 1920s, the most frequent violations of federal criminal statutes involved interstate transportation of stolen vehicles, white slavery, peonage (forcing someone to work out a debt), violations of civil rights, fraud against the government, and antitrust violations. But the Bureau was handicapped by not being allowed to initiate on its own any investigation of civil rights violations, government fraud, or antitrust cases. Agents had to get authority from the head of the criminal division of the Justice Department involved.

Agents were allowed to initiate investigations of bankruptcy, white slavery, motor theft, theft of interstate shipments, thefts of government property, crimes on Indian reservations, and crimes on high seas, but any violation with political or public policy implications required approval. FBI agents were not given power to make arrests or carry firearms until 1932. "I can remember [calling] policemen when a wanted fugitive is at such-and-such place," Clegg later recalled:

> The policemen will tell me, "Well, you guard the back and I'll go in the front. You don't have a gun, so I'll go in." I've stood at the back door of a house, had [only a] brickbat in my hand, hoping the [fugitive] would not come out that way. . . . If he'd come out shooting, I had no defense at all, no weapons, no offensive weapons, and you're just at his mercy.[31]

In his early days with the Bureau, Clegg made an immediate impression on his colleagues and supervisors, and after he had completed thirty days service in the New York office, he was considered to be an "exceptionally capable agent."[32] In a memo to Hoover, Clegg was praised for his work on International Arms and Fuse cases by the attorney general's office.[33] Hoover was impressed and recommended a transfer, promotion, and a salary increase to $3,300. Two weeks later Hoover wrote Clegg to inform him of the promotion and raise and his designation as junior administrative officer in the Bureau.[34] Yet Clegg was soon inundated with the agency's bureaucracy, the prevailing mood among federal agencies being the more paperwork the better.

Clegg's relationship with Hoover during the former's career with the FBI was perplexing. Although he had gained Hoover's respect, he also was a victim of Hoover's ire time and time again. Examples of the "love-hate" relationship during Clegg's early years with the Bureau abound. Hoover chastised Clegg for neglecting three cases while he was assigned to the Atlanta office and demanded an explanation.[35] Clegg responded by indicating that he was absent from the Atlanta office from November 12, 1926, to December 24, 1926, and from January 13, 1927, to March 4, 1927, and did not have the files in these cases and was thus unacquainted with the status of each one. He apologized for not notifying the Atlanta office that he was not in a position to render status reports in these cases. He informed the director that his records did show that he prepared or dictated status reports on one of the cases on December 29, 1926, and also on March 24, 1927, but he was absent on the dates the reports were due in January and February 1927. He ended his response with a pledge that he would make every effort to prevent a recurrence of omissions and to make proper status reports.[36]

Soon after Clegg's appointment as junior administrative officer, Inspector James S. Egan filed a report indicating that there were 363 reports on Clegg's desk dating back to September 12 that had not received any attention. Egan stated that he had been informed by Clegg that he was out of the city and did not return until September 15. Egan thought Clegg was capable and could develop into a good supervisor but that he "should have spent Saturday afternoon and Sunday on this work when he was so far behind, or nights, since his return to the city."[37] Hoover was irritated by Egan's report and sent a memorandum to Agent Harold "Pop" Nathan complaining about the accumulation of work on the desks of Supervisors Clegg and Frank Baughman to such an extent as to impair the efficiency of the Bureau. Hoover acknowledged that both were away from the office but stated that supervisors should put in overtime to clear their desks. He instructed Nathan to take this matter up with the supervisors to prevent a repetition. Hoover noted he did not think that the assignment of work was so heavy that they could not keep abreast of it. Then he turned around and commended Clegg for establishing an excellent card record system for each field office in the Bureau "on which is made a notation of each letter written to such field office with regard to errors in reports submitted" and recommended that each supervisor in all of the divisions adopt this system.[38]

Five months later, Hoover reminded Clegg "that in every instance where a piece of mail matter remains on your desk 48 hours after receipt and without a reply having been dictated, that I desire to be informed in person for said delay."[39] Yet fieldwork continued to conflict with all the required paperwork, because eight months later the problem persisted. Inspector J. M. Keith sent Hoover a status report on four agents who had reports on their desks for a period of more than forty-eight hours (Nathan, Clegg, Baughman, and McFarland). Clegg was found to have seven matters he had already reviewed that were in his dictation basket awaiting a stenographer. He had four matters yet to be reviewed. But Keith noted that Clegg's stenographer had been working on dictation taken from McFarland and other agents in the division because of the absence (annual leave, sick leave) of two of the five stenographers available.[40]

There were numerous occasions of correspondence between Inspector Egan, the director, and Clegg. Most were harsh criticisms by Egan that Clegg had failed to file reports in a timely manner. Clegg responded at length with explanations and corrections of fact.

Issues other than paperwork continued to get Clegg in hot water with the director. Inspector Egan provided Hoover with the scores of six agents who had taken an examination on the Manual of Rules and Regulations. Three of the agents missed two of the ten questions asked—including Clyde Tolson, who would later become the number 2 man in the FBI and Hoover's close associate—while two others missed three of the questions. Even worse, one agent, E. K. Thode, missed half the questions. Hoover chastised Clegg, saying he expected supervisors in the Bureau to make a perfect score and directed Clegg to make further study of the Manual of Rules and Regulations. One can only imagine the letter that Agent Thode received from Hoover.[41]

With the criticism, however, came the praise. Before the end of 1928, US Attorney Thomas J. Hawkins of Asheville, North Carolina, wrote Hoover to express his appreciation for the cooperation of the FBI and to congratulate Clegg, whose "investigation was most thorough and able," and to report that "his assistance most valuable in the actual trial" in *US vs The Wonder Furniture Company*. The case involved concealing assets in violation of the Bankruptcy Act. All five defendants were convicted on every count.[42] Less than a week later, Hoover wrote Clegg acknowledging Hawkins's letter and praising Clegg for his work on the case.[43]

One month later, Hoover would again express his appreciation for Clegg's devotion to duty and regard for the interest of the Bureau because Clegg had requested and been accorded only sixteen days and two hours of annual leave.[44]

Despite the bureaucratic problems Clegg encountered, he continued to make progress in the Bureau. In July 1929, Hoover sent a memo to Mr. Sornberger, an appointment clerk, directing him to prepare a letter transferring and promoting Clegg from assistant chief of Division No. 2 to special agent in the Bureau at a salary increase to $4,600 per annum.[45]

And Clegg knew how to please Hoover. He would often draft letters of response for Hoover's signature. Once Clegg drafted a letter for Hoover addressed to Congressman Will B. Hood of Indiana, who had recommended and provided a letter of introduction for Edward W. Parker for a position as special accountant in the Bureau. Hood thought he could use his influence to have the Bureau hire Parker. Clegg's letter for Hoover indicated that because the Bureau anticipated a deficit in appropriations, there would be no openings in the foreseeable future. Hoover responded to Clegg that he "liked the phraseology of your reply" and the issue apparently went away.[46]

As the 1920s came to an end, Clegg's career was highlighted by his involvement in two major cases: a scandal involving a commissioner on the US Shipping Board and an attempt to break up an important disarmament conference in Europe. President Herbert Hoover requested a special investigation involving a commissioner on the US Shipping Board. Although Congress had appropriated four billion dollars to the US Shipping Board, there was little accounting for the expenditure of these funds. A commissioner of the shipping board, a New York native, was, according to Clegg, a "jack leg labor leader and was placed on the board." The commissioner made a salary of $10,000 a year and after six or seven years he and his wife had $7,500 maximum savings deposits in every savings and loan office in town. At the time, New York law prohibited an individual from having a savings account in excess of $7,500 in any one institution, so the commissioner and his wife diversified their maximum accounts. The investigation also revealed that the commissioner owned a yacht on the Potomac and three Cadillac automobiles. Also, the commissioner and his family lived in a suite of rooms at Washington's swankiest hotel at the time.

Clegg learned the name of the commissioner's tailor and was told that the commissioner would buy two $125 suits and one $150 overcoat from two to three times a year—an expensive lifestyle for an individual who had no reported income aside from his commissioner's salary. Clegg prepared a report of his findings and sent it to President Herbert Hoover. Unfortunately for Clegg, Hoover sent it to the president of the Shipping Board who, in turn, sent it to the commissioner under suspicion. This was unfortunate for Clegg, because his sources in the shipping industry had not talked to him except under strict confidence. He had given his word that he would not disclose his sources.[47] Clegg did not discuss the final outcome of the investigation.

The second major case in which Clegg became involved in the late 1920s was related to special operations. Munitions manufacturers hired a public relations expert, William B. Shearer, to sabotage the 1927 Three Power Geneva Naval Conference at which the United States, Great Britain, and Japan were to meet and consider limitations to, and even elimination of, their naval forces. President

Coolidge had called upon the Five Powers who had signed the 1922 treaty limiting the size of their navies to consider expanding the scope of those limitations. The United States, Great Britain, and Japan accepted the invitation but France and Italy declined. The 1927 conference was a failure.

Shearer had the reputation of knowing everyone of importance in world capitals, and some suspected that without the help of William Randolph Hearst, he would not have had the resources to become involved in the conference.[48] Senator William Borah of Idaho introduced a resolution in the US Senate directing the Naval Affairs Committee to investigate Shearer's activities at that conference and appropriated ten thousand dollars for the investigation. The committee appointed a subcommittee comprised of Senators Henry Allen of Kansas, Joseph Robinson of Arkansas, and Samuel Shortridge of California to conduct the hearings. Four shipbuilding officials were summoned to appear before the committee to determine if they had been conducting propaganda to force the government to build more ships than it intended or desired and if they had hired Shearer to disrupt the 1927 conference. Clinton Bardo, president of the New York Shipbuilding Company, stated that

> in 1927 the uncertainty of the American shipbuilding industry was such as to make it of the utmost importance that the company be advised of the trend of the shipbuilding as indicated by the Geneva Conference and not shown in the press reports. There were many serious questions then as to whether or not the company could continue its shipbuilding activities. Shearer was commissioned by New York Shipbuilding Co. and others to act as an observer only at the Geneva Conference. Such observation was the sole question of Shearer's appointment. If Mr. Shearer, while in Geneva, twisted such limited employment into a broad commission to indulge in other activities, he did so without the knowledge of the New York Shipbuilding Co.[49]

Shearer had received $425,000 from Bethlehem, Newport News,

and American Brown-Boveri (of which the New York Shipbuild-ing Co. was a subsidiary) and then sued them for $225,000 more.[50] Shearer's involvement in putting covert pressure on the delegates at the conference might not have come to light had Shearer not filed that suit.[51]

A correspondent of the *New York Times*, Wythe Williams, said of Shearer, "If, as he says, he was employed to help wreck the Confer-ence, the opinion at Geneva would be that he earned his money." However, an investigation initiated by the State Department indi-cated that Shearer had "scant influence on American delegates and technical advisers at the conference."[52] The collapse of the gather-ing was a boon to the shipbuilding and steel industries. Shearer was quoted as saying, "As a result of my activities . . . eight new 10,000 ton cruisers are now under construction."[53] The FBI had also investi-gated the relationship of Shearer with the National Security League, an organization that promoted a strong military, among other na-tionalistic proposals, but found there were no strong ties between the two. Clegg played a major role in gathering information relating to Shearer's involvement in the 1927 Conference and attended all of the Senate hearings. The upshot was that Shearer's career as a lobby-ist ended, and he failed in his attempt to earn money by presenting lectures on the entire episode, as he could not attract decent-sized audiences.

The 1930s represented one of the most turbulent periods in the country's history, dominated by the economic Depression, the emer-gence of gangster-driven violence, and preparations for World War II. Clegg had completed almost five years at the Bureau at the turn of the decade, and his most important cases were yet to come. Many of his initial assignments involved the mundane process of interview-ing applicants and nominees for the positions of US attorney and US district judge. One of the major problems inherent in this process was that of confidentiality. Senators attempting to get someone ap-pointed put pressure on the attorney general, who would then re-veal to the senators negative information obtained from the Bureau about the nominee's life. The senators would share this information with the nominee, who was often told the source of the negative information, thus creating serious problems for the Bureau. But Clegg was adamant that the leaks did not come from within the Bureau, that all members of the staff were thoroughly screened. At Hoover's insistence, and with the support of Attorney General Harlan Stone, Bureau employees were now selected and investigated with deeper scrutiny.

Another task Clegg took quite to heart was recruiting new agents. For years, Clegg would spend the spring traveling to universities up and down the Atlantic Coast speaking to seniors in law school or accounting school about the rewards, challenges, and hazards of the job. His travels would take him as far south as Louisiana State University in Baton Rouge and would also bring him to the University of Mississippi and Mississippi State University. He always presented the job of an agent in the Bureau as being worse than it was in order to weed out applicants who might later become disgruntled.

In 1930, Clegg was designated as one of twenty-nine or thirty special agents in charge, meaning he was in charge of a field office. Clegg anticipated being transferred to the Kansas City office, but the peace conference and disarmament conference breakups and the shipping board fraud cases caused a change in plans. He became agent in charge of the Atlanta office.

Clegg's seemingly lackadaisical handling of paperwork, a deficiency noted in his first evaluation as an agent, continued to bring admonitions from the director. Clegg's FBI files contain numerous memos from Hoover admonishing him at every opportunity on matters that ranged from significant to petty. In every case Clegg would respond, usually apologizing for the problem and accepting blame. Hoover blamed Clegg for problems in the Atlanta office such as totally neglecting several cases when in fact the problems existed before Clegg arrived to take charge of that office.[54] Clegg promised to improve the situation at once.[55] When Clegg later become special agent in charge of the Atlanta office, Hoover complained that "the average number of cases closed per Agent in your district was 11.60, which is one of the lowest of the field offices."[56] Clegg responded by noting that it would take at least thirty days to correct this matter.[57]

However, the above issue must not have been too irritating to Hoover, because four days later he transferred Clegg from the Atlanta office to the one in Washington and told Clegg that he was "eminently qualified to perform the duties of Agent in Charge in that district."[58] Clegg did not remind Hoover that only a week or so earlier he liked being in the Atlanta office and hoped to remain there. Within a week, Hoover chastised Clegg again for the number of problems in the Atlanta office.[59] A month after Clegg was transferred to Washington, Hoover informed him that a number of similar problems were found in the Washington, DC, office.[60] Clegg responded that corrective measures had already been taken and noted that he needed more stenographic assistance.[61]

Despite the problems Clegg encountered with his paperwork, his evaluations continued to improve, and he received praise from Inspectors J. S. Egan and J. M. Keith and Agent C. A. Tolson, all of whom observed in a March 31, 1930, evaluation that "we feel that this Agent in Charge is fully qualified to handle an office of any size. He is conscientious, well informed, a hard worker, and a capable executive. We have placed him second in the Excellent group."[62]

Clegg did not fare as well when conducting his own evaluations of those for whom he was responsible, since these evaluations were judged to be too soft. Hoover complained that an agent who had been reported as unqualified to perform bankruptcy work or who performed in an unsatisfactory manner on the test ratings for the Bureau's manuals in the previous six months cannot be considered to be in either the Satisfactory or Excellent class and is not entitled to these ratings. Clegg responded with an apology.[63] The merry-go-round continued. Following an inspection of the Washington field office, Inspector Keith brought to Clegg's attention eighteen instances in which agents under Clegg's supervision had failed to file reports on cases on which they had worked. One instance involved the failure to submit fingerprints of a fugitive to the Identification

Division. Clegg pointed out that these fingerprints were received in the Washington office before he was assigned there. (Keith did note that Clegg made a grade of 99 percent on a test of the Manual of Instructions and 100 percent on the Manual of Rules and Regulations.[64]) The issue was not as important as Keith felt, since the 18 neglected cases represented a small percentage of the 546 cases the Washington field office had pending at the time. Less than a week later, Keith would retract his criticism and rated the situation of the Washington field office as being in excellent condition except that that there was a deplorable shortage of stenographers.[65]

Although no mention is made in his files, Clegg was moved to Chicago around 1930 as special agent in charge. Former acting agent in charge Melvin Purvis—who had a penchant for seeking publicity—was one of those serving under Clegg. An inspection of the Chicago office revealed problems similar to those that existed in Washington. Clegg was admonished by Hoover, but the criticism focused on the large number of typographical errors that appeared in Clegg's correspondence.[66]

Clegg's inability to adequately evaluate applicants again aroused Hoover's anger. Clegg had interviewed two potential agents and pointed out several deficiencies but nevertheless recommended them, saying they could become "better than average" agents. Hoover ridiculed him, pointing out that Clegg considered one of the candidates as "temperamental or almost effeminate in personal appearance" and yet recommended that he should be favorably considered. Hoover also noted that one candidate scored 60 percent on the special agents test and the other scored only 41 percent. Yet Clegg recommended them as agents.[67] In another instance, an inspector interviewed an applicant and found him to be "one of the poorest specimens he had ever interviewed." Clegg interviewed the same candidate and gave him a good recommendation, angering Hoover once again.[68]

Clegg's inability to evaluate applicants was a deficiency that plagued him throughout his FBI career. It is difficult to assess Clegg's relationship with Hoover. Clegg was always loyal to the director and was the recipient of glowing praise on several occasions. However, Hoover also admonished and chastised Clegg for blunders in handling paperwork. It is obvious that pushing paper was not one of Clegg's strong points.

Despite Clegg's problems with administrative paperwork, Hoover continued to place his trust in him and put him in charge of several projects and programs that would greatly enhance the Bureau's ability to fight crime and enhance the confidence that the public had in the FBI. Among Clegg's responsibilities was bringing efficiency and economy to FBI operations in areas such as organization, administration, investigation, personnel, and public relations.

In 1930 President Herbert Hoover established the US National Commission on Law Observance and Enforcement to perform the first federal review of law enforcement in the United States. Although its initial focus was on the effects of Prohibition on criminal activity, it was also charged with identifying causes of criminal activity and suggesting ways to deal with the problem. The commission recommended that law enforcement training be centralized and a set of standards for training be established throughout the nation. Because the Bureau of Investigation had established its own formal training of agents in the late 1920s, it became the obvious choice to establish a police training school. Director Hoover was quick to put the Bureau at the forefront in the training of law enforcement officers.

In December 1934, Attorney General Homer S. Cummings, appointed by President Franklin Roosevelt a year earlier, convened a National Crime Conference in Washington, DC, to generate public support for the Roosevelt administration's program on crime. The conference raised the issue of police professionalism and singled out small police departments for increased training in order to meet the threat posed by the existing crime problems of that day. One suggestion resulting from this conference was the idea of developing a structure that would deal with all aspects of crime and become a focal point for the dissemination of information regarding crime prevention and law enforcement techniques of value in eliminating crime to all parts of the country.

Reacting to this conference, Director Hoover created the first Police Training School, later named the FBI National Academy, whose main objective was to raise the level of police professionalism nationwide by training local police officers. The announcement of the formation of the academy received immediate support from law enforcement organizations such as the International Association of Chiefs of Police. Hoover conceived the idea of a National Academy to train police and new agents in the latest law enforcement techniques. While the principal objective of the academy would be to raise the level of professionalism in law enforcement nationwide, it would also establish the Bureau as a model of professionalism for local and state police.[69]

In the late spring of 1934, Hoover called Clegg to his office and assigned him the responsibility of designing a training curriculum, recruiting a teaching faculty, securing FBI agents to constitute the core faculty, and organizing and operating the education and training activities of the FBI. He was also given the responsibility of establishing the academy.[70] Hoover gave him one month to develop the plan. Since Clegg had served the Bureau as assistant director in charge of training and inspection, he was the logical candidate to head the new training school.

Clegg set out to recruit leading criminologists, law professors, and other law enforcement experts to create a faculty. He traveled up and down the East Coast and was successful in recruiting personnel from institutions such as Yale, Harvard, Vanderbilt, Columbia, Johns Hopkins, the City College of New York, Georgetown University, the University of Cincinnati, and Northwestern.[71] Clegg also recruited experienced state and local police and executives. He worked closely with the International Association of Chiefs of Police to establish the curriculum.

In 1935 Congress authorized the establishment of the FBI National Police Training School. The school was renamed the FBI

National Police Academy in 1936 and the FBI National Academy in 1945.[72] On July 29, 1935, just seven months after the attorney general's conference, the FBI's National Academy program started when Special Agent Hugh H. Clegg greeted a class of twenty-three eager police officers for the first session of the FBI National Police Training School.[73] The school soon moved from the Department of Justice building into the Old Post Office building. Later it was moved to Quantico, Virginia. The curriculum offered by the academy soon grew to include courses in law, management, communications, behavioral science, terrorism, money laundering, scientific and technical methods of controlling crime, statistics, report writing, international crime, and ethics and conduct.[74] During World War II, courses were added in combating espionage and sabotage. By the time Clegg left the FBI, one hundred thousand policemen had been given the benefits of training in these programs. The first FBI Manual of Rules and Regulations was published by the academy. Despite concerns expressed by some members of Congress, the FBI never urged the formation of a national police force. Clegg would always emphasize that "there's no place in America for a national police force."[75] An FBI training building consisting of an indoor firing range, an armory, a dining room, kitchen, five classrooms, and a gymnasium was eventually constructed on the Marine base at Quantico to house future classes of the academy.

The academy was selective in accepting participants and picked only the best and the brightest applicants. Enrollment was limited to two hundred students a year. The school offered a twelve-week training course that educated the participants on the latest law enforcement techniques and equipment. Each graduate of the school was provided a diploma signed by the director, an inscribed photograph of the graduate posed with Hoover, and automatic membership in the alumni association of the school, the FBI National Academy Associates. A key benefit of the school was that the contact which graduates maintained with local FBI field offices and their FBI contacts provided Hoover with a direct connection to local police organizations. With time, the number of graduates rose each year, and about

30 percent of those who completed the training program assumed executive leadership positions in local law enforcement. While the rewards of attending the school were great, the cost of attendance was significant, so each student selected originally received a thirty-five-cents-per-day living allowance. Clegg considered the organization and establishment of the FBI National Academy to be his most satisfying achievement during the time he was at the FBI.[76]

Another of Clegg's major accomplishments was authoring the FBI Pledge for Law Enforcement Officers, although he would receive little credit for it. In 1937, the Executive Congress of the FBI recommended that the pledge be named after Director Hoover and be referred to as the J. Edgar Hoover Pledge. However, Assistant Director Clyde Tolson, a close friend of Hoover, felt uncomfortable and suggested that the pledge be referred to as the FBI Pledge for Law Enforcement Officers. Hoover concurred.[77]

Because of his ability to establish and maintain close relationships with many key political figures, Clegg became a valuable weapon in the lobbying efforts the FBI had to wage to achieve legislative support and to pass bills of interest to the Bureau. Clegg was, in fact, the legislative liaison for the FBI. Prior to the Lindbergh baby kidnapping and the consequent expansion of FBI jurisdiction by making kidnapping a federal crime, the Bureau lobbied and otherwise fought against expansion of its jurisdiction into certain other crimes. For example, Clegg used his political contacts to kill ensuing bills such as a measure that would have required chickens to be tattooed under one wing or the other so they could be identified if they were stolen and transported in interstate commerce. The bill never passed.[78]

In the 1930s, Hoover loaned Clegg to the House Appropriations Committee for several months. But not all of his work with the committee involved matters affecting the FBI. Clegg was often directed by the committee to investigate a request made by a department to determine if the request was vital or useful, necessary or unnecessary. For example, the Rural Electrification Administration (REA) had a request before the committee for millions of dollars to purchase copper wire. Clegg put together a team of investigators that found eighty million dollars in copper wire stored by a previous administration in warehouses for which the REA had no record.[79]

Clegg took particular pride in establishing a retirement program for FBI agents. Despite many efforts by the attorney general and Director Hoover to establish a program, their requests had been denied by Congress because FBI agents did not fall into the class of civil service personnel. Clegg was acquainted with radio reporter Walter Winchell and told him of the efforts of the Bureau to reward its agents. Winchell bought into the need for such a program and brought the issue to the attention of his radio audience on several occasions. The public relations effort reached the attention of Congress, and when Clegg and Attorney General Tom Clark appeared before the Senate and House appropriations committees, they were successful in securing a retirement program.[80]

Clegg's career with the FBI was marked by a continuing battle with minor health problems. The extensive annual physical examinations that he and other agents were required to undergo reflected the interest Director Hoover had in maintaining the health of his agents. Hoover would directly inform Clegg of most of the examination results. In 1936, his examination disclosed the following defects in his health: athlete's foot, a slight varicocele in his left side, and bronchitic changes in both lungs that did not affect strenuous physical exertion and did not interfere with the use of firearms. Clegg admitted to smoking cigars and cigarettes and indulging in alcohol on occasion. His vision was excellent and needed no correction. He stood five feet nine inches tall and weighed 192 pounds. His blood pressure was 130/78. Following another examination, Hoover wrote Clegg chiding him for being seven and one-half pounds overweight and ordered him to lose that excess weight within the next six months.[81] Clegg met that goal, but his weight subsequently increased. By January 1952 it was up to 225 pounds and his blood pressure had climbed to 186/98.[82] Clegg visited his own physician a month later and his blood pressure measurement had dropped considerably by that time.

Clegg was a team player and was a good company man. In response to a Bureau memo to its agents requesting suggestions regarding existing rules of the Bureau, he sent several memos to the director expressing ways the efficiency and performance of the FBI could be improved. Hoover acknowledged receipt of the suggestions and commended him on his interest in the Bureau's work.[83] To Hoover's pleasure, Clegg submitted suggestions for amendments of the Manual of Rules and Regulations and the Manual of Instruction. Clegg paid attention to minute detail, one time informing Hoover that the locks on the briefcases used by Bureau accountants could be opened with a simple paper clip with little difficulty. He urged Hoover to furnish more substantial locks, and the director responded with enthusiasm.[84]

Clegg continued to perform well, and he was promoted to the important position of an assistant director of the FBI; his salary gradually increased as well. Clegg had established himself among the hierarchy of the Bureau and would become involved in many interesting cases and situations as he continued to serve the Bureau.

Chapter Three

Making Important Contacts

If you haven't got anything nice to say about anybody,
come sit next to me.—Alice Roosevelt Longworth

CLEGG'S BACKGROUND IN DECLAMATION AND PUBLIC
speaking would serve him well in both his FBI and Ole Miss
careers. He had an easygoing, southern style of speaking
that enabled him to establish rapport with his audiences. People
tended to like him upon first meeting. He became a popular public
speaker and gave hundreds of speeches to community civic groups,
law enforcement organizations, state bar association meetings, high
school and college groups, and alumni meetings. He was an effective representative of the Bureau, and his files are full of letters and
messages praising him for his speaking engagements and thanking Hoover for sending him to represent the Bureau. Charles A.
Freiberg, president of the Judges and Police Executive Conference,
wrote Hoover praising Clegg for addressing a banquet, stating that
Clegg delivered a "masterful address."[1] Marston T. Bogert, president
of the combined meeting of the Institute of Arts and Sciences and
the Sigma Xi Scientific Honor Society devoted to a discussion of science in the detection of crime, wrote Hoover praising the "splendid
address" Clegg delivered to 1,200 attendees.[2] The *Hartford Courant*
ran an article describing Clegg's speech to the University Club of
Hartford in which he dispelled several myths regarding the FBI, for
example, its ostensible "shoot to kill" policy and the Bureau's attitude
in kidnapping cases where the family negotiates the release of a hostage on its own.[3]

Clegg made a presentation before the 20th Century Club of the Daughters of the American Revolution and received a letter from the committee secretary, Paul Scharf, praising him for his "splendid address." Scharf went on to say that "you are doing a marvelous educational work for the welfare of this country and we wish the sob-sisters could hear all of it. Interest was keen every moment and an exhilaration surpassing the reading of the finest detective story [*sic*]."[4] John Maude of the British Embassy wrote Hoover to thank him for allowing Clegg to address an audience of "the '41–'42 group" of Britons and wished that Hoover had been there to hear "the prolonged applause going on and on, and seen the warmth of feeling as well as the appreciation."[5] A memorandum from a J. S. Rogers to Clegg recalled a visit the two had in the lobby of a hotel. Rogers indicated that after Clegg departed, an unidentified individual remarked to him, "There is a fine man. I have never heard anyone say anything that wasn't good about Mr. Clegg."[6]

Through these speaking opportunities, Clegg made many important contacts. One of Clegg's major strengths was his ability to establish close relationships with influential appointed or elected national and state politicians and jurists, in particular Vice President Charles Curtis, Attorney General Homer Cummings, and Justices Earl Warren and Tom Clark. He would use these contacts to promote the FBI or resolve problems affecting the Bureau.

One of his solid contacts was Charles Curtis, the thirty-first vice president of the United States. Clegg was in Phoenix, Arizona, when he received a telephone call from Hoover telling him to come to Washington at once. Clegg had never flown in an airplane but flew to Dallas for the night. The next morning, he flew to Cincinnati and caught a train to Washington. He arrived in DC at 8:30 the next morning and went straight to Hoover's office to be briefed and was told to go to Vice President Curtis's office. President Herbert Hoover had been invited to go to Los Angeles to address the Motion Picture Academy of Arts and Sciences Banquet at which the Oscars were presented. President Hoover sent Vice President Curtis to attend in his place, and Clegg was to accompany Curtis to prevent any attempt to use the presence of the vice president in a promotional scheme of some sort.

Curtis was the nation's only vice president to have Native American ancestry, and he had lived with his maternal grandparents on the Kaw reservation in Kansas. Up to that time, he was the only candidate of known mixed race to win on a presidential ticket. As of this writing, he was also the last vice president or president to don a beard or mustache. Although lacking formal education, he passed a bar examination at the age of twenty-one. In an age when political correctness was an unknown concept, he was called Indian Charlie. Despite being in a powerful position in Congress to address issues affecting Native Americans, Curtis often took positions on issues that were not in their best interests. He proposed a law giving away Native American mining rights, a law that he would claim as one of his greatest achievements. He believed that it was in the best interest of Native Americans to assimilate into the white man's society, drop their Native languages, and abandon all their customs.

His half-sister, the controversial Mrs. Edward Everett Dolly Gann, was part of the entourage that went to Los Angeles for the Academy Awards. Dolly was purported to be the first woman to actively campaign during a presidential election.

Curtis's wife, Annie Elizabeth Baird, died of pneumonia in 1924, and when Curtis was elected vice president as Herbert Hoover's running mate in 1928, he assumed that Dolly would take on the responsibilities of being his official hostess, fulfilling the role of the wife of the vice president. She had helped Curtis campaign as far back as his election to the House in 1893 and had even acted as his secretary for over twenty years.

Dolly Gann was the subject of a public controversy with Alice Roosevelt Longworth over issues of protocol. Alice was married to Nicholas Longworth, Speaker of the House of Representatives. Both Longworth and Gann were outspoken, so a clash appeared to be inevitable. Dolly was well-known in Washington, and since Curtis was a widower, he designated his sister to be the Second First Lady of the White House.

A feud between Dolly Gann and Alice Roosevelt Longworth began when Curtis was elected.[7] Alice, wife of Speaker of the House Nicholas Longworth and daughter of former President Teddy Roosevelt (and thus also known as Princess Alice), was a significant player in the Washington social scene, and she also claimed the right to be called the second first lady.[8]

Clegg had to handle protocol delicately for Dolly Gann when he accompanied Vice President Curtis on the trip to Los Angeles. Curtis brought her along on the trip. He liked Clegg and told him of his background and how he was raised on the Kaw reservation and raced ponies when the Indians would come into a town. Curtis bragged that his horse almost always ended up the winner.

The entourage arrived in Los Angeles and was met by Louis B. Mayer of the Metro-Goldwyn-Mayer movie studio and a Republican leader in southern California. Clegg, Dolly, and Curtis spent the night at Mayer's home in Santa Monica, and the next day they went to the banquet held at the Biltmore Hotel. Clegg helped Curtis practice his speech, which turned out to be about forty-five minutes long. Curtis had not been advised what he was to talk about and had little to do with the awards themselves. Instead, he covered topics in which the audience had no interest, so it was bored and inattentive, showing him little respect. In private conversations, Dolly Gann expressed her outrage regarding the disrespect shown to the vice president.[9] The whole program lasted so long that the nine-year-old actor Jackie Cooper, nominated for best actor for his role in *Skippy*—the first child actor to be nominated for an Academy Award—fell asleep.[10]

Ten days later, Curtis wrote Hoover thanking the director for sending Clegg with him and praising Clegg for making Curtis's trip pleasant. "I cannot speak too highly of his splendid service," Curtis said. Hoover wrote Clegg on November 25, advising him of the letter from Curtis and thanking him for the way he handled this assignment.[11]

Clegg and Curtis hit it off so well that word got back to President Hoover. In 1932, Hoover asked Curtis to represent him at the Opening Ceremony of the X Olympiad in Los Angeles to officially open the Olympic Games. This marked only the second time in the modern games that an elected sitting head of government of the host country did not appear. The president was too busy campaigning for his reelection and was advised by his campaign manager that since the games never attracted large crowds, his appearance there would be a waste of time. Earlier that year, Hoover had not attended the Winter Olympics held in Lake Placid, New York. President Hoover was not well liked by Curtis and the feeling was mutual, but they never revealed their personal relationship in public. Curtis battled Hoover for the Republican nomination in 1928 but lost. Hoover turned to Curtis for his running mate, hoping Curtis could help get the vote in the Midwest farm states. The strategy worked, but president Hoover consulted his vice president only on rare occasions, and the two never enjoyed a close relationship. Curtis asked Director Hoover to allow Clegg to accompany him to Los Angeles. Dolly Gann did not make this trip.

Because of the economic Depression affecting the country and the world, only half the number of athletes who had participated in the 1928 Olympics were able to afford the trip. International relations were quite tense, especially between Japan and China following Japan's takeover of Manchuria. Yet over 105,000 spectators attended the opening ceremony and President Hoover missed a much-needed opportunity to appear before a large crowd. Despite economic conditions, the Olympics ended with a clear profit. Curtis had prepared a speech but did not present it because it was not part of the customary ritual. Instead, he simply declared, "I proclaim open the Olympic Games of Los Angeles, celebrating the tenth Olympiad of the modern era." Not surprisingly, this speech was much better received than his presentation at the recent Academy Awards banquet. These two trips bonded Clegg and Curtis and they became reasonably good friends.[12]

Clegg also became a close friend of Attorney General Homer

Cummings, who was appointed to that office by the new president, Franklin D. Roosevelt. Cummings was born in Chicago, received a law degree from Yale, and became actively involved in the Democratic Party, obtaining the post of chairman of the Democratic National Committee. Earlier in his career as a state attorney in Connecticut, he earned a reputation as an advocate for prison reform. Roosevelt rewarded Cummings's service and commitment to the Democratic Party by selecting him to serve as the governor-general of the Philippines, but when Roosevelt's initial choice for the attorney general post, Senator Thomas J. Walsh of Montana, passed away from a heart attack suffered on his way to attend Roosevelt's inauguration, Roosevelt appointed Cummings to head the Justice Department.

Cummings made an immediate impact on the Bureau of Investigation, strengthening it by expanding its authority. On July 1, 1933, he created a Division of Investigation that merged the Bureau of Investigation (renamed the United States Bureau of Investigation in 1932), the Prohibition Bureau, and the Bureau of Identification. But confusion regarding the title of the division led to changing its name in 1935 to the Federal Bureau of Investigation, which was more descriptive.

The period of 1933–1934 was a tumultuous time for crime in the United States. In addition to the pursuit of John Dillinger and other notorious gangsters such as Pretty Boy Floyd, Baby Face Nelson, Machine Gun Kelly, and Alvin Karpis, prominent kidnapping cases were being investigated, including the kidnappings of Texas oilman Charles Urschel, Minnesota brewery owner William Hamm, and Minnesota banker Edward Bremer Jr. The Bureau credits Cummings with coining the term *Public Enemy Number One*, thus popularizing the pursuit of criminals.[13]

Clegg was involved in coordinating activities of the Bureau by directing the search for Dillinger and investigating two of the prominent kidnappings (those of Bremer and Hamm). He had been assigned to the St. Paul, Minnesota, office because of reports that John Dillinger was thought to be in that area.

Director Hoover interrupted Clegg's St. Paul assignment to inform him that he was wanted as soon as possible back in Washington. Attorney General Cummings had informed Hoover that he was about to take a six-week trip and wanted Clegg to accompany him. The stated purposes of the trip were to inspect penitentiaries at Fort Leavenworth in Kansas, McNeil Island in Washington state, and Alcatraz in California; to inspect land that the government was going to acquire to enlarge the Pearl Harbor Naval Base; and to inspect national parks in Hawaii along with Yellowstone Park, primarily in Wyoming, and Glacier Park in Montana. In truth, the trip was a six-week junket lasting from July 22 until September 5, 1934. Among those making the trip with Cummings and his wife were Stanley Reed, general counsel for the Reconstruction Finance Corporation and later an associate justice of the Supreme Court, and his wife, and Mrs. Emily Newell Blair, a writer for and editor of *Good Housekeeping*, and her husband, Harry Wallace Blair, who was an assistant attorney general in the Lands Division of the Justice Department under Cummings.

Emily Blair was from Missouri and was a founder of the League of Women Voters. She also served as national vice chairman of the Democratic Party.[14] She was much better known than her husband, Harry, who was appointed assistant attorney general in 1933. Cummings appointed Harry Blair to this position when the previous nominee, George Sweeney, was reassigned to the Claims Division of the attorney general's office. Emily Blair had let it be known that she hoped that her reward for working so hard for the Democratic Party and the election of FDR would be a federal appointment for her husband. Also making the trip was Hugo Carusi, executive assistant to the attorney general. While the government paid for most of the expenses of the trip, only Cummings's were totally covered. For example, Harry Blair was given six hundred dollars traveling expenses and the trip cost him an additional five hundred dollars. Emily Newell Blair had been paid one thousand dollars for an article she wrote for *Liberty* magazine, which helped cover her expenses.

Although Stanley Reed was a Democrat, Herbert Hoover appointed him to be the new general counsel of the Federal Farm Board in 1929, and just as Hoover was leaving office he appointed him as the new general counsel of the Reconstruction Finance Corporation. Roosevelt retained him in that position when he became president. Reed was appointed solicitor general in 1935 and won many important cases (e.g., upholding minimum wage laws, the National Labor Relations Act, and the taxing power of the Social Security Administration). He earned the reputation of being one of the strongest solicitor generals since the creation of the office in 1870. Roosevelt later nominated him to the Supreme Court to replace Justice George Sutherland, and he was confirmed in ten days. Reed and Cummings became close friends when the Roosevelt administration appointed Reed as a special assistant to the attorney general to assist Cummings in writing the brief for the government and also to assist him in oral arguments in the controversial Roosevelt Gold Clause Cases regarding President Roosevelt's decision to remove the United States from the gold standard. Within one month following the government's victory in these cases, Reed was appointed solicitor general.[15]

Cummings was careful to plan his trip to Hawaii so it would not conflict with the July 24–28, 1934, visit of President Roosevelt, the first sitting president to visit Hawaii. Roosevelt had appointed Joseph Poindexter, a fellow member of the Benevolent and Protective Order of the Elks, as the territorial governor of Hawaii earlier that year. The president had taken a twelve-thousand-mile vacation cruise aboard the USS *Houston* starting on July 1 at Annapolis, a cruise that took him to the Virgin Islands, Puerto Rico, Colombia, through the Panama Canal, and then on to Hawaii.

Cummings's entourage began the trip by taking a train from Washington to Kansas City. Clegg was the first to arrive at the station, followed by Cummings and his wife. Cummings said that Edgar, as he called J. Edgar Hoover, told him to tell Clegg that John Dillinger had been shot in front of a theater in Chicago. The first destination after the delegation left Washington was Chicago, where a large number of photographers and reporters met the train to get Cummings's reaction to the Dillinger killing.

The group then went on to Kansas City to inspect Leavenworth prison, located nearby. Clegg carried a snub-nosed pistol all through the tour, although it was against prison rules and regulations. When the group was asked if any of them carried firearms, Clegg did not lie—he just did not answer. Cummings knew Clegg was carrying a pistol and told him that he was establishing a bad precedent. Clegg, however, felt his major responsibility was to protect the attorney general, especially when the group visited the prison shoe shop where prisoners worked on leather with knives.[16]

The group's members then proceeded to Los Angeles, where they were met by Harry Warner of the Warner Brothers movie studios. The Warner brothers (Harry, Albert, Sam, and Jack) worked hard for Roosevelt in California in the 1932 election. As Clegg recalled it, Harry Warner took the group to the studios to watch Ann Sothern and James Cagney shooting a film.[17]

After the movie tour, the group boarded a ship to San Francisco and spent a day inspecting Alcatraz. Alcatraz became a possession of the United States as a result of the treaty with Mexico ending the Mexican war in 1848. The US Army used the island as a fortified military site from 1859 to 1933, when it was transferred to the Department of Justice. The army first used it as a prison in 1861 to house Confederate Civil War prisoners, knowing escape from the island would be impossible. From 1909 to 1911, the prisoners built a new prison on Alcatraz that became known as The Rock. Because it was not able to sustain the cost of operating the prison, the army decided to close the facility in 1934.

In the early 1930s, there were only three federal prisons in the country: at Leavenworth, Kansas; McNeil Island in Puget Sound, Washington state; and Atlanta, Georgia—all of which were almost as well known for famous escapes as for their ability to safely incarcerate hardened criminals. Cummings is credited with originating the idea of using Alcatraz as a special maximum security federal prison to house dangerous gangsters spawned by the crime wave of the Depression era. In 1933 Cummings suggested creating "a special prison for racketeers, kidnappers, and others guilty of predatory crimes" located in a remote place or island.[18] He jumped at the opportunity to obtain Alcatraz from the War Department.

When the entourage arrived at Alcatraz, it had just been converted to a federal prison. The government then fortified Alcatraz into a maximum-security prison, a step designed to let the American public know it was serious in its fight against the crime wave of the 1930s.[19] When the attorney general inspected the prison, no prisoners were yet housed there. The first group of fourteen prisoners from the McNeil Island penitentiary arrived at Alcatraz on August 11, 1934. Soon famous gangsters were imprisoned there. Later that month, the prison's most famous inmate, Al Capone, arrived in a group of fifty-two other prisoners. Cummings and Sanford Bates, head of federal prisons, had made arrangements to have Capone transferred from the Atlanta penitentiary where Capone was able to flaunt his power and manipulate the system.

On this point there seems to be some confusion. Many sources say the first prisoners, including Capone, arrived on August 11, 1934. However, a book about Capone states that Cummings made a final inspection on Saturday night, August 18, 1934, and that Capone was transferred from Atlanta aboard a special train among the fifty-three shackled prisoners that arrived on August 22.[20] Capone was among the early prisoners to be incarcerated at the "new" Alcatraz, but not in the first group. He was assigned prison number AZ #85. Frank Bolt, convicted of sodomy, was given the dubious honor of being AZ #1![21]

James A. Johnston, the first warden of Alcatraz, conducted the tour, and the entourage was given freedom to move about the prison. Cummings was pleased that his idea of creating a prison for the nation's most dangerous criminals had become a reality. When the tour was complete, the group boarded the Matson Navigation Company's flagship liner, the SS *Lurline*, and set out for Hawaii. William Matson, a US shipping executive, built four fast, luxurious vessels to make the West Coast–Hawaii run. The *Lurline*, named after Matson's daughter, Lurline Berenice, was the third. Matson also owned the Royal Hawaiian Hotel, where the group planned to stay. Two and a half days after the group was out to sea, Cummings received a cablegram from Warden Johnson that read "FIFTY THREE CRATES OF FURNITURE FROM ATLANTA RECEIVED IN GOOD CONDITION INSTALLED NO BREAKAGE," the prearranged code indicating that Al Capone and the rest of the prisoners from Atlanta had all arrived.[22]

While the group was aboard the *Lurline*, Clegg ingratiated himself with the attorney general by working out a reduced lodging fee at the Royal Hawaiian Hotel. Clegg met with the hotel representative who was aboard the liner and later related the following conversation:

> Listen, here's the Attorney General of the United States, a member of the President's cabinet, he could be making hundreds of thousands of dollars as a lawyer practicing; he had a large practice out of Connecticut; here are these other people who are serving their government, Mr. Blair and Mrs. Blair, Mr. Reed and Mrs. Reed and so on. I said, "Is there any way that you could arrange for us to have a special rate at the hotel? These people are, at great sacrifice, serving the nation."
>
> The attorney general had reserved the Presidential Suite, which I think was thirty-five dollars a day, which was a high price in those days. The next day the representative called me to one side and said, "I've heard from my hotel. You know, you'll get meals included with the price of the rooms and would it be too much if we suggested the nominal sum of five dollars a day for each person?" So, we had the Royal Hawaiian and each had his room or suite . . . five dollars a day including three meals. Of course, we took a lot of meals outside, the people entertained us. That was an interesting experience.[23]

Five dollars a day for a suite with sitting rooms between their rooms was not a bad price, indeed.

When the group arrived in Hawaii, it was met by the governor, an admiral, and an army air force general and was invited to their homes. Cummings insisted he had a policy of "we accept for all eight of us or none." The group was entertained by the Democratic Party at a luau. Clegg recalled hearing Cummings say he was glad that he could be "at a strictly nonpolitical, objective, fair minded, one hundred percent democratic meeting." The group's members were treated to "all the advantages seldom given anybody."[24] They would not let the opportunity of visiting Hawaii pass by without making side trips to some of the other islands.

After completing its Hawaii "business," the group went to Portland, Oregon, and then on to McNeil Island, located south of Seattle, Washington, to tour the McNeil Island Corrections Center. This, the oldest prison facility in the Northwest, opened in 1875 on a site of more than twenty-seven acres of land. Cummings inspected the facility as a prelude to his announcement in 1935 that the federal government would seek to condemn and purchase land on McNeil Island and build another "American Devil's Island" similar to that at Alcatraz.[25] McNeil Island thus became home for the largest prison in the country. The entire island would be under federal control. The facility closed in 2011 after housing prisoners for more than 135 years.

The group then inspected Glacier National Park and Yellowstone National Park on the flimsy basis that the Lands Division of the Justice Department did the legal work for the Department of Interior for all national forests. One of the members of the entourage, Harry Blair, was, conveniently, an assistant attorney general in the Lands Division under Cummings's jurisdiction. When they arrived at Glacier, they were met at the train station by a fleet of three Rolls-Royces owned by a wealthy person in Butte, Montana, whom Clegg did not identify (although it was reported that the group would be the guests of influential Democrats Mr. and Mrs. J. Bruce Kremer).[26] Needless to say, the group was entertained almost like royalty, and

Clegg claimed that this was one of his most memorable experiences at the FBI.

Homer Cummings was one of the most effective attorneys general while Clegg was in Washington. He increased federal jurisdiction without overextending police power and was responsible for enhancing the effectiveness of the FBI through the kidnapping law, the bank robbery law, and by gaining the approval of Congress for agents to carry firearms and to make arrests. Cummings merged the Justice Department's Bureau of Investigation, the Prohibition Bureau, and the Bureau of Identification into the renamed Federal Bureau of Investigation, all under the direction of J. Edgar Hoover.

Among other important contacts, Clegg developed a close business relationship and personal friendship with Senator Everett McKinley Dirksen of Illinois. Dirksen, the Republican Senate minority leader, was an important and imposing figure in American politics, serving in the US House of Representatives for sixteen years and then in the US Senate from 1951 until his death in 1969. Two of his major accomplishments in the Senate were helping write both the Civil Rights Act of 1964 and the Open Housing Act of 1968.[27] Dirksen was a member of the House Appropriations Committee when Director Hoover sent Clegg there as the committee's first chief of staff. Senator Dirksen also became well-known for his famous quote regarding the out-of-control federal spending: "A billion here, a billion there, and pretty soon you're talking real money."

Clegg conducted investigations requested by the committee and recruited investigators from all government services to assist him. He worked hard to establish contact with the cabinet officer or administrative assistant of each department. As Clegg's friendship with Dirksen developed, the congressman would bring personal problems as well as official problems to Clegg's attention, often asking Clegg for advice. Once Dirksen approached Clegg with a problem that he became aware of while serving on the board of trustees of an unnamed midwestern university. (Dirksen did not want his university affiliation known when discussing these problems.) Dirksen had received reports that narcotics and other unauthorized drugs were being sold at a designated spot on the university campus and asked for Clegg's help in investigating the reports. Clegg informed Dirksen that the FBI did not investigate illegal drugs but would refer the matter to the Bureau of Narcotics. Clegg did not discuss the outcome of that investigation. On another occasion, Dirksen informed Clegg that he had received information that a prominent Illinois citizen was a homosexual who would often accompany the university basketball team on road trips and was accused of making "improper approaches" to some of the players. Dirksen asked for Clegg's counsel in that matter, but again Clegg did not discuss the outcome of that investigation.

Years later—around the time of the Meredith integration crisis at Ole Miss—Clegg accompanied University of Mississippi's chancellor, J. D. Williams, on a business trip to Washington. Williams knew of Clegg's relationship with Senator Dirksen, so they paid Dirksen a visit and pleaded with him, knowing Dirksen's opposition to segregation, "Senator, we are harassed in Mississippi over this integration situation. Give us some breathing room, please sir!" Dirksen told them he would go to Senators Eastland and Stennis, "and I'll tell them that I haven't changed my philosophy, but I'll do my timing in collaboration with them." Clegg credits Dirksen, an avowed integrationist, with giving Mississippi some breathing room.[28]

Another important contact for Clegg was Earl Warren, who would later become chief justice of the Supreme Court. Warren served as the district attorney in Alameda County, California, as the state attorney general, and then as a three-term governor of California. He was a candidate for vice president as Tom Dewey's running mate against Harry Truman in 1948 and was a favorite son candidate for the Republican nomination for president in 1952, when Dwight Eisenhower was nominated and elected. Eisenhower selected Richard Nixon to be his running mate but promised Warren the position of solicitor general and would later nominate him to the Supreme Court. Eisenhower would hold true to his promise, and when a position to the nation's highest court opened in 1953, he selected Warren as a recess appointment. Warren's liberal bent would later cause Eisenhower to second-guess his decision, but Warren would earn the reputation of being one of the most important jurists of the twentieth century. Clegg first met him when Warren was a district attorney, and they attended law enforcement conventions, judicial conferences, and US attorney's conferences. Prior to rulings by the so-called Warren Court after Warren became chief justice, the FBI was in doubt as to exactly what constituted a civil rights violation. In the 1920s, the Bureau was not allowed to initiate on its own any investigation of civil rights violations.

Clegg told a story about a case he had been involved with in Georgia that seems almost unbelievable. A farm owner had blacks working for him and he made sure they would become in debt to him by sending them to his commissary as soon as they began working—a violation of peonage laws. The owner got word after a period of time that some of the blacks were going to report him for making them stay on and work against their will to pay off their debt. The farmer's lawyer advised him that what he was doing was against the law. So the owner unbelievably began to kill workers. According to Clegg, the farmer would chain two workers together and throw them off a bridge that crossed a river on his land, thinking this would count as one murder rather than two. He would toss the heaviest one first so the lighter one would be dragged into the river. He killed several of his workers in this fashion. The farmer was found guilty and sentenced to ninety-nine years in prison and his associates, some of them blacks, also were sentenced to ninety-nine-year prison terms. The agency, however, was not allowed, under orders of the Justice Department, to initiate any investigation of violations of civil rights.[29]

Hoover assigned Clegg to go to California, and he stayed in Sacramento for six weeks to inspect and analyze audit details regarding one of the subagencies under Hoover's supervision. Clegg and Warren served on the criminal law committee of the American Bar Association (ABA), and they were the only two committee members who attended the panel's meetings. Later, when Warren came to Washington as the California attorney general, the two would get together to exchange suggestions regarding law enforcement. Warren would write up the suggestions and submit the notes to the ABA as the report from their committee.

Clegg used his contact with Chief Justice Warren when he went to the University of Mississippi after retiring from the FBI. On one occasion he was in Washington with his boss, Chancellor J. D. Williams, and the president of the Ole Miss alumni association, Bill Griffin. Showing off his influential contacts, Clegg asked them if they would like to meet the Chief Justice. Clegg sought an appointment to see Warren but was told that he was out of the office. Later that afternoon, the chancellor and Griffin were in the lobby of the Supreme Court building when they heard an announcement over the loudspeaker, "Mr. Clegg, the Chief Justice calling Mr. Clegg."[30] An arrangement was made for an appointment the next day. Clegg, Williams, and Griffin had a congenial forty-five minute meeting with Warren, but Clegg did not disclose the topics covered.

Pushing its good fortune, the delegation then went to meet with Associate Justice Tom Clark. Clark had been appointed to the Supreme Court by President Truman in 1949, an appointment Truman would call the biggest mistake of his presidency.[31] He had been appointed attorney general by Truman in 1945. Clegg attended US attorney conferences on a regular basis; so did Clark, and they struck up a friendship. Clark was more politically oriented than Clegg, who was more reticent. Clark would give a big party at each of these seven or eight conferences. Clegg took Williams and Griffin to see Clark, who was in the Supreme Court building gymnasium at the time. When he was advised that these visitors wished to meet with him, Clark got dressed and rushed upstairs. The chancellor and Griffin were impressed by Clegg's connections and hoped those contacts would benefit the university.

Clegg came to know several justices of the Supreme Court in addition to Warren and Clark, including Stanley Reed, whom he met during the Cummings trip to Hawaii, and Robert H. Jackson, who was the chief US prosecutor at the Nuremberg trials.

Clegg forged contacts with key leaders at all levels of government.

Another valuable connection was Fiorello LaGuardia, then mayor of the City of New York. Clegg met LaGuardia while attending a meeting of the Sheriff's Association of North Carolina held in Wilmington, where Clegg made a presentation to the group. LaGuardia was present, a fact that did not go unnoticed by Clegg, who in his speech referred to the statesmanship of the mayor and mentioned how Director Hoover had referred to LaGuardia's support for the Bureau on many occasions when LaGuardia was in Congress. Clegg also referred to the role LaGuardia played in the development of the Bureau. After the speech, LaGuardia sat beside Clegg and praised Hoover for the fine work the Bureau was doing under his direction. LaGuardia asked Clegg "that his love be extended to Edgar."[32] Clegg assured LaGuardia that the feeling was mutual.

Following the meeting, LaGuardia, his wife, and Clegg were, by chance, on the same train heading to Washington. LaGuardia invited Clegg to join them in their stateroom and "after a few highballs" insisted that Clegg join them for dinner. The mayor was in a good mood and began discussing the Louis "Lepke" Buchalter case. Buchalter (his nickname Lepke was Yiddish for "Little Louie"), whose only known occupation was that of being a criminal, was considered the bloodiest Jewish gangster of all time and one of the most powerful figures in organized crime. LaGuardia had been elected as a reformer and took on the gangsters. New York City was offering a $25,000 reward for the capture of Buchalter on a murder charge. The federal government matched the reward offer on narcotics charges. New York City special prosecutor Thomas E. Dewey wanted to incarcerate him for his activities in The Syndicate, as it was called. LaGuardia was concerned that some difficulties might arise in getting cooperation from the FBI, the New York City Police Department, the New York State Police, and in particular, Dewey's office, in exchanging information when Buchalter was apprehended. Buchalter was known to be politically involved with Dewey and offered Dewey his support if the latter should run for president in the future. Dewey rejected the offer. LaGuardia was confident that an exchange of information could be arranged between the New York City Police Department and the FBI, leaving the New York State Police and Dewey's outfit out of the arrangement. LaGuardia told Clegg in confidence that he hoped Buchalter would never be arrested and that it might be necessary "to kill him at the time of the arrest."

Under intense pressure from the US attorney, the FBI, and other law enforcement groups, Lepke turned himself in on August 24, 1939, expecting a soft sentence. Buchalter was wary of Dewey, so he made an arrangement to turn himself in to popular radio newscaster and newspaper columnist Walter Winchell who, in turn, handed him over to J. Edgar Hoover. Dewey was completely left out of the surrender scenario. However, Buchalter made a fatal mistake in coming out of hiding and giving himself up, because no deal was forthcoming. Dewey knew that a murder indictment would result in a harsher penalty than a federal conviction of narcotic trafficking.[33] Buchalter had been tricked. The federal government tried and convicted Buchalter on narcotics charges, and he was sentenced to fourteen years in prison. But after the trial, Hoover turned Buchalter over to Dewey to stand trial for murder. An informant for the state of New York, Abe Reles, named Buchalter as being involved in four murders. On the day the trial was to begin, Reles, who was guarded by six policemen, fell from a sixth floor window in what was mysteriously described as a suicide. Nevertheless, Buchalter was convicted of first-degree murder for ordering his gang to murder Joseph Rosen, a candy store clerk who threatened to rat on Buchalter, and he was ultimately executed by electrocution in Sing prison in upstate New York.[34]

LaGuardia also talked to Clegg about Lucky Luciano. In the early 1930s, Buchalter and Lucky Luciano had formed what was called the National Crime Syndicate, and along with mobsters Bugsy Siegel and Meyer Lansky would form the notorious Murder, Inc. LaGuardia told Clegg that although Luciano was convicted in 1936 on charges of leading one of the largest prostitution rings in America—a conviction credited to Dewey's relentless pursuit of Luciano—Luciano did not profit from his White Slave Act violations. LaGuardia said that all profits from the prostitution ring went to members of his mob. Luciano was convicted on sixty-two counts of Compulsory Prostitution and was sentenced to from thirty to fifty years in prison. Clegg told a surprised LaGuardia that the preliminary information enabling Dewey to pursue prosecution came from the FBI.[35] However, it was believed by many that Dewey actually framed Luciano, since the syndicate normally did not bother with prostitution, and according to Dewey, David Betillo, a loan shark, was in charge of the prostitution ring in New York.[36]

Clegg said that LaGuardia then asked him if he knew the extent to which the "third degree" was practiced in the South. Clegg said that it was practiced "too frequently" in some departments and against blacks in particular. Clegg was opposed to hitting any suspects unless they resisted arrest. LaGuardia "affably failed to agree" with Clegg and expressed the opinion that "it was a splendid thing" to beat up criminals, in particular those guilty of sex violations, and thought "the tough babies" deserved a "good working over." LaGuardia went on to say that he admired the police in Turkey, who were trained to be judges, act as judges in police court, and oftentimes prosecute those cases in court.

The conversation ended with LaGuardia repeating that he was fond of Edgar and again urging Clegg to extend his best wishes to the director. Hoover congratulated Clegg on his contact with LaGuardia and wrote, "I am very happy that Clegg made this contact & laid such a fine foundation for future approach."

Clegg's easygoing, Mississippi-style demeanor served him well throughout his life. He was able to befriend, and be trusted by, key people. Later in his life his colleagues, in particular those at Ole Miss, would call him a "name dropper," but Clegg did not just drop names; he really knew the people he named.

Chapter Four

The Tumultuous '30s: Kidnappers and Gangsters

To the generations of Americans raised since World War 2, the identities of criminals such as Charles 'Pretty Boy' Floyd, Baby Face Nelson, 'Ma' Barker, John Dillinger, and Clyde Barrow are no more real than are Luke Skywalker and Indiana Jones. After decades spent in the washing machine of popular culture, their stories have been bled of all reality, to an extent that few Americans today know who these people actually were, much less that they all rose to national prominence at the same time. They were real.—Bryan Burrough

THE 1930S WAS A TURBULENT PERIOD, not only for the nation but also for the FBI. The Great Depression caused many of the unemployed (estimates of a 25 percent unemployment rate were common) in the United States to turn to lives of crime, as evidenced by a dramatic increase in the rates of all types of crime. In order to survive, many of those unable to find a job turned to a life of crime, either acting independently or as members of gangs or mobs. Organized crime established its roots in the United States in the late nineteenth and early twentieth centuries and flourished with the failed experiment of the Eighteenth Amendment to the US Constitution. That amendment, ratified in 1919, prohibited the manufacture, sale, or transportation of intoxicating liquors. Prohibition in the 1920s is thought to be the single most important factor giving rise to the formation of organized crime syndicates. Although the amendment was repealed in 1933, the damage to American society had been done. Crime and criminals flourished, and many mobsters became national pop figures. Some Americans came to regard criminals such John Dillinger, "Machine Gun" Kelly, Pretty Boy Floyd, Baby Face Nelson, Bonnie Parker and Clyde Barrow, Ma Barker and her gang, and Alvin "Creepy" Karpis as heroes since they robbed banks, the same banks that were foreclosing on their land and seizing their property for lack of payment. At the same time, kidnappings came to be viewed as an easier way to grab money than robbing banks.

Prohibition provided the impetus for the emergence of organized crime and mobsters, the most well-known being Al Capone, Lucky Luciano, Dutch Schultz, Meyer Lansky, and Bugs Moran. The most famous, and perhaps most notorious, gang at the time was led by Al Capone and his mob in Chicago, but other big cities such as New York and Detroit also sprouted violent gangs. Crime seemed to be immune to the Depression, and with the ending of Prohibition, organized crime began to diversify to overcome the expected drop in revenue from the sale of illegal alcohol. In addition to their illegal activities in gambling, narcotics trafficking, labor racketeering, and robbing banks, criminals turned to kidnapping prominent rich individuals as a source of revenue. Small gangs began to grow in number and popularity. Organized crime involved Italian, Jewish, and Irish gangsters, and black gangs also sprouted, in Harlem in particular. Newspapers and movies added to the myth of these criminals being "Robin Hood" characters. The Public Enemy era, that period perceived as primarily occurring between 1931 and 1935, captured the attention of the American public. Movies in particular depicted crime in a fashion that caused the public to find gangsters entertaining and popular, making them folk heroes. Classic films of the early 1930s such as *Little Caesar*, *The Public Enemies*, and *Scarface: The Shame of a Nation* made stars of Edward G. Robinson, James Cagney, and Paul Muni, while Humphrey Bogart and George Raft emerged as stars portraying gangsters in other films.

The FBI was faced with an enormous challenge early in this era as it confronted these murderers unarmed—unless agents carried a personal weapon. Spurred on by Attorney General Homer Cummings, the FBI's War on Crime peaked from 1933 to 1936. The FBI tried to fight all forms of crime but had its hands tied behind its back. The lack of authority to make arrests and to carry weapons to match those of the criminals was rectified in the early 1930s under Cummings's leadership. Congress passed a federal kidnapping law and other federal crime laws while federal crime-fighting agencies were combined. Just as important, Cummings gave the agents the authority to carry weapons. The War on Crime had begun, and Hugh Clegg played a major role in the pursuit of many of these gangsters.[1]

The inability of federal agencies to coordinate their attacks on crime was a big advantage for the criminals. Attempts to bring the most widely known mobster, Al Capone, to justice is a good example. Clegg was with the Chicago field office when the Bureau of Internal Revenue (BIR) was investigating Capone. The BIR had a witness whom it wanted the FBI to guard. The US attorney and the head of the Chicago branch of the BIR met with Clegg and asked the FBI to guard the witness. Clegg refused, stating that each government agency should be responsible for its own actions, and Hoover backed him up.[2]

The FBI, however, did get involved in investigating Capone's activities before and after the date he was subpoenaed to appear before a grand jury in Chicago regarding his racketeering and gambling activities. Capone submitted a physician's statement by Dr. Kenneth Phillips recommending that he not be forced to appear since he was ill with bronchial pneumonia. In the opinion of the physician, Capone should not be required to undertake the trip from his home in Miami Beach. The judge agreed and Capone was excused. Because he avoided a federal grand jury subpoena, however, Hoover took a personal interest in incarcerating Capone.[3] FBI agents learned that on the day he was to appear before the grand jury, Capone was attending horse races on Bimini. The agents located the airline pilot who flew Capone to Bimini, the policeman who helped him park his car at the Hialeah racetrack in Miami when he was supposed to be confined to bed, and an officer on a boat who talked to Capone while he was aboard a Nassau-bound pleasure craft.[4] This information was reported to a Chicago grand jury, and the grand jury indicted Capone for contempt of court. He was tried, convicted, and sentenced to six months in jail. This sentence was to run concurrently with the eleven-year sentence he received for income tax evasion when he was convicted in 1931 for failing to pay tax on his profits from illegal liquor trafficking. Capone at first pled guilty to Prohibition and tax evasion charges, thinking he had worked out a deal for a two-and-one-half-year sentence. But the judge said he was not bound to any deal. Capone then changed his plea to not guilty but was convicted nonetheless.

Although alcohol consumption declined dramatically at the start of Prohibition, the public's desire to consume alcoholic beverages had not diminished greatly. Alcohol consumption began to increase to near pre-Prohibition levels over the next several years because organized gangs found ways to quench the public thirst. An unforeseen consequence of Prohibition was the creation of an underground industry of widespread criminal activity. The federal government expressed little interest in enforcing Prohibition in a rigid way, and so speakeasies proliferated. Organized gangs to distribute illegal beverages waged territorial wars.

The St. Valentine's Day Massacre in 1929 marked the beginning of public awareness of the heightened criminal activity and led President Hoover to create the National Committee on Law Observance and Enforcement. He appointed George Wickersham, who had served as attorney general in the Taft administration, as head of the commission, which later became known as the Wickersham Commission. The committee was charged with studying the entire problem of enforcing existing laws and the ways for improving the judicial system. It was also tasked with studying the abuses of the prohibition laws. It was thought that the commission would recommend the repeal of the Eighteenth Amendment, but instead it made recommendations that encouraged more aggressive law enforcement while overlooking the fact that enforcement of Prohibition was impossible, for all intents and purposes, considering the profitable rewards of violating the law.

It became obvious that those charged with law enforcement nationwide had little formal training and that enforcement was inconsistent. Experienced criminals had a distinct advantage over local police. The Wickersham Commission recommended the establishment of what it called a Federal Police Training School, whose purpose was to standardize law enforcement. But the FBI had little to do with enforcing Prohibition; rather, enforcement was the responsibility of the Treasury Department, which was doing an inadequate job. The public's confidence in law enforcement had broken down. Newsreel stories featuring bank robbers and kidnappers had the effect of making these outlaws the heroes and the police the villains. Clegg described efforts of the FBI to stop filming of the 1935 movie *G-Men*, starring James Cagney, playing the role of James "Brick" Davis, a lawyer with racketeer connections turned G-Man. The Bureau feared it would show the agency as a bunch of gunfighters. However, the movie had just the opposite effect and depicted FBI agents as the heroes, as action detectives. All of a sudden, agents of the FBI became heroes. Clegg admitted that the FBI was mistaken in trying to stop the making of the movie since it changed the image of the Department of Justice.[5] Hoover and the Bureau became icons of American culture.

Public confidence in the FBI began to increase as bank robbers and kidnappers were captured and imprisoned or killed. President Roosevelt and Homer Cummings submitted a Twelve Point Crime Program to Congress in 1934 and it was enacted into law. The program was designed to coordinate a strategy combining public awareness and legislation, as well as police power, to eradicate crime. The enacted law made bank robbery, interstate flight of felons, murder or assault of federal officials, extortion, and racketeering federal crimes.[6] Due to the success of *G-Men* and other films about the FBI, the public gave credit to the Bureau alone, ignoring the impact Homer Cummings had in curbing criminal activity. The agency became so popular that sightseers requested tours of its Washington headquarters, particularly to the crime laboratories and firing ranges.

In 1934, Congress enacted the Bank Robbery and Incidental Crimes Statute, making it a federal crime to rob any national bank or bank that was a member of the federal Reserve System. This statute was later expanded to include bank burglary and bank larceny and similar crimes committed against federally insured savings and loan associations and Federal credit unions. The investigative jurisdiction under this statute was delegated to the FBI, which today probes bank crimes concurrent with local law enforcement. Prior to the enactment of this law, bank robberies averaged twenty-two a week. Within eleven months of the law's enactment, that figure was reduced to one and one-quarter bank robberies per week.

Gangsters began looking for easier ways to make money, and many turned to ransoms from kidnapping ranging from $1,500 to $200,000. The new federal laws did not include kidnappings, so they became quite common during this period. Depending on the source of kidnapping data, kidnappings in the United States during the period of 1930–1932 numbered from three hundred to two thousand. The most widely publicized kidnappings were those of the Charles Lindbergh baby in 1932, oilman Charles F. Urschel and Hart & Son Company department store heir Brooke Hart in 1933, and millionaire Minnesota brewer William Hamm and Minnesota banker Edward Bremer Jr. in 1934. Clegg became involved in most of these kidnapping investigations.

The kidnapping in New Jersey of twenty-month-old Charles Augustus Lindbergh Jr., the son of American hero Charles Lindbergh and Anne Morrow Lindbergh, on the evening of March 1, 1932, shocked the nation. The federal government did not have official jurisdiction in kidnapping cases at the time. Clegg remembered that President Roosevelt called Hoover to the White House. Hoover found the president lying in bed, resting. He always called Hoover "Johnny." Roosevelt said, "Johnny, we've got to solve that Lindbergh case. Get in it. Do whatever needs to be done to solve the case."[7]

On May 13, 1932, Roosevelt directed all federal government agencies to assist law enforcement agencies in New Jersey on the Lindbergh case and designated the FBI as the clearinghouse and coordinating agency for investigations conducted by federal agencies. On October 19, 1933, Roosevelt assigned the FBI exclusive jurisdiction in handling the Lindbergh kidnapping investigation.

The search for the kidnapper took two years and involved the work of several law enforcement agencies, including the FBI, New York City Police, New Jersey State Police, and the Newark Police Department. On September 19, 1934, Bruno Hauptmann, a carpenter and former convict born in Germany, was arrested and charged with the kidnapping and murder of the Lindbergh baby. Within eighteen months, Hauptmann was tried, convicted, and executed.

Just prior to Hauptmann's arrest, Clegg was sent to New York to join another Mississippian, Percy E. "Sam" Foxworth, to inspect that city's field office. Foxworth had an interesting background and an interesting career with the FBI.[8] Clegg and Foxworth reviewed thousands of pages of material collected by squads of agents who were working on the Lindbergh case. When Clegg observed the extensive work done by the New York–based FBI agents, he had a gut feeling that the investigation was about to bust wide open, so he called Hoover and said he thought the case would be solved within the next twenty-four hours. He urged Hoover to come to New York. Hoover asked, "Well, what do you want me to do?" Clegg said "I want you to get up here and work with the police chief and the state police superintendent and coordinate the administrative control of the handling of the case."[9] Bruno Hauptmann was arrested soon thereafter. When Hoover arrived, he placed Clegg in control of public relations, but Hoover could not resist the opportunity for publicity and handled questions relating to the substance of the case.

Clegg reviewed the Hauptmann evidence and had "no doubt in the world but that Hauptmann was guilty."[10] Others, however, including FBI agents, doubted his guilt or that he had acted alone. The FBI chief agent in the investigation, Thomas Sisk, argued that others may have also been involved since the ladder used in the crime was divided into three sections and could not be handled by one person. Sisk also believed that Hauptmann would have had trouble getting through the window because of his broad shoulders. Others who were convinced that Hauptmann was involved thought he had an accomplice or accomplices. Even New Jersey governor Harold Hoffmann doubted Hauptmann's guilt. Hoover admitted that Hauptmann's fingerprints did not match those found on either the ransom note or the ransom money and remarked in a secret memo, "I am skeptical as to some of the evidence."[11] On the day the Bureau withdrew from the case, Clegg summed up the divergent views among the agents assigned to it, noting "there are logical reasons which would point to the presence of someone else but there are an equal number of reasons why there is only one person." Clegg surmised that if anyone else was involved, he guessed it would be Hauptmann's wife, but he dismissed even that possibility because "Germans don't cozy up to their womenfolks [sic] like most people do. So, he probably kept it a secret from her."[12]

Long after Clegg's retirement from Ole Miss, he still maintained that he never had any doubt—and never would—about either Hauptmann's guilt or the fact that he had acted alone. Clegg was present when Hauptmann was picked out of a lineup and was there when ransom money was found in Hauptmann's garage. Clegg also was convinced that Hauptmann's handwriting was found on the kidnap note and that the wooden ladder found at the kidnap scene matched the lumber found in Hauptmann's attic. Clegg maintained that the controversy was similar to the conspiracy theories related to the murders of President John F. Kennedy and his brother Robert, and were simply made for the sake of publicity.

When Clegg took over the public relations aspects of the case, fifteen or twenty reporters at a time besieged him, wanting a press conference or a statement. To throw the reporters off, Clegg said that he knew little about the case.

I'd have some of our prettiest secretaries with large numbers of files out, but accurate files; they were actually the files.

We'd count the drawers involved and the number of files, and estimate the total number of sections, and the total number of pages, and the total number of words. I kept giving them that sort of stuff with pictures of the pretty girls and the substance would be given out by Mr. Hoover and the chief of police and the state police of New Jersey.[13]

Despite the doubts of some, Hauptmann was the only person who was formally accused in the kidnapping. He was found guilty in February 1935 and electrocuted on April 3, 1936.

In 1933, millionaire Minnesota brewer William Hamm Jr. was kidnapped by the Alvin Karpis-Ma Barker gang. The ease with which Hamm's ransom of one hundred thousand dollars was collected appealed to the Karpis-Barker gang, and six months later they kidnapped Edward Bremer Jr., a St. Paul, Minnesota, banker and heir to the Schmidt Brewery fortune. A Russian immigrant, Harry Sandlovich, known as a political henchman and a bagman for the mob, held a grudge against Bremer and convinced the Karpis-Barker gang to kidnap him and try to double the amount of ransom money they got for the Hamm kidnapping.

Bremer possessed an abrasive personality and was even disliked by many in his family. The Bremer family had an association with gangster elements and even supplied them with "near beer" during Prohibition. On the morning of January 17, 1934, Bremer dropped his daughter off at school and was on his way to his office when the gang ambushed him, took his black Lincoln, and pistol-whipped him to a state of semiconsciousness. Bremer was driven to Bensenvile, Illinois, blindfolded, and bound. By the time his abandoned car was discovered by the police, it had been wiped clean of any fingerprints. St. Paul was swarming with government agents. After a series of notes to Bremer's family and friends, the ransom of two hundred thousand dollars was paid twenty-two days after the kidnapping, despite pleas from Hoover and the FBI to continue to hold off payment. Bremer was dropped off on Highway 52 between Rochester and Chatfield and told to take a bus back to St. Paul. Hoover had ordered a massive search for the house in which Bremer was held captive, requiring hundreds of work hours. The Chicago office, of which Clegg was agent in charge, was the central point of the investigation and search. Half of the agents there were tracking down John Dillinger while the other half stayed on the road searching for the combination of trains, church bells, and factory whistles Bremer heard while being held captive. Despite their intensive efforts, the agents failed to turn up any significant leads and became tired of the search, considering it to be a useless exercise. Clegg went to St. Paul to lead the investigation, and in frustration suggested that they hire Boy Scouts to canvass their hometown.[14]

Edward Bremer's father, Adolph, was a friend and fund-raiser for President Roosevelt, who, during one of his famous radio Fireside Chats, called the kidnapping "an attack on all that we hold dear" and issued a statement deploring the kidnapping of the son of a friend. Roosevelt ordered Hoover to fix the wave of criminal activity caused by the gangster element in the country. As a result, the FBI and local police became more determined to catch the kidnappers and captured them five months later. A federal grand jury in St. Paul indicted Karpis, Doc Barker—Ma Barker's son—and others for conspiracy to kidnap Bremer. Karpis avoided trial for the Bremer kidnapping by pleading guilty to the Hamm kidnapping.[15]

The indictment of members of the Karpis-Barker gang and the solving of these kidnapping cases was evidence that the federal kidnapping laws transcending state lines, adopted after the Lindbergh kidnapping, were justified. The FBI played a major role in solving kidnappings and had a great record of success. Little information is evident in Clegg's FBI files, but he was involved with coordinating the efforts of the FBI in the investigation of the Hamm and Bremer kidnappings during his assignment to the St. Paul FBI office. Clegg said that of the hundred or so kidnapping cases in which the FBI was involved, all but one had been solved.[16]

Because the FBI had been granted wider authority, the search for popular gangsters of the day intensified. A key participant in the War on Crime was FBI special agent Melvin Purvis. Clegg and Purvis would find themselves intertwined in the hunt for gangsters, despite different approaches to their jobs. Purvis became a national media figure for his exploits in the massive search for criminals such as John Dillinger, Baby Face Nelson, and Pretty Boy Floyd. Like Clegg, Purvis was a product of the South, having been born in South Carolina. Purvis received his law degree from the University of South Carolina Law School and joined the FBI in 1927. Director Hoover placed Purvis in charge of the Chicago FBI office in 1932 although he had little experience in dealing with criminals, having been involved mostly in investigating white-collar crime. Al Capone took advantage of Purvis's inexperience by using his contacts within the office of the prosecutor to frame his rival, Roger Tuohy, for the kidnappings of Jake "The Barber" Factor and William Hamm.

Purvis's crime-fighting skills improved, and he was far from shy in accepting the fame heaped upon him and in using his southern charm to promote himself through the media. Purvis and Hoover developed a close friendship at first, but in time Purvis's penchant for publicity would earn him Hoover's wrath.

Clegg was one of Hoover's favorite agents, as much for his law enforcement skills as for his loyalty and widely proclaimed high opinion of Hoover's leadership. Unlike Purvis, publicity was not Clegg's main objective in serving Hoover. His loyalty to the director led to his promotion to an assistant director of the Bureau in 1932 after only six years with the FBI.

Although the Bureau's agents were heavily engaged in the pursuit of the criminal element, they were at a disadvantage when it came to the use of firearms against the likes of Dillinger, Floyd, and Nelson. On February 4, 1934, Hoover wrote several agents, including Clegg and Purvis, that they had not qualified as marksmen with a pistol and urged them to qualify at the earliest possible date. When the famous botched raid on the Little Bohemia Lodge in 1934 began, the leaders of the raid, Clegg and Purvis, were, amazingly, not qualified in the use of firearms.[17]

The Kansas City Massacre of 1933 sparked the War on Crime.[18] Prior to the massacre, and despite the uproar caused by the Lindbergh baby kidnapping and the subsequent adoption of the Lindbergh Kidnapping Act, Congress was reluctant to amend the law to include more severe penalties for crimes. Congress was also reluctant to legalize FBI agents carrying weapons to offset the advantage that the gangsters enjoyed at the time. The attitude in Congress changed with the massacre that occurred on the morning of June 17, 1933, at the Union Station railroad depot in Kansas City, Missouri. The shoot-out resulted in the deaths of four law enforcement officers and their prisoner.

Several law enforcement officers were transporting gangster Frank "Jelly" Nash back to the Leavenworth, Kansas, federal prison. Nash, a convicted murderer and burglar, had been sentenced to twenty-five years at the Leavenworth prison for assaulting a mail custodian. He was given his nickname because of his ability to use the explosive nitroglycerin. He managed to escape in 1930 and later aided seven other prisoners, including noted bank robber Harvey Bailey, in their breakout from the same prison.

As the result of a massive search, FBI agents Frank Smith and Joseph Lackey, along with McAlester, Oklahoma, police chief, Otto Reid, captured Nash in Hot Springs, Arkansas, and transported him on a Missouri Pacific train to Kansas City. They notified the Kansas City special agent in charge, Reed Vetterli, of their prize catch and made arrangements for Vetterli, FBI agent Ray Caffrey, and Kansas City policemen Frank Hermanson and W. J. Grooms to meet them at the Union Station. However, friends of Nash—Frank Mulloy, Richard Galatas, Herbert Farmer, and "Doc" Louis Stacci—learned of his capture and the plans to bring him to Kansas City, most likely because of an Associated Press news release describing Nash's capture and details of plans to transport him to Kansas City. These friends designated fellow gangster Vernon Miller, Nash's best friend, to help Nash escape.[19] Miller then sought the help of Kansas City mob boss Johnny Lazia, who recommended two gunmen, Adam Richetti and Pretty Boy Floyd, to help. Floyd and Richetti met at Miller's home in Kansas City the evening of June 16, where they devised their plan and then went to the train station to await the arrival of the Missouri Pacific train bearing Nash.

When the train arrived, Agent Lackey left Smith, Reed, and Nash on the train and went onto the train platform to meet Vetterli, accompanied by Caffrey, Grooms, and Hermanson, who had arranged for two automobiles to meet the group. When the group saw nothing to arouse their suspicion, Lackey returned to the train to collect Smith, Reed, and Nash. The entourage then escorted Nash through the station to the waiting cars. Although the FBI lacked the authority to carry firearms, many did so anyway as a means of self-protection. Lackey and Chief Reed carried shotguns, while many of the others bore pistols.

When they reached their cars and climbed in, Agent Lackey observed a green Plymouth parked nearby. Two armed men, one carrying a machine gun, approached the agents in the cars, and one of them—generally assumed to be Pretty Boy Floyd—shouted to the group, "Hands up!" A third gunman, who also carried a machine gun, joined them. The gunmen opened fire before any of the law enforcement contingent had time to react. The Kansas City policemen were killed immediately, and Vetterli was shot in his left arm and fell to the ground. Agent Caffrey was killed by a shot to the head and Frank Nash and Chief Reed were shot to death inside their car. Agent Lackey was critically wounded by three gunshots to his back. When the three gunmen ran to their car, they thought that everyone was dead. However, a Kansas City policeman, Mike Fanning, came running out of the station, saw what had happened, and began firing at the killers. Floyd was hit but all of the gunmen managed to escape.[20] When the massacre ended, Agent Caffrey, Kansas City policemen Grooms and Hermanson, and Chief Reed were dead and Agents Vetterli and Lackey were wounded. Only Agent Frank Smith was unscathed. Of the three gunmen—Miller, Richetti, and Floyd—only Floyd was wounded, and all three managed to get away. The subject of the planned escape, Jelly Nash, was dead from gunshot wounds to the head fired by his would-be rescuers.

Despite being wounded and bleeding, Vetterli rushed to the Kansas City FBI office and called Director Hoover to tell him a massacre at the train station had occurred and that Agent Ray Caffrey was killed. Hoover began what he considered to be the most important investigation in the history of the Bureau.[21] But since it was not a federal crime at the time to kill a federal agent, the Bureau had no jurisdiction to conduct the investigation.

The FBI later determined that Miller, Richetti, and Floyd were involved in planning the escape. Many theories about the shooting surfaced among agents of the Bureau. Some of them felt that Floyd was not involved and categorized him as a bank robber, not a wild gunman. Yet another theory that surfaced pinned the massacre on a group of gunmen headed by Harvey Bailey that included gangster Wilbur Underhill, supposedly attempting to rescue Nash in return for his help in their escape from Leavenworth. Vetterli would later identify an Oklahoma bank robber, Bob Brady, as wielding a machine gun during the massacre.[22] Brady was among those who escaped from the Leavenworth prison with Harvey Bailey. Underhill would go to his death denying that either he or Bailey had anything to do with the massacre.

The War on Crime had begun. The public was outraged at both the gangsters and the government, which was blamed for allowing gunmen to run around the country at will. Director Hoover was also outraged, in particular at the loss of one of his agents, and vowed to spare no effort to bring the killers to justice. Less than two weeks after the massacre, Attorney General Cummings announced plans designed to toughen the government's war on crime, including the enactment of a law making it a federal crime to kill a federal agent and the establishment of Bureau task forces assigned to major crimes.[23] However, Congress did not pass such a law until the following spring, in 1934.

Disregarding the other theories of who was responsible for the massacre, Hoover focused on the involvement of Pretty Boy Floyd, elevating him to the number 2 spot on the FBI's Ten Most Wanted list behind John Dillinger. Hoover, without hesitation, announced that Floyd had carried out the massacre and named legendary agent Gus Jones to head up the investigation.[24] Hoover also rescinded the unofficial ban on agents carrying firearms.

Clegg would play a significant role in the investigation. Despite a major effort to identify and capture the perpetrators of the massacre, the probe had had difficulty gaining momentum. Several agents in the Bureau who worked on contrasting theories were not hesitant to argue their case and began bickering among themselves. Hoover was irate and ordered Clegg to step in and resolve the disputes and end the quarreling. He wasted no time following up on Hoover's order. Clegg telephoned Acting Agent in Charge M. C. Spear of the Kansas City office, who brought Clegg up to date on the various theories agents in that office were proposing. Clegg told Spear that it was not Bureau policy for agents to get involved in disputes over various theories and that friction among agents was not acceptable. Clegg then wrote Hoover that afternoon to inform him that he told Spear that the director was

> very much displeased with the reported lack of vigor in this investigation of the Kansas City Massacre case; that it appeared that they had let this case fall by the wayside and it was being handled off and on by any one of a number of agents and it was not being pursued vigorously toward a logical conclusion.[25]

Hoover was angry with Spear and the bickering agents and responded to Clegg's memo by telling him to stop the Kansas City bickering immediately.[26]

Whatever the involvement of Pretty Boy Floyd, Hoover used him as the centerpiece for the government's War on Crime. Less than six months after the massacre, Vernon Miller's body was found in a ditch outside of Detroit. This gave rise to theories that the massacre had been carried out by gangland-type henchmen who had silenced Frank Nash. Floyd, who was shot to death a year later by FBI agents, denied to his dying day that he had any part in the massacre. Richetti was later captured, convicted of the Kansas City murders, and executed by means of a gas chamber in 1938. Mulloy, Galatas, Farmer, and Stacci were later apprehended and convicted of conspiring to aid and abet the escape of a federal prisoner. They were sentenced to two years in prison. Hoover's War on Crime was gaining momentum.[27]

One of the most famous of the Public Enemies of the era was a gangster named Baby Face Nelson, born Lester M. Gillis in Chicago. Nelson entered the criminal world as a youngster, learning to steal automobiles, a crime at which he became adept. His youthful appearance led to his nickname Baby Face. At the age of fourteen he was convicted of auto theft and sent to a boy's home. At the age of twenty-three, he was sentenced to the Illinois State Penitentiary on bank robbery charges. He, his wife, Helen Gillis, and a criminal cohort, John Paul Chase, joined the John Dillinger gang.

Four months after Dillinger was shot and killed in 1934, FBI special agents Sam Cowley and Herman "Ed" Hollis, who had been given the assignment of hunting down Nelson, received word that a Ford coupe stolen by Nelson and containing two men and a woman had been spotted near Barrington, Illinois. Two carloads of agents spotted the stolen car and gave chase. Hollis and Cowley, in a black Hudson sedan, passed a car but failed to spot Nelson although he was in it. The stolen car swerved onto a side road and the woman passenger, Helen Gillis, jumped out and hid in a ditch. The Hudson came to a stop 150 feet past the Nelson vehicle. Then the two men in the car, Nelson and Chase, began firing machine gun bullets at Cowley and Hollis before the agents could get out of their car. Nelson flamboyantly fired at the agents while standing on the car's running board. Cowley and Hollis returned fire from behind their sedan and emptied their weapons at the gangsters. Cowley fired over fifty bullets from his machine gun and Hollis discharged ten shotgun shells. Cowley shot Nelson six times in the chest and stomach, but Nelson returned fire and shot Cowley twice in the stomach. (He was not wearing a bulletproof vest that might have saved him.) Hollis then emptied his shotgun at Nelson, hitting him in both legs. Yet Nelson was able to shoot Hollis in the head, fatally wounding him. Despite his wounds, Nelson continued to fire, and Chase helped him get in the Hudson that had been driven by the agents. Cowley leaped out of the Hudson and began firing while crouching beside the car. Helen Gillis climbed out of the ditch and jumped into the car as well. Cowley was taken to a hospital in Elgin and refused an operation until he could assure his famed chief, Melvin Purvis, that his opponent had indeed been Baby Face Nelson. A few hours later, Cowley also died.[28]

When word reached Hoover that Sam Cowley was on his deathbed and, knowing Purvis's inclinations to seek publicity, he called Clegg, who was in Pittsburgh on another investigation, and told him to take a plane that evening for Chicago and "take charge of the entire situation."[29] Hoover warned Purvis not to issue any statement to the press, nor did he want Purvis to continue running the Chicago office. Yet Purvis, having seen Cowley's wife crying at his bedside, could not resist an opportunity. He was approached by a Chicago reporter, Elgar Brown of the *Chicago American* newspaper, who asked for a comment regarding the shooting. Purvis blurted out, "If it's the last thing I do, I'll get Baby Face Nelson—dead or alive. Nelson ought to know he hasn't a chance at eventual escape. . . . We aren't particular whether we get him alive or dead."[30] Purvis returned to the Chicago office, against Hoover's wishes, to coordinate the search for Nelson.[31]

Hoover heard about Purvis's vow to get Nelson and was furious. He told Clegg, "I stated very emphatically that I am displeased with the publicity. I do not want to send Mr. Purvis out of Chicago unless absolutely necessary, but I may have to in order to take care of the publicity situation." Hoover went on to say that Purvis "exercises poor judgment in appearing publicly, putting him in a position to be quoted by newspapermen," and told Clegg to keep Purvis out of the action to find Nelson.[32]

Nonetheless, Clegg stood by Purvis and suggested to Hoover that Purvis continue to work on the hunt but restrict himself to the back of the Chicago office. Hoover was not receptive to the suggestion.[33] Clegg tried again to persuade the director and suggested that Purvis stay out of the public eye by accompanying Herman Hollis's body on its way back to Des Moines. Hoover, however, was adamant and told Clegg that Purvis was "not to accompany raiding parties. He is not to come to the office or accompany the bodies of either Cowley or Hollis to their homes, and is to remain in the background." Hoover further stated that Purvis "should remain at home until such time as we can work out something for him to do."[34] Hoover then put Clegg in charge of the investigation. The press was concerned about Purvis's absence, but Clegg was ordered not to offer an explanation. Rumors persisted that Purvis had been replaced by Clegg and would not return to the Chicago office.

Clegg directed the hunt for Nelson by thousands of federal, state, and local officers. At that time, Nelson was the only man to kill more than one Department of Justice agent. Cowley and Hollis's Hudson was found abandoned in suburban Winnetka. The front seat was caked with blood. A Chicago undertaker received an anonymous call regarding the location of a body. He called the police and gave them directions that took them to a muddy ditch outside a cemetery in Niles Center, Illinois, where they found a small, naked corpse wrapped in a blanket. There were eight bullet wounds in its legs and one in its stomach. Using the Bureau's new technique of fingerprint identification, it was determined that the corpse was that of Baby Face Nelson.

Nelson in fact died early the same afternoon of the shootout, and Chase and Gillis disposed of his body. Chase was captured a month later in California and was subsequently found guilty of murdering Agent Sam Cowley. He was also indicted on the charge of killing Agent Ed Hollis as well but was never tried for that crime. Two days after Nelson's body was found, Helen Gillis surrendered and was sentenced to a year and a day at the Women's Federal Reformatory for aiding and abetting her husband. She lived for fifty years after Nelson was killed.

News rapidly spread that Nelson had been killed. Clegg gleefully announced the FBI killing of Nelson to journalists waving a Nelson "wanted" poster. But Clegg was not the only braggart. Attorney

General Homer Cummings told newsmen: "Our men got him! Our men got him!" But Hoover was more reflective, bemoaning the fact that although the FBI did get Nelson, it cost the agency the lives of two of its agents, Sam Cowley and Herman Hollis.[35] Upon receiving news of Hollis's death, an unnamed federal agent in Chicago blurted, "Damn them! Hollis killed Dillinger, and now they get him."[36] Hoover told Clegg that credit for killing Nelson should not be given to either Cowley or Hollis. Rather, Clegg should tell the press that both agents fired their weapons, and as a result Nelson was killed.

The FBI war on the gangsters was paying off. Three of the four most wanted public enemies were killed within a four-month period in 1934—John Dillinger on July 22, Pretty Boy Floyd on October 22, and Baby Face Nelson on November 27, 1934. Only Alvin Karpis remained on the loose.

Alvin "Creepy" Karpis, born Alvin Karpowicz in Montreal, Canada, began his criminal life before reaching his teen years. Later, he was sentenced to a ten-year prison term at the age of nineteen for an attempted burglary. He escaped from the Hutchinson, Kansas, reformatory but was captured a year later after stealing an automobile. He was returned to the reformatory but was later transferred to the Kansas State Prison in Lansing, where he met Freddie Barker—one of the four sons of Ma Barker. The two teamed up to establish the Barker-Karpis gang that became known for its brutality and cunning. Karpis was considered to be the brains of the operation and was thought to possess a photographic memory. He masterminded the Hamm and Bremer kidnappings and numerous bank and train robberies. Karpis blamed Hoover for killing Ma and Freddie Barker in a Florida shootout and threatened to kill Hoover himself.

The FBI's hunt for Karpis took an important turn during a US Senate hearing in 1936. Tennessee senator Kenneth D. McKellar publicly criticized the FBI for its performance and embarrassed Director Hoover by accusing him of being a law enforcement officer who had never arrested anyone. Although the feud between Hoover and Senator McKellar surfaced at this Senate hearing, it had actually begun in 1933 when McKellar ran for reelection to the US Senate. He had promised numerous constituents, mostly Memphis policemen, appointments to the FBI. When McKellar was elected, he proposed to Hoover that the FBI hire several of these individuals. Hoover refused on the basis that they were not accountants or lawyers and that even if they were, they would have to pass several written examinations before being appointed. McKellar complained to Attorney General Cummings, and Hoover retaliated by firing three Tennessee special agents. The feud had begun.

Clegg recalled that Hoover appeared at a hearing of the Senate Appropriations Committee, chaired by Senator McKellar, with a request for an appropriation of five million dollars—double the previous appropriation—after Hoover bragged about the success of his agents in solving numerous kidnapping cases. McKellar criticized the publicity Hoover was given in the movie industry and publicly criticized the FBI for claiming these successes when, in actual fact, the real credit belonged to law enforcement agencies other than the FBI. McKellar even criticized the Bureau for being allowed to use guns and claimed that only eight criminals had been killed since approval was granted while the FBI lost four of its own agents. McKellar then questioned Hoover's qualifications for the job as director, charging him with never making an arrest. "Here is a man that never captured a criminal in his life, never solved a case in his life," McKellar ranted.[37] Hoover had to admit that he did not make arrests but bragged that he had led several investigations. Hoover bristled at the McKellar criticism and made a commitment that he would personally capture then-Public Enemy No. 1, Alvin Karpis. According to Clegg, Hoover began going out on cases and taking the lead and staying on the case until he got results.

When FBI agents located Karpis in New Orleans and informed Hoover that they knew where he was hiding out, Hoover flew in to personally direct the arrest, bringing Clyde Tolson along. Hoover claimed that Karpis left the house in which he was hiding (located at the intersection of Canal Street and Jefferson Davis Parkway) and got into his car. Hoover then said he approached Karpis and told him he was under arrest. Hoover further claimed that he stopped

Karpis from reaching into the backseat as he tried to grab a rifle. Karpis would later write that Hoover emerged on the scene only after the agents had grabbed him, and he claimed that his car had no backseat. Karpis asserted that "the story of Hoover the Hero is false. He didn't lead the attack on me. He waited until he was told the coast was clear. Then he came out to reap the glory." Hoover's public reputation, and the reputation of the FBI, received a large and much-needed boost, fueled even further by the movie *The FBI Story* (1959), in which Hoover walks up and arrests Karpis single-handedly. This was reported to be the first arrest ever made in person by Hoover, and he denied the account given by Karpis. Hoover's account is backed up in FBI files.[38]

FBI agent Earl J. Connelley's version is perhaps more accurate.[39] Connelley served as the main FBI operating boss throughout the hunt for Karpis. Connelley reported that he and Agent Clarence O. Hurt were posted on the opposite corner of Canal Street and Jefferson Davis Parkway, followed by a car occupied by J. Edgar Hoover, Agent W. L. "Buck" Buchanan, and Special Agent in Charge Dwight Brantley when subjects Karpis and Fred Hunter came out of the apartment and started to enter the Plymouth coupe. Agents Connelly and Hurt immediately drove across the intersection, crossed Canal Street, and blocked the coupe into the sidewalk. Hoover and agents Brantley and Buchanan moved across Canal Street at the same time that Agents Hurt and Connelley covered them. According to Connelley, the field agents moved in just as Karpis settled behind the wheel of his car. Connelly swerved his car in front of the Plymouth coupe and blocked it against the sidewalk. Connelly and Hurt leaped from their car with guns drawn, and Karpis quickly found himself staring into about five gun barrels. Hoover was present but not in the forefront.

The FBI version claims that Hoover reached into the car and seized Karpis before he could reach a rifle on the backseat.[40] However, Karpis's car, a Plymouth coupe, had no backseat. Hoover himself bragged that he rushed up to Karpis as Karpis sat behind the wheel of his car and threatened him with a gun, saying "put the cuffs on him, boys." But none of the agents carried a pair of handcuffs; they tied Karpis's hands with agent Hurt's necktie.[41]

This entire incident has been controversial for a long time. It has been said that Hoover himself never claimed he single-handedly captured Karpis, adding that he did lead the raid, but it was a "we" thing for the FBI, not an "I" thing. Nevertheless, Hoover became a folk hero in the public eye. Less than a month after being criticized in public by Senator McKellar, Hoover "led" the successful raid that resulted in Karpis's capture. Hoover's national popularity soared. Later that year, McKellar tried to reduce the FBI budget by $225,000 but was opposed by Senator Arthur H. Vandenberg of Michigan. The FBI's proposed budget was approved by voice vote, and while Hoover was director, the Senate never opposed a House-approved FBI budget.

Clegg reviewed the circumstances leading up to Hoover being present at the arrest of Karpis and supported Hoover's account. Hoover and Senator McKellar reconciled their feud after the capture of Karpis. Clegg recalled a later occasion at the commencement exercises of the FBI National Academy when a reporter for the Memphis newspaper, the *Commercial Appeal*, entered the ceremony accompanied by Senator McKellar. Two extra chairs were brought onto the stage as the featured speakers, Norman Vincent Peale and Secretary of the Navy Claude Swanson, gave their addresses. McKellar rose to make his remarks, causing much concern to Clegg and Hoover, who feared further criticism. McKellar, however, said, "I surrender! J. Edgar Hoover is the greatest American we have today. I was mistaken." He continued to praise Hoover and became a strong supporter of Hoover and the FBI and led budget fights to enhance the agency.[42]

After the earlier confrontation with Senator McKellar, Hoover became more aware of public relations as opposed to blatant publicity. An annual publication called the *Federal Bureau of Investigation* gave credit to the Senate and the Appropriations Committee of the House of Representatives for their support of the Bureau. The names of every member of that committee were listed, which pleased the committee members. This approach paid off, because the Bureau always received an appropriation greater than requested. Public confidence in the war against gangsters improved. As Hoover campaigned by using the press to publicize any FBI success, congressional appropriations increased, the salaries of FBI agents increased, and the youth of the country began to consider FBI agents rather than the gangsters as their heroes.

Chapter Five

John Dillinger and Little Bohemia

All my life I wanted to be a bank robber. Carry a gun and wear a mask.
Now that it's happened I guess I'm just about the best bank robber
they ever had. And I sure am happy.—John Dillinger

T HE HIGHLIGHT OF CLEGG'S INVOLVEMENT in the FBI's War
on Crime was his role in the search for John Dillinger, a role
that merits thorough discussion. There have been several er-
roneous depictions of Clegg's participation in the hunt for Dillinger.
For example, the movie *Public Enemies* (2009) spotlights agent Melvin Purvis as being solely in charge of the FBI raid at the Little Bohemia Lodge.[1] In fact, however, the raid was coordinated by both
Purvis and Clegg, and Clegg was the agent in charge.[2] And despite
some reports to the contrary, Clegg was not involved in the killing
of Dillinger outside the Biograph Theater in Chicago. The botched
raid at the Little Bohemia Lodge represented the darkest incident in
Clegg's tenure with the Bureau.

The most famous criminals of the 1930s were Al Capone and
John Dillinger. While Capone was feared, Dillinger, who was named
by the FBI as America's first Public Enemy No. 1, was considered
by the American public to be a Robin Hood and was thus, despite
his criminal activities, a public idol. Several movies and numerous
books recounting Dillinger's life and exploits have appeared, further
enhancing his notoriety.

Dillinger was born in Indianapolis, Indiana, in 1903 to middle-
class parents. His mother died when he was three years old and he

drifted into a life of crime at an early age, leading a neighborhood gang at the age of sixteen. He soon joined the US Navy but went AWOL and was dishonorably discharged. Dillinger was first convicted of a felony in 1924, when he robbed and assaulted a local grocery store owner and was sentenced to a prison term of from two to fourteen years in the Indiana Pendleton Reformatory. He developed his talents at escape, attempting twice in his first few weeks at Pendleton to make a break.[3] Embittered with his situation, he established friendships with several hardened criminals, including Harry Pierpont and Homer Van Meter, and developed a more hardened criminal mindset. Five years into his sentence Pierpont and Van Meter were transferred to the Indiana State Prison at Michigan City. In 1929, Dillinger's wish to be transferred with them was granted, and his relationship with the two was firmed up. Dillinger was paroled in April 1933 and his life as a bank robber started soon thereafter.

During the Great Depression, banks were not popular among ordinary Americans because of the role they played in foreclosures on homes and farms. In 1934, a movie company featured the manhunt for Dillinger and audiences cheered when his photo flashed on the screen, despite the fact that he had shot and killed a police officer while robbing a bank in East Chicago. He was captured and jailed in the Crown Point prison in Indiana but escaped, stole a car, and drove back to Chicago. The FBI was able to enter the investigation because driving a stolen automobile across state lines had become a federal crime.

The popularity of criminals, bank robbers in particular, infuriated Hoover. He was determined to bring Dillinger, Baby Face Nelson, Bonnie Parker and Clyde Barrow, Pretty Boy Floyd, Machine Gun Kelly, and others to justice. Dillinger was such a popular bank robber he was even photographed with his arms around law enforcement officials who eagerly posed with him. There was a need to turn around public opinion about crime, especially among the youth of the country, and the FBI was determined to do just that. But Dillinger was shrewd and proved hard to capture, and when he was captured, he escaped custody. The FBI was criticized for its failure to stop the Dillinger gang, and the criticism reached new heights with the shooting of Eddie Green, a member of the Dillinger gang.

In April 1934 Dillinger and his gang, which now included Baby Face Nelson, hid out at the Little Bohemia Lodge in Manitowish, Wisconsin, where they were tracked down. Clegg and Melvin Purvis assembled a number of agents and raided the Lodge. The raid turned out to be an embarrassment for the agency when both Dillinger and Nelson made their getaway. FBI agent W. Carter Baum was shot dead by Nelson, the fifth agent to be killed in the line of duty. In addition to the embarrassment, the raid at the Little Bohemia Lodge became a major point of controversy.

The events that led to the Little Bohemia raid are almost as interesting as the raid itself. Eddie Green, a former member of the Barker-Karpis gang, had become disenchanted with it and joined the Dillinger gang in early 1934. Known as a "jug marker," Green was adept at casing vulnerable banks to rob, thus endearing himself to Dillinger.

On March 30, FBI agents Rufus Coulter and Rosser "Rusty" Nalls, along with St. Paul, Minnesota, policeman Henry Cummings, had Dillinger trapped in an apartment but failed to secure the rear entrance. A shootout developed and Dillinger was wounded, hit by a ricochet from his own gun. He and his girlfriend, Billie Frechette, just walked out the uncovered back door and drove to Eddie Green's apartment to get help finding a doctor. Green provided Dillinger with a safe house in St. Paul. When Hoover learned of the bungled attempt to capture Dillinger, he was livid and set out to make the capture of Dillinger the top priority of the Bureau.

An FBI team led by Inspector William Rorer was able to locate the safe house as an apartment rented by a "Mr. Stevens." Suspecting this was the apartment in which Dillinger was hiding, they entered and found bank robbery paraphernalia but not Dillinger. As the agents waited for the return of Mr. Stevens, Rorer issued instructions over the telephone to agent Ed Notesteen to kill him on sight if and when the black maid, who initially described "Mr. Stevens" to the FBI, made a positive identification of him. After a while a car, a fancy

Essex Terraplane 6, occupied by Green and his common-law wife, Bessie (Beth) Skinner, pulled up to the house. The black maid identified the driver and agents fired several shots into the Terraplane to prevent anyone from using it to escape.[4] As the man lay wounded, it became obvious that he was not Dillinger, but Eddie Green.

The FBI received strong criticism from the American public for the cold-blooded shooting of an unarmed man. Hoover called upon Clegg to try to pacify the press. Clegg came to the defense of the agents involved, claiming that Green had "assumed a threatening attitude accompanied by menacing gestures" and had gone for his gun, forcing the FBI to shoot him.[5] But the press, unconvinced, increased its criticism of the FBI. Clegg did everything in his power to discourage a detailed investigation into the Green shooting and would not name any specific agent as the shooter to avoid having the agent involved in the shooting being called to testify in any probe. Clegg's tactics gained the immediate approval of Hoover, who would adopt this tactic in future incidents such as this. Hoover would credit the team, rather than any single agent, and publicly stress teamwork in the War on Crime.[6] Hoover held Clegg as a model for other agents, circulating throughout the Bureau his report on how the Green shooting was publicly handled. Clegg would return the admiration and became known as one of Hoover's favorite "yes men." Because of Clegg's efforts to cover up the shooting, the coroner ruled the killing justified despite pleas from reporters for further investigation.

As Green lay dying, he was tricked, under intense interrogation, into revealing the address of an apartment where he claimed Dillinger was hiding. Green first claimed Dillinger was at 635 Park Avenue, but agents were unable to find that address. Green then said the correct address was Apartment 4 on 1835 Park Avenue. Clegg had just arrived from Washington to supervise the hunt for Dillinger and was given the address where Dillinger was thought to be hiding. Clegg ordered every available agent to surround the apartment building, but no activity was detected. An impatient Clegg, carrying a submachine gun, ordered the apartment to be raided but it turned out to be the wrong apartment. Dillinger's hideout, which he had vacated the previous night, was in fact located on the floor below Apartment 4. Dillinger continued to outfox the FBI as he and his girlfriend, Billie Frechette, made their way out of St. Paul.[7]

Eddie Green died seven days after the ambush. Clegg had begun interrogating Bessie, but she yielded no information until she learned of Green's death. She then provided Clegg and the FBI with the names of members of the Dillinger and Barker-Karpis gangs. Bessie also confirmed the involvement of Alvin Karpis and Doc Barker in the Bremer and Hamm kidnappings.[8]

After getting out of St. Paul, Dillinger and his gang made their way to the Little Bohemia Lodge in Manitowish, Wisconsin. Thus began one of the Bureau's most famous failed raids that set the stage for Senator McKellar's later scathing attack on Hoover's credentials and law enforcement background and the ability of the FBI to get the job done. An embarrassed Hoover ordered an intense investigation of the events that took place before, during, and after the disastrous raid on the Lodge.

Many accounts of the raid on the Little Bohemia Lodge have appeared over the years in movies and books. In the most recent movie, *Public Enemies*, released in 2009, Clegg is erroneously portrayed as playing a minor role in the raid.[9] Two of the most important reports detailing the raid were prepared for Director Hoover, one by Clegg just days after the raid took place and dated April 25, 1934,[10] and the other by agent Harold "Pop" Nathan, dated June 1, 1934.[11] While Agent Nathan's report has been considered to be the more complete version because it was based on interviews from several agents and private citizens involved in the raid, his report had the luxury of time on its side. On the other hand, Clegg's detailed report was submitted to Director Hoover within a few days of the raid and offers a timelier version of the events that took place. To gain a fuller understanding of the actions of the FBI agents involved, including those of Clegg and Purvis, both accounts should be read. Interspersed in the Nathan report are additional known facts about the raid, acquired weeks after it took place, which were not included in Clegg's initial report.

Clegg's report provided details that attest to the meticulous approach he took in matters of this type. The botched raid at the Little Bohemia Lodge under his leadership would come to be known as one of the FBI's most controversial actions. Because this entire episode represented the most significant case Clegg was involved in during the gangster era of his tenure at the FBI, his report to Hoover regarding the raid takes on special significance. Included in the following synopsis of Clegg's report are excerpts from the Nathan report and other sources when clarification is necessary.

Melvin Purvis was in charge of the Chicago FBI office and was enjoying a rare day off on Sunday, April 22, when he received a telephone call at one o'clock in the afternoon. Chicago US marshal H. C. W. Laubenheimer told Purvis that he had received a call from a man identifying himself as Henry Voss of the Birchwood Summer Tavern in Wisconsin indicating that Dillinger, six other men, and a woman were in that area.[12] Purvis called Clegg and asked him and agents William Rorer and Werner Hanni to meet him at the Rhinelander airport. Director Hoover also instructed Clegg to meet Purvis.

Clegg chartered a plane at a cost of thirty-five cents per mile, and he and agents Rorer, John E. Brennan, Sam Hardy, and T. G. Melvin took off for Rhinelander. Certain weaponry, such as gas gun equipment, was not permitted on the chartered flight. Agent Hanni, accompanied by Agents O. G. Hall, G. F. Hurley, and Thomas Dodd, loaded the equipment in an automobile and set out for Rhinelander. Hanni had a fear of flying. When Clegg's airplane arrived at the airport, the first to arrive, three individuals in two automobiles greeted him. One of the individuals, Lloyd LaPorte, introduced himself to Clegg and then introduced Clegg to Henry Voss. Clegg was informed that Dillinger was believed to be at an inn fifty miles north of Rhinelander owned by Emil Wanatka.[13]

The arrival of Clegg's airplane attracted a large crowd, so Clegg, LaPorte, and Voss moved to a quiet location where Voss told Clegg the group staying at the inn included six men and four women.[14] Clegg showed them photographs of individuals the FBI was searching for, and although Voss could not identify Dillinger, he did identify photographs of Dillinger gang members Tommy Carroll and Patricia Cherrington. Emil Wanatka and his wife told Voss they were convinced those members of the group were mobsters, and Wanatka's wife was convinced that Dillinger was a member of the group.

Voss then prepared a diagram of the building, including seven or eight outhouses, a cabin, and closed and open garages. Voss further informed Clegg that there was a lake at the rear of the lodge, but that making an escape over the lake was impossible, since there was no boat and a thin coat of ice covered the lake. Because Agent Hanni's group could not possibly arrive at Rhinelander until later in the evening, Clegg began locating automobiles to transport his team to the lodge. He found a Ford dealer in town who owned a number of vehicles. The owner of the agency told Clegg he had no license to rent automobiles and was reluctant to rent out his new ones. He did tell Clegg that a coupe was available but would not let him use it if the federal agents were involved in pursuing liquor law violations; he did not want his name connected to rendering aid against liquor law violators. Clegg assured him that they had other purposes in mind but did not disclose their real purpose. The owner then told Clegg he could have two automobiles that his salesmen were out demonstrating, but that the cars would not be available for another hour or two.

Clegg had seen an airplane headed for the airport and he assumed the plane carried Melvin Purvis and his group, so he headed back to the airport. Purvis's group had actually arrived in two planes. Voss and one of the agents were instructed to proceed to the Voss home to obtain information regarding the latest plans of the gangsters. Fifteen minutes later, Voss and the agent returned to the airport and told Clegg they had encountered Mrs. Voss. She was on her way to the airport to inform her husband that the group had changed plans and would be leaving the lodge as soon as they finished dinner. Clegg and Purvis had to speed up their plans for the raid. The original plan was to surround the lodge and wait for daylight to conduct the raid, but the latest news from Voss forced the teams to head straight to the lodge some fifty miles away.

The car of one of the spectators in the crowd at the airport was commandeered, and three agents went back into town to obtain as many cars as they could find. The agents soon returned with several cars that were then loaded with the guns and machine guns needed for the raid. By this time it was about 7:30 p.m., and Clegg and the agents headed for the lodge in five vehicles over bad roads covered with melting snow, holes, and mud. Other than the diagram given him by Voss and LaPorte, Clegg had no information as to the layout they would encounter. Clegg said two automobiles were disabled by the rough rides, so the agents in those cars rode the last fifteen or twenty miles on the running boards of the other three vehicles.

When they arrived at a point two miles from the Lodge they stopped, and Voss explained that Mrs. Wanatka and her child had left the inn, the gangsters had not yet left, and the only other occupants of the inn were Emil Wanatka and two or three assistants who worked for Wanatka. Clegg was also advised of the location of the garage where the cars of the gangsters were located.

At 9:00 p.m., the lead automobile in which Clegg was riding approached the lodge with its lights off. As Clegg got out of the lead car, dogs belonging to Mrs. Wanatka began barking and, fearing the mobsters would be alerted, he ordered the agents to empty the cars and surround the house. No one had mentioned the presence of dogs at the lodge. The agents quickly got out of their cars and began to surround the house. Rorer led a group to one side of the lodge, other agents went to the other side, and Clegg, Purvis, and Baum were located in the center, blocking the only road exiting the lodge.

An automobile (a 1933 Chevrolet coupe) parked in the front of the house started up. Its three passengers were John Hoffman and two Civilian Conservation Corps (CCC) workers, Eugene Boisneau and John Morris. Clegg, Purvis, and others identified themselves in loud voices, saying that they were police and federal officers and ordering the car to stop. The car radio had been turned on so loud the occupants could not hear the order to stop and rather than stopping, the car sped up.[15] Clegg said that he and Purvis, assuming that Dillinger was in the coupe, simultaneously gave orders to shoot the tires out.

They then heard machine gun fire coming from the rear of the house by the lake and Clegg assumed Rorer had cornered the gang. Meanwhile, the automobile in front of the house continued its efforts to get away but suddenly stopped with the motor still running.

An elderly man (John Morris) got out of the car and sat down beside it. He was ordered to put his hands up and come forward, but he sat down by the garage, pulled a flask out of his pocket, and took a drink instead. Rather than approaching the officers, he turned and went back into the house. Clegg could not tell if the man was drunk or injured. Later it was discovered that Morris had been shot four times.

Rorer returned to the front of the lodge and informed Clegg that agents had been deployed all the way to the lake. Rorer then said he returned fire coming from men on the roof of the lodge and that one man jumped off the roof. Rorer assumed this man went back into the house. He also said he saw another man running alongside one of the cabins, firing his gun in the direction of Clegg, Purvis, Baum, and the automobile in which those later identified as the CCC workers were found, so he fired at the shooter. This man, assumed to be Baby Face Nelson, got away. Clegg assumed that the others were still in the house. About this time, the elderly man who had returned to the house came out, followed by Emil Wanatka and two employees with their hands up. They approached Clegg and Purvis, who searched them and found them to be unarmed. A deputy sheriff arrived on the scene and identified the four men.

An ambulance arrived, and the two Civilian Conservation Corps workers were then put in it and, accompanied by agent Ken McIntire, taken to a hospital. Boisneau was dead and Hoffman was wounded.

Just before the ambulance arrived, another car, with its headlights on, came down the road that led off the highway. The car was ordered to stop but instead sped away and was fired on by agents who were covering the road from the rear. The occupants of this car were Pat Cherrington and Pat Reilly, who were returning from a trip to

St. Paul. The car backed off the premises and, it was later learned, stopped at a service station a mile away and had a shot-up tire replaced.

When the shooting subsided, Clegg told agents Newman and Baum to go to the Voss residence two miles away and call the airport to leave directions for agent Hanni on how to get to the lodge. When Newman and Baum returned to the lodge, Clegg told Newman to go back and telephone the sheriff to let him know about the raid and make sure the federal agents were not attacked from the rear by mistake. Newman asked Clegg if Baum could accompany him, and Clegg agreed (a decision he would regret).

Emil Wanatka had been allowed to go to his father-in-law's house to get a coat. When he returned, he told Clegg that a house two miles away was being robbed and that the bandit was holding two agents and members of a family at gunpoint. Clegg then dispatched other agents to the house, but they returned with some bad news: Newman and Baum had been shot and Baum killed. Nelson, who had escaped from the lodge, stopped to rob a house and held an elderly couple hostage. Just as he was leaving with his hostages, Baum and Newman drove up and Nelson ordered them to get out of the car. Nelson thought one of the agents was reaching for a pistol and began firing, killing Baum instantly and wounding Newman in the head. By this time, Hanni had arrived at the scene of the fatal shooting and took Newman and a constable who had also been wounded to a hospital in Ironwood, Michigan, several miles away.

Meanwhile, Clegg feared that someone might have escaped from one of the garages or outhouses. Therefore, he sought reinforcements and ordered one of the agents to assume a position between the house and the entrance to the roadway that led off the highway to the house. Another agent was ordered to a spot deep in the woods to prevent any surprise attack from the rear. The rest of the agents held their positions, waiting for daylight. A light went out in one of the rooms on the first floor—the only sign of life in the house. Just before daybreak, the sheriff and his posse arrived and were told the location of the agents around the house so they would not be fired on by mistake. Although the sheriff was in charge, several members of the posse were hotheads and wanted to burn the house down.

Clegg informed the sheriff that he was about to order tear gas to be thrown into the house to rouse the gangsters rather than blindly walk into the house and give the gangsters an advantage. Several canisters of gas were fired by the gas guns toward the house, but because of their lack of accuracy, they bounced back after hitting the windows, so an agent threw a gas grenade into the house by hand. Members of the posse fired rifle shots through the windows. A woman's voice was heard coming from the building, pleading for the shooting to stop. Clegg told the people in the house to come out with their hands up, and three females emerged. When the gas subsided, the agents entered the house only to find that the rest of the occupants, including Dillinger, had gotten away.[16]

Clegg's report ends with Clegg and Purvis going to the Voss home to inform Hoover of what had taken place and provide him with information Clegg had been given concerning the shooting of agents Baum and Newman. They were advised to return to their St. Paul and Chicago offices, leaving agent Rorer in charge.

The Clegg and Nathan accounts have similarities as well as differences. Clegg appears to downplay the role Purvis played in planning and conducting the raid without reflecting credit or blame upon Clegg himself. Neither report mentions the fact that as of April 23, 1934, Clegg, Purvis, and Clyde Tolson had not been qualified in the use of firearms,[17] and that on February 16 of that year, Hoover wrote Clegg and nine other agents that they had not qualified as marksmen with a pistol and urged them to qualify at the earliest possible date.[18]

This raid represented one of the greatest debacles in FBI history (unmatched until the FBI siege in Waco, Texas, in 1993). One FBI agent was killed, another seriously wounded, an innocent CCC worker killed, and two others wounded. Despite being surrounded by twelve or thirteen highly trained FBI agents, Dillinger escaped the lodge through an unguarded back door. Other gangsters slid down the steep bank located at the rear of the lodge and escaped. Except for the women in the lodge, all of Dillinger's mob made a clean getaway. Dillinger had once again escaped from the FBI, the fourth time he had done so in less than four weeks' time.[19]

Hoover was upset with the events that took place at the Little Bohemia Lodge. He wrote a memo dated April 26 to Attorney General Homer Cummings stating that "Mr. H.H. Clegg, Assistant Director, was in charge of this particular investigation, and not Mr. Purvis." Yet more blame for the failure of the Little Bohemia raid fell on Purvis, and he later resigned. On May 8, 1934, Hoover wrote a memorandum regarding events that had taken place at Little Bohemia. The memo was not addressed to anyone; however, in the upper left corner was the designation "JEH:HCB(mtr)."[20]

Hoover had met with Justice Department prosecutor Joseph Keenan in his office, after which he telephoned Harold "Pop" Nathan. Keenan told Hoover he had two things to tell him that would anger him, but that he would not disclose his source unless Hoover insisted. Keenan said that at Little Bohemia, agents mutinied against Clegg, Rorer, and Purvis, telling them they didn't know how to handle the situation. Then, Keenan continued, they locked the three in a shack adjacent to the inn, holding them there until the shooting was over. He also said it was untrue that agent Carter Baum had shot the federal work camp man, Eugene Boisneau, despite what was stated in Nathan's report. In fact, Keenan said, Baum's gun was found to be locked when it was found at the place where Baum was killed. No shots were fired from Baum's gun. Keenan said his source told him that Rorer was the agent who killed Boisneau. Furthermore, Clegg, Purvis, and Rorer agreed, "it [the shooting of Boisneau] could be fixed up another way." The source claimed the supposedly mutinous men were out of control.

Keenan further claimed that when Dillinger was located at the Lincoln Court Apartments on Lexington Avenue in St. Paul in March 1934, a shootout occurred during which Dillinger and Billie Frechette managed to escape. When agent Rorer was informed of Dillinger's location, he attempted to call the St. Paul police chief,

Thomas Dahill. Rorer could not reach him by phone so rather than calling another police officer, he went to police headquarters, thus wasting time. Keenan said that his source told him that by the time Rorer arrived at the Lexington Avenue apartment with the police, Dillinger and his gang had escaped.

Keenan told Hoover he was reluctant to tell this story since it was none of his business, but thought that if "my Agents" were not telling the truth, Hoover would want to know rather than have the story revealed from the outside. Keenan said he had no plans to tell the story to the attorney general. Hoover said he had no objection to his doing so but that he could not believe that three officials of the division were locked in a shed by the other agents, and he could not believe that if the agents had lost respect for the three, they managed to keep it quiet for so long. Hoover also corrected the Lexington Avenue story. He told Keenan that Rorer did try to call Chief Dahill to no avail and that Rorer had sent two agents to police headquarters to pick up reinforcements, while Rorer himself rushed to the Lexington Avenue address.

Hoover insisted that Keenan tell him the name of his source, and Keenan named former agent Thomas F. Cullen in Chicago. Keenan was convinced that Cullen had obtained this information from an agent attached to the St. Paul office.

Hoover called Nathan, who told the director that he had a dinner engagement with Cullen that night. Hoover directed Nathan to tell Cullen he had been told the story and that the Bureau would not try to cover anything up. He then told Nathan to ask Cullen to reveal the source of his information. Hoover promised not to fire the agent who told Cullen the story. He also told Nathan to drop everything else at Chicago and find out the exact condition of Baum's gun. Hoover further requested Nathan to obtain statements from various agents as to the exact facts with respect to first, the allegation that the agents mutinied and locked three officials in a shack; second, the statement that agent Baum's gun could not have fired the shot that killed the CCC man; and third, the statement concerning Rorer's actions in the Lexington Avenue incident. Hoover told Nathan about a statement a sergeant of the Michigan State Police gave to a Mr. Olander about the Little Bohemia incident, and that this version was "entirely different from the version given by Messrs. Clegg, Rorer and Purvis." Hoover then stated, "There doesn't seem to be a very strong degree of accuracy in the descriptions of what transpired at Little Bohemia."[21]

The issue would not go away. On July 5, 1934, Hoover wrote Clegg regarding the recent Little Bohemia raid.[22] He stated that it had been alleged prior to this raid that Clegg said to special agents assigned to the raid that he "had never before conducted a raid and had never, in fact, participated in a raid." Hoover said it was further alleged that "because of your inexperience you would welcome any advice or suggestions which might be offered." Hoover was concerned not that Clegg would solicit advice, but that a division official, about to direct subordinate personnel, would indicate to those subordinates a lack of knowledge concerning the activities about to be conducted.

Hoover wanted Clegg to respond to this latest allegation, and on July 9 Clegg wrote Hoover that prior to April 22, 1934—the date of the raid—he had participated in at least three raids that he could recall and denied making the statement cited.[23] Clegg stated that during the first week of his arrival in St. Paul, he heard complaints that raids had been made without the agents being informed of the definite objective or the importance of the raid. Clegg said that prior to the raid, he called a meeting of all agents in the St. Paul office (Hanni and Rorer were both present) and informed them that those participating in raids hereafter would be informed as to the purpose of the raids, that a definite program of action would be first prepared and followed, and that he would be pleased "to receive any suggestions or recommendations which any of the Agents might desire to make." Furthermore, he said that "it is entirely possible that I might have stated at this time that I had not had a great deal of experience and therefore did not want to tell them precisely what must be done in every raid, because each raid would have different problems arising," and hence the request for suggestions. He did not recall any other time in which he directly or indirectly referred to his lack of experience. He assured Hoover that with regard to the Little Bohemia raid, "such a remark was not made, immediately prior to that raid or at any other time."

It is not surprising that jealousies among agents arose. Clegg was basically in charge of the dreaded Training and Inspection Division of the Bureau—dreaded mainly because the division was responsible for the inspection of the Bureau itself—and was considered a Hoover favorite. Despite Melvin Purvis's penchant for seeking publicity, many agents aligned themselves with him, so at least two camps existed: the pro-Clegg camp and the pro-Purvis camp. Events at Little Bohemia further separated the camps. What is surprising is that Clegg was very supportive of Purvis and refrained from any open criticism.

The division became more evident when fellow agents criticized Clegg prior to the Bohemia raid. On May 2, 1934, Special Agent in Charge Edward A. Tamm wrote a personal and confidential memo to Hoover regarding an investigation at New Castle, Pennsylvania.[24] Tamm quoted agent W. V. McLaughlin as saying that he admired and respected agents Clegg and Rorer, but based on his observations of their activities in the Chicago district, he did not believe that they had a sufficient amount of experience in conducting raids and, furthermore, they did not give consideration to suggestions made by agents under them. At the same time, McLaughlin noted that agents Purvis and Hanni had much better attitudes toward hearing and paying attention to suggestions made by agents.

Agents continued to squabble over the botched Little Bohemia raid and Clegg's leadership of it. Agent Werner Hanni of the St. Paul office was especially frustrated. As special agent in charge, he resented Rorer and Clegg's commandeering of his office. Clegg found a memo Hanni had written but had not sent to Hoover stating that the raid was staged with little organization and lack of knowledge and judgment. Hanni claimed that he and other agents had been led into a death trap. No preparations had been made, he wrote. Hanni had a bad word for almost everyone. He even criticized Clegg, though not by name, for hindering the earlier pursuit of Dillinger by pestering his men with questions during the investigation into the death of Eddie Green.[25] Hanni had written Clegg on May 1 criticizing him and claiming it was evident that the raid was staged with little organization.[26] Clegg was incensed and in turn suggested that Hanni was upset because despite the fact that Hanni was in charge of the geographical area in which the Little Bohemia raid was conducted, he was not chosen to lead the raid. Clegg also pointed out that since Hanni had a fear of flying, he drove, rather than flew, with Clegg's group to northern Wisconsin. He was the last agent to arrive on the scene and did not appear at Little Bohemia until after Dillinger had escaped. When agent Nathan defended the Bureau's actions in his report, he excoriated Hanni, calling his allegations absurd. Hanni was quietly transferred from the St. Paul office to the office in Omaha.[27]

On June 1, 1934, Agent Nathan submitted a document in addition to his detailed report of the raid at Little Bohemia.[28] Responding to allegations and rumors in connection with the raid, Nathan had interviewed Clegg, Purvis, Hanni, Rorer, and twenty-four other agents from the Chicago and St. Paul FBI offices who were either at the lodge when the first assault took place or arrived later that night or early the next morning. The following questions were asked of those interviewed and the results summarized:

Q. Was there any mutiny or disobedience of orders by the Special Agents there that was either observed by you or was heard of by you then or at any other time?
A. In each and every instance the answer to this question was in the positive negative. Not the slightest evidence of any mutiny or disobedience or disregard of orders was indicated by any of those interviewed.

Q. Is it a fact that the Division executives in charge of this expedition, Messrs. Clegg, Rorer, and Purvis, were seized by Special Agents and placed in a shack or any other building, or in any manner ordered or taken by any Agent or Agents from the scene of this affair?

A. The answers to this question indicated unanimously that there was absolutely no foundation to the foregoing allegation. In fact, it was looked upon as ridiculous by the majority of those interviewed, as indicated by their smiles and manner of answering the question. It may safely be assumed that this statement is without the slightest basis in fact.

Q. Had you occasion to observe who killed Eugene Boisneau, the Civilian Conservation Corps man there?

A. [in part] No direct evidence was secured indicating the individual who killed Boisneau. It is quite possible that he was killed by the late Special Agent Baum.

Q. Did the Agents act on their own responsibility without orders at any time?

A. Each and every one of those interviewed indicated that the Agents acted under specific orders and they did not act on their own responsibility other than, of course, firing when fired upon or at gun flashes, during the entire episode. Instructions were issued by Inspectors Clegg and Rorer and Special Agent in Charge Purvis at various times during the evening. The men were stationed under their direction and appeared to be closely and directly controlled during the entire time.

Hanni's allegations were later dismissed by the Bureau, suggesting that Hanni was suffering from fatigue when he made the charges.[29] When Hoover completed his final report on the raid at the Little Bohemia Lodge, he attributed the failure to capture Dillinger not to negligence or poor tactical decisions by Purvis or Clegg but rather to the "extremely unfortunate incident whereby three drunken or at least drinking members of the Civilian Conservation Corps were in the Little Bohemia when our agents arrived there and departed hastily, ignoring instructions to stop."[30] The FBI did a poor job during the entire episode, both at the raid itself and with regard to the resulting internal bickering and backbiting.

Although the FBI became the object of ridicule, it would restore much of its lost respect when Dillinger was eventually shot and killed. After escaping from the Little Bohemia Lodge, Dillinger made it back to Chicago, where Purvis was put in charge of the renewed manhunt. On July 22, Dillinger emerged from the Biograph Theater and was shot anywhere from two to four times by a contingent of FBI agents led by Melvin Purvis that included Bob Gillepsie from Meridian, Mississippi, with whom Clegg had worked in the past. Purvis was hailed as a hero, but the actual shooter is still a mystery. Purvis did, however, follow the Clegg press tactic that Hoover appreciated by saying two or three agents fired the fatal shots.[31]

Despite rumors and claims to the contrary, Clegg was not involved and was not even on the scene.[32] He was preparing to board a train in Washington, DC, when Attorney General Homer Cummings informed him that Dillinger had been shot in Chicago. Clegg and Cummings were leaving for the six-week Cummings junket discussed earlier.

Dillinger's crime spree lasted only fifteen months, but the effects on the nation were long lasting. During this brief period he was charged with, but never convicted of, the murder of an East Chicago, Indiana, police officer during a shoot-out— his only alleged homicide. His gang robbed two dozen banks and four police stations and Dillinger twice escaped from jail. Among all of the public enemies of the time, Dillinger was the most famous.

The raid at the Little Bohemia Lodge would not rank among Clegg's finest achievements while at the FBI. It is, however, without a doubt among the most well-known.

Chapter Six

Family Life

URING THE 1920S AND 1930S, Clegg's life was almost totally devoted to serving the FBI. There is little documentation
of his social life during this period, although he dated several women from time to time. All that would change in 1937, when
he met his future wife. Clegg recalled that a group of Mississippians, including a contingent from Anguilla, Mississippi, and Sharkey
County, came to Washington for the second inauguration of Franklin Roosevelt, which took place on March 4, 1937. Included in the
group were Clegg's sister Irene, her husband, and a beautiful woman
from the Mississippi Delta who caught Clegg's eye, Ruby Kathryn
Fields. Clegg would brag that no one ever caught his attention like
Ruby Kathryn, who often went by the nickname Kat. She was once
engaged to the son of the owner of a lumber mill in Picayune but
later broke off the engagement. Hugh and Kat were free to pursue
a relationship, and they did. They had a small town background in
common, a factor that may have attracted them to each other. In the
1930 census, Mathiston and Anguilla had populations of 484 and
467, respectively.

Ruby Kathryn was born in Anguilla, Mississippi, in 1909 and attended Millsaps for two years before transferring to the University
of Mississippi, where she graduated. She was a member of the Phi
Mu sorority. Kat was the equivalent of today's Miss Hospitality and
went to the Chicago World's Fair as Mississippi hostess. She was also
honored as an Ole Miss favorite. Kat had fallen in love with Oxford
and Ole Miss and the old traditions and longed for the day when she
would somehow return.[1]

After graduating, she accepted a job in social services in Clarksdale, Mississippi, and then returned to Anguilla to take care of her ailing father. When she joined the delegation from Sharkey County on the trip to Washington, DC, for the inauguration and met Clegg, her life changed forever.

Ruby Kathryn's grandfather, Captain H. J. Fields, came to Anguilla after the Civil War. Her great-grandfather had opened the territory to agriculture. Captain Fields married Kate Sullivan and they had thirteen children in a period of twenty-six years. Ruby's father was Grover Cleveland Fields, who became a county supervisor and the president of the Bank of Anguilla. Her mother was Ruby Lynn Wray from Pope, Mississippi, who lived for a while in Greenville and New Orleans before coming to Anguilla as a music teacher and marrying Grover.

Clegg was smitten with Kat and they began seeing each other more and more often. While many regarded Hugh as a stern leader and administrator, in private life he was a romantic. He often sent Kat two dozen roses at a time. He wrote her romantic letters and pursued her with vigor. When Hugh returned from England in 1940, where he had gone to study the British intelligence system before the US involvement in World War II, he proposed to Kat, and she accepted. They were married on June 11, 1941, in Anguilla, and the event was considered a big happening for a small town. Hugh's brother, James Ellis, was his best man. Hugh and Kat honeymooned in Atlantic City and New York City. Director Hoover gave the couple a sterling silver bowl and tray engraved with the FBI shield as a wedding gift.[2] Hugh and Kat had one daughter, born on December 11, 1943, in Washington, DC. They named her Ruby Kathryn after her mother and grandmother.

When Hugh and Kat moved to Oxford, their daughter attended University High School—which later became Oxford High School—and then went to Ole Miss. She made excellent grades and was elected president of the Pan-Hellenic Council. Like her mother, she joined Phi Mu sorority and became president of the pledge class. She was also a member of Mortar Board, a national senior honorary society. In addition to being as beautiful as her mother, she was also a talented singer and sang in choirs in Oxford and Tupelo. She began dating Aubrey B. Patterson Jr., and they continued to date while they were both students at Ole Miss. Ruby Kathryn would recall that her father was protective of her not only when they were in Washington, but also when they lived in Oxford. Clegg had told her that she could not marry Aubrey until she was either twenty-one years of age or had graduated from Ole Miss.

On December 12, 1964, when she was both twenty-one years old and an alumna of Ole Miss, she and Aubrey married at the First Baptist Church in Oxford. Aubrey was in the ROTC at Ole Miss and joined the air force upon graduation. He received a bachelor's degree in business administration and was commissioned a second lieutenant. His first assignment was in St. Louis, and according to Clegg, it involved some sort of intelligence work. Aubrey was then selected for the master's degree program in accountancy at Michigan State University and graduated first in his class. The couple then moved to Karamürsel, Turkey, where Aubrey served as comptroller of several bases in the area. He later completed work at the Graduate School of Banking at the University of Wisconsin. Ruby Kathryn and Aubrey had two sons and a daughter. Aubrey became vice president of the Bank of Mississippi at Tupelo and then executive chairman and chief executive officer of BancorpSouth Bank.[3] He was later appointed to the Mississippi Board of Trustees of Institutions of Higher Learning (IHL). Ruby Kathryn has fond memories of Webster County and calls her father's hometown warm and cozy.[4]

Clegg's service with the FBI yielded an unexpected friendship for his daughter. For three years, from 1939 to 1942, Margaret Elizabeth "Betty" Turner served as his secretary before becoming the secretary of J. Edgar Hoover. She was quite attractive, and agents would pass by Clegg's office just to steal a glance at her. One of those agents, William A. "Bill" Murphy, was well liked by Clegg, so he introduced the pair and they later married. Clegg gave Betty away at the wedding. Murphy had joined the FBI in 1936 and retired in 1959.

Like Clegg, Bill Murphy was loyal to Director Hoover. Bill and Betty had a daughter, Betsy (Betsy Dyke), who had planned on going to an Ivy League university that admitted female students, the University of Pennsylvania. But her father was worried for her safety in a big city like Philadelphia and called his good friend, Hugh Clegg, who was at Ole Miss at the time, and expressed his concern. Clegg suggested to Murphy that his daughter come to Ole Miss. When she flew to Oxford to visit the university in June 1961, Clegg met her at the airport and Betsy met her father's long-time friend for the first time. She liked Ole Miss at first sight and decided to enroll there rather than go east for school. She and Clegg's daughter, Ruby Kathryn, became immediate friends.[5]

Clegg called his daughter his "ace."[6] She had suffered from various allergies in her youth and was allergic to changes in temperature. She missed a considerable amount of school due to sinus problems, which were a major concern for her parents. A pediatrician feared her allergies could progress to asthma, so the Cleggs began to explore other job opportunities in warmer climates than Washington, DC.[7] Many times Ruby Kathryn would take their daughter to Anguilla during the winter to give her some relief from the cold. During the winter, their daughter attended Anguilla Elementary School, and her mother would then bring her back to DC for the second semester of school in the spring and early summer.[8]

Clegg was asked if it was true that during the war years his life was hectic and if he had much of a home life. He said that it didn't matter whether it was wartime or peacetime; he would get to his office precisely at nine o'clock and didn't leave before 7:40 p.m. Hoover would leave his office at 7:40 and out of courtesy and respect no one would leave before Hoover. Even at this late hour, Hoover was known to call a conference on some matter. Clegg and the other agents were free to leave, but they voluntarily stayed until Hoover had left the office, when one of the secretarial staff would announce, "Mr. Hoover has departed for the evening." If Clegg and others had left early, Hoover would perhaps not have said anything, though.[9]

In Washington, the Cleggs lived in an apartment on Connecticut Avenue with their daughter. He felt comfortable about his housing and the atmosphere of the nation's capital. Unlike Kat, who was outgoing and made friends easily, Hugh—influenced by the nature of his job with the FBI—was wary in developing social relationships. But Clegg would occasionally mix the two. Cartha D. "Deke" De-Loach, who served the FBI for twenty-eight years and was to become a member of Director Hoover's inner circle, recalled a time when Clegg visited Akron, Ohio, to give a speech. DeLoach at the time was a resident agent based in Cleveland. Clegg visited DeLoach's home following his speech and one week later recommended DeLoach's promotion to agent supervisor at the FBI headquarters in Washington. He and Clegg became fast friends and would enjoy many long talks when the two were in Washington. DeLoach remembered that he and his wife had dinner in Clegg's home where he met Kat and their small daughter Ruby Kathryn. They maintained correspondence for many years, and after Director Hoover's death, Clegg encouraged Deke to become director of the FBI. DeLoach considered Clegg to be "a man of great ability, an excellent representative of the FBI and a fine person."[10]

Clegg did have regrets that his work took him on the road so much, but his wife and daughter did not complain.[11] His later decision to retire and move to Ole Miss was difficult. After all, he spent thirty-one years, including law school, in DC, so leaving the Bureau and the city was not an easy decision.[12] While the Cleggs enjoyed their time in the nation's capital, working for the FBI was not without its drawbacks and dangers. Clegg warned his wife and daughter that their telephones might be tapped by at least two different organizations and that they should exercise caution in discussing anything related to Clegg's work.[13]

Chapter Seven

The FBI and World War II

We are not afraid to entrust the American people with unpleasant facts, foreign ideas, alien philosophies, and competitive values. For a nation that is afraid to let its people judge the truth and falsehood in an open market is afraid of its people.—John F. Kennedy

THE WAR ON CRIME, including the hunt for John Dillinger and the subsequent fiasco at the Little Bohemia Lodge, was among the highlights of Clegg's FBI career during the 1930s. As America was moving toward its involvement in World War II, Clegg, by then an assistant director of the FBI, was placed in charge of the Training and Inspection Division and directed several investigations from his Washington, DC, administrative office. However, he was also in charge of field operations in many major cases. In addition, Hoover sometimes sent him to a national or regional office to assume leadership of an operation because of his faith in Clegg and because of Clegg's strong loyalty to Hoover.

His loyalty to Hoover was challenged in 1938 by Special Agent Angus W. Taylor, who made inflammatory charges against Clegg in a June 30 memo to Clyde Tolson.[1] Taylor alleged, among other things, that the Bureau comprised two factions, one working for the director and the other headed by Clegg, which was at odds with the director and was desirous of seeing the director replaced; that when stories appeared in the press "some years ago" indicating that the director would resign to accept a position at DuPont, Taylor heard stories that Clegg "was desirous of securing the Director's position"; and that he recently heard that Clegg "is still seeking the position of the Director." Taylor went on to say he did not recall where he heard this information but that it came from Bureau employees. In a letter to Hoover four months later, Clegg categorically rejected all of these allegations and declared "I want to go on record as stating that they are separately, collectively, and individually false." He claimed that Taylor was "an unmitigated liar" and that there had been "no word or act on my part which could even with the wildest stretch of imagination be interpreted in any way as to form a basis for such statements and they are utterly ridiculous and false from beginning to end." Clegg went on to state that Taylor had borne animosity toward him since the latter was in training school and furthermore conjectured that Taylor had not even heard anyone making the comments he claimed to have heard.[2] If Hoover doubted Clegg's loyalty, he did not indicate it.

During the years from 1937 to 1939, the Bureau grew to about nine hundred agents. When the war started, the agency increased by several thousand agents. Clegg was deeply involved in training these new agents, sometimes scheduling sixteen classes with fifty agents in each class. At various times there were from 100 to 150 experienced agents brought back for retraining. The agency offered inspector schools, executive schools, special agents in charge schools, and assistant special agent's schools, all taking place at the same time. Efforts were made to train agents in Spanish so they could go to South America to train police forces there and to prepare agents for intelligence gathering in the Western Hemisphere. Preparing for war, the FBI published numerous booklets, such as *War Duties of Police* and *War Duties of Public Executives*. Before Clegg became involved, only sporadic training programs had existed.

As the decade came to a close, the FBI turned most of its attention to the events taking place in Europe, and in preparation for the outbreak of a world war, President Roosevelt assigned to the FBI the responsibility for intelligence operations in the entire Western Hemisphere. Clegg would later be placed in charge of organizing the domestic intelligence division. His interest in intelligence matters was evidenced by his earlier application in 1935 for an appointment as a major in the Intelligence Division of the Officers Reserve

Corps of the US Army. Clyde Tolson, who considered Clegg to be eminently qualified, supported his application.[3] Eventually it was approved, and in 1938 he received a commission as a major.

Archibald MacLeish, the librarian of Congress and a speechwriter for President Roosevelt, participated in a conference held in Hoover's office in which language was drafted to give the FBI jurisdiction over intelligence field operations in the entire Western Hemisphere, while the Office of Strategic Services (OSS) was assigned intelligence operations in the rest of the world. In addition to his duties as librarian of Congress, MacLeish directed the Office of Facts and Figures for the War Department and was assistant director of the Office of War Information. The US military had its own intelligence programs.

In July 1941, as events in Europe and the Pacific precipitated America's entrance into World War II, President Roosevelt appointed William J. "Wild Bill" Donovan—called the Father of Central Intelligence—as the Coordinator of Information (COI) whose purpose was to lead America's first peacetime intelligence organization. The COI soon evolved into the Office of Strategic Services (OSS) and shared responsibility for foreign intelligence with the FBI. The establishment of the OSS provoked hostility from the FBI and other war agencies.[4] The OSS was viewed by Hoover as a competitor of the FBI intelligence program. In 1945, the OSS was technically abolished and its collection, analysis, and counterintelligence activities were taken over by the State and War Departments. The Central Intelligence Agency (CIA) was created under the National Security Act of 1947. The CIA was given intelligence jurisdiction over the entire world outside the United States, thus leaving the FBI with responsibility for domestic intelligence. However, the FBI would continue to compete for a role in all intelligence responsibilities.

In 1940, the strength of the US Communist Party and pro-Nazi organizations and the open activities of these political groups caused much national concern. The underground activities of the Communist Party caused particular concern in Washington. Attorney General Robert Jackson, appointed in 1940, called on the FBI to infiltrate these organizations and created a national defense investigation unit within the FBI. The FBI coordinated all governmental investigations that affected national defense. Hoover put Clegg in charge of a new investigational unit at a time when the United States had not yet become involved in the war in Europe. Clegg became assistant director in charge of the domestic intelligence division, but Director Hoover thought it would be beneficial for the FBI to send a mission to Britain to study and learn its intelligence operations. Hoover discussed this idea with Britain's foreign intelligence branch, MI6. Their MI5 branch handled domestic intelligence similar to the FBI's role in the United States. The MI6 representative to Washington was in constant contact with the FBI and Clegg. The two met every Tuesday afternoon at two o'clock in Clegg's office. The United States and Britain were cooperating in intelligence matters even though the former was not directly involved in the war at the time. Hoover used his persuasive powers to obtain an invitation to the FBI to go to England and study its intelligence operations. The British agreed to work with its counterparts. Hoover wanted the FBI to work with MI5, MI6, Scotland Yard, and whoever else was involved in intelligence operations and study those operations under wartime conditions. The United States was expected to enter the war shortly, and since America had no experience in deploying a foreign intelligence system, it would soon have to implement such a structure. Hoover also saw this visit as an opportunity for the FBI to expand its areas of responsibility and to put himself in the position of being the US central intelligence guru.

On November 12, 1940, Hoover wrote agents Tolson, Clegg, and Tamm that the attorney general had approved his October 30 memorandum that he (Hoover) send representatives of the Bureau to London "to make a survey not only of intelligence matters but all matters dealing with functions of police in times of national emergency."[5] After all, the British had a long history in military intelligence and espionage.[6]

Hoover designated Clegg and agent Lawrence Hince to proceed upon this mission at once. The attorney general then suggested that the work of the FBI in London be extended to include a complete file of British laws and regulations that would come into effect in a national emergency. The delegation was to detail their report so the information could be incorporated into the curricula of the FBI training schools. Clegg suggested to Hoover that the time had come to more closely coordinate intelligence and investigative work in the field and recommended the establishment of field superintendent areas.[7] However, on December 10, Clyde Tolson informed Hoover that the Executives Conference was opposed to the suggestion since it would create a superstructure in the way of authority and therefore decentralize the activities of the bureau. Hoover agreed with the Conference's opposition.[8]

On November 23, 1940, Clegg and Hince departed from New York for London by way of Lisbon, Portugal. They traveled to Lisbon aboard the *Excalibur*, operated by American Export Lines, to await a British Overseas Airways flight to England. Their presence on this flight was supposed to be confidential, but one of the passengers aboard the plane was the American newspaper correspondent Ernie Pyle. The trip was dangerous and the plane had to fly low to avoid German patrol planes, but Clegg and Hince arrived safely in London on December 1.

Clegg and Hince spent December and January in England, confirming the role that the FBI would establish a high standing in all intelligence matters.[9] Clegg studied British foreign intelligence, domestic intelligence, communications, postal censorship, civil defense, security, and customs censorship operations. They scrutinized the MI5 and MI6 operations in detail. The US Embassy housed them at the Claridge Hotel, one of the top two hotels in England—The Savoy being the other. Clegg was given access to operations headquarters and a secondary headquarters "near some old Roman ruins" where they were guests of Lord Gorhambury. Clegg and Hince experienced a German air raid the first night they were in England. They heard the air raid sirens blowing and headed for the shelter located in the basement. Then they heard German planes and the British antiaircraft batteries firing on them by using sound detection devices that picked up the noise of the unsynchronized motors of the German aircraft. Clegg marveled at the way the British characteristically understated everything about the war. An air raid was often referred to as "a bit of noise" or a damaged house described as "being touched with a bit of bomb." Clegg was surprised that the Germans did not bomb London over the Christmas holidays.[10]

British intelligence officers schooled Clegg in all matters related to intelligence gathering and security, including the tracking and detection of spies, air raid defense techniques, blackout systems, and the protection of manufacturing plants and shipping ports. British intelligence also compiled and maintained lists of aliens and suspect citizens and developed procedures for censorship, law enforcement, the installation of hidden cameras to take surveillance photos, and the opening of mail without detection. They also placed undercover agents at embassies and consulates.[11]

On January 20, 1941, Clegg and Hince telegrammed Hoover through the American Embassy in London:

> We are today finishing the study in detail of the method by which matters of intelligence and counter-intelligence are organized and operated, including censorship, methods of evacuation, all methods of safety measures against air raids and all defense measures aside from those under full military control, a study of the police functions, of the control of foreigners, of the safeguarding of factories and public services, of the means of communication for emergency work and for transmission of intelligence, the method of investigating selective service, the special functions of the police under war conditions, the process of internment, and the handling of so-called Fifth Column activities and the relation of these to civilian activities for defense, including home guard, monitoring activities, and the organization of fire fighting. Have secured copies of the statutes, the regulations, and the instructions relative to the above. Awaiting transport home.[12]

When he returned, Clegg submitted reports to Hoover on everything he and Hince had studied and learned. He also directed specific reports to specific agencies. For example, his civil defense report was sent to Fiorello LaGuardia, whom Roosevelt had appointed as the first director of the Office of Civilian Defense and his censorship report to the attorney general, who sent it on to the president.

Clegg's visit was not without its critics. Fellow FBI agent Robert Lamphere disliked Clegg and would later say in reference to a subsequent trip he and Clegg took to England that Clegg "had been in London for the FBI in 1940, and had not endeared himself to British intelligence at that time. In fact, many of the M-I5 people disliked Clegg and were unable to separate what he had done in 1940 on Hoover's explicit instructions from Clegg's own personality."[13] However, Clegg was used to receiving criticism as well as praise and considered both to be part of the job.[14]

On December 7, 1941, Clegg was attending a Washington Redskins football game at Washington's Griffith Stadium and was watching the Redskins beat the Philadelphia Eagles 20-14 when the public address announcer paged high-ranking government and military personnel who were in attendance and told them to report to their duty stations. He did not mention the attack on Pearl Harbor. Curious reporters were told to check with their offices and given no information. The remaining fans in the stadium were among the last to learn of the attack.

That night Clegg and other agents assembled at FBI headquarters. At about 12:35 the following Monday morning, Hoover called Clegg into his office and showed him a message, in President Roosevelt's handwriting, notifying Hoover that he had been designated as "American Censor" until other arrangements were made. Then Hoover turned over the reins to Clegg, saying, "You got me into this and now you are the censor."[15] So Clegg became the American Censor for what proved to be just a few days.

During his short time in this new role, Clegg took the approach that censorship regarding issues such as whether newspapers ought to publish reports of enemy activity that are not documented should be matters of judgment for the newspapers. Despite the experience Clegg gained from observing the ways the British handled censorship issues, he was not comfortable with his new role. Clegg's appointment did not last long because two weeks later, Byron Price was appointed director of the Office of Censorship.[16] Price was a newspaperman and acting general manager/executive news editor of the Associated Press when appointed by President Roosevelt. Price's successful philosophy generally was to let the media voluntarily censor itself by asking whether the information at hand was something the enemy would like to have. Nevertheless, the Allied plans to invade North Africa, the D-day invasion of Normandy, and the successful effort to develop the first atom bomb were censored by Price's office.[17]

The Office of Censorship had about 15,000 employees monitoring all American media. Price was awarded a Pulitzer Prize Special Award in 1944 for the creation and administration of the radio and newspaper codes and was awarded the Medal of Merit by President Truman in 1946 "for exceptionally meritorious conduct in the performance of outstanding service as Director of the Office of Censorship." In 1948, King George VI named him an honorary Knight of the British Empire. After the war, Price was appointed vice president of the Motion Picture Association of America, and in 1947 he was appointed assistant secretary general for administrative and financial services of the United Nations. Price had offered Clegg the position of assistant to the censor but Clegg declined, saying that he did not like censorship although it was a necessity in time of war. He wanted no part of the job.[18] From a career point of view, Clegg seemed to have made the right decision, since the Office of Censorship was abolished as of November 15, 1945.

The issue of censorship has always been controversial and sometimes had fatal consequences. In May 1945, the War Department, over the protests of Censor Price, insisted on censoring reports of the arrival of Japanese balloon bombs—Japan's so-called fire-balloon campaign—on the West Coast. The issue reared its ugly head on May 5, when a Sunday school teacher and five of her students were picnicking in eastern Oregon and kicked a downed balloon, not knowing what it was. The resulting explosion killed all six.

Roosevelt himself was accused of misusing the Office of Censorship during the war. There were very few if any photographs showing his infirmity from his bout with polio. The press also kept his affair with Lucy Page Mercer Rutherfurd a deep secret.[19] One wonders how Clegg would have handled these censorship issues.

Clegg was able to handle some normal FBI duties during the war. In January 1942 he received his committee assignments in the Bureau: Intelligence Coordinating Committee for Facilities Security, Departmental Advisory Committee on Revision of Criminal Procedure, American Bar Association Committee on Police Standards and Training, and Civil Service Commission Committee to Select Special Investigator for the Washington Police Department.[20] Six weeks later, Hoover sent a letter to Clegg regarding the dissolution of the US Army Reserve Pool in which Clegg had served. The War Department had issued a ruling that all officers holding reserve commissions would be considered eligible for active duty. Hoover said that a discussion was held between the secretary of war and the attorney general regarding Clegg's status, and it was agreed that Clegg's employment on civilian matters in the FBI "is of such a vital nature to the national defense" as to necessitate his continuing in his existing capacity. Clegg was directed to resign his commission, and on March 9 he submitted his resignation as a major in the Intelligence Division of the US Army Reserve. He would later receive an occupational deferment from his local Selective Service Board, which listed his principal service as "investigation of violations of Federal Statues including espionage, sabotage, sedition, etc.," and his draft status was thus classified as 2-B (indicating a registrant who is deferred because of an occupation in a war industry). On October 29, 1943, his draft classification was changed to 4-A (indicating a registrant who completed military service).[21]

During 1943 he was assigned for several months to be the first chief of staff of the House Appropriations Committee to make studies of the economy, explore ways to improve the efficiency of the government, and study the functions of various departments. He also served as a member of the Advisory Council of the Senate Civil Service Subcommittee. He strengthened his many Washington contacts by visiting the cabinet officer or administrative assistant of every department, informing them of his role on the committee. Clegg became personally acquainted with every member of the Appropriations Committee and these friendships proved helpful at the time and in the future.[22] Clegg would be directed by the committee to investigate requests made by the executive departments to determine if the requests were necessary or unnecessary.

Clegg earned a strong reputation in the training of law enforcement officers through his work with the FBI National Academy and his work in training agents during the war. His efforts caught the attention of those involved in preparing to administer postwar Germany, and on April 9, 1945, Clegg wrote Hoover to inform him that he had turned down an offer to become a civilian consultant on the selection and training of German police following the end of the war.[23]

By all accounts, Clegg played a major role in the defense of his country during World War II. Intelligence operations of the FBI were enhanced by his study of the British intelligence system, and he helped established the role of the FBI in domestic intelligence.

James Clegg home, built in 1898, and inset photograph: James Clegg, Hugh Clegg's father. (Lavelle McAlpin Private Collection)

Young Hugh Clegg, circa 1905.

Hugh Clegg (left), James Ellis Clegg (center), and Irene Clegg (right). Taken in 1909.

College photo of Clegg, circa 1920.
(Ruby Kathryn Clegg Patterson
Private Collection)

Mathiston High School, circa 1908. (Lavelle McAlpin Private Collection)

Mathiston Depot, circa 1934. (Lavelle McAlpin Private Collection)

Bank of Mathiston, circa 1908. (Lavelle McAlpin Private Collection)

Downtown Mathiston, circa 1905. (Lavelle McAlpin Private Collection)

Detail of downtown Mathiston, circa 1905. Henry Clegg and James Clegg (right). (Lavelle McAlpin Private Collection)

Aerial view of Mathiston, 1940. (Lavelle McAlpin Private Collection)

Little Bohemia Lodge following failed Dillinger raid, 1934. (FBI file photo)

Wanted poster for Baby Face Nelson,
photograph taken November 29, 1934.

Clegg FBI photo, 1947. (Library of Congress)

Clegg checking out "black out" automobile. (*Reno Evening Gazette*, October 17, 1941)

"Infamous" photo of Clegg with his foot on a chair, prompting a complaint from Dr. Harriet M. Doane of Pulaski, New York. (*Post Standard*, Syracuse, New York, 1938)

Clegg with nephews Jimmy Clegg and Jimmy Gardner at the FBI National Academy at Quantico, Virginia, 1948. (ancestry.com)

Clegg and Robert Lamphere arrive at Idlewild Airport in New York (subsequently John F. Kennedy Airport) after returning from Klaus Fuchs's interrogation in England, 1950. (© Bettmann/CORBIS)

Clegg (center) and two unidentified agents at the FBI National Academy. (Ruby Kathryn Clegg Patterson Private Collection)

Clegg and Kat at the wedding of their daughter, Ruby Kathryn Clegg Patterson, December 12, 1964. (Ruby Kathryn Clegg Patterson Private Collection)

To Ruby and Hugh Clegg
In Appreciation of a valued
friendship   J. Edgar Hoover

1·27·54

Clegg, Kat, and FBI director J. Edgar Hoover at the ceremony marking Clegg's retirement from the FBI, January 27, 1954. (Ruby Kathryn Clegg Patterson Private Collection)

Ole Miss Marching Band at the 1958 Brussels World Fair. (University of Mississippi Archives and Special Collections)

Clegg at Ole Miss as director of development and executive assistant to the chancellor. (Ole Miss Yearbook, 1960)

University of Mississippi Lyceum Circle, circa 1954. (Deborah Freeland Private Collection)

US marshals arriving at the University of Mississippi, September 30, 1962. (Deborah Freeland Private Collection)

US marshal at the University Oxford Airport,
September 30, 1962. (Deborah Freeland
Private Collection)

Clegg during retirement at Anguilla, Mississippi, 1976.
(Lavelle McAlpin Private Collection)

Clegg Field at the airport at Ole Miss, 2014. (Deborah Freeland Private Collection)

Postwar Communism and Espionage: Emil Julius Klaus Fuchs and Harry Gold

I joined the Communist Party because I felt I had
to be in some organization.—Klaus Fuchs

T HE FBI WAS INVOLVED IN HUNTING DOWN Communi
in America almost from the beginning of Hoover's dire
torship. Hoover had been involved as a special assistant
the attorney general just after graduating from George Washingt
Law School in 1917. In that post, he prosecuted subversives for vi
lating federal laws and sought to deport undesirable aliens. Cle
considered Director Hoover to be "one of the best informed me
in the country on communists" and ranked him as the expert o
Communism in the agency.[1] Soon after Hoover joined the Justic
Department, he was promoted to head the new General Intelligenc
Division (GID) in 1919.

In the summer of 1919, bombs were detonated in seven American
cities (Boston; Cleveland; New York; Paterson, New Jersey; Philadelphia; and Washington, DC), including the home of then–Attorney
General A. Mitchell Palmer in the nation's capital. The coordination
of these detonations led to the country's realization that it faced a
new enemy, the onset of Communism, which led to what is known
as the Red Scare. Palmer responded by forming the GID and choosing his assistant, J. Edgar Hoover, to lead a crackdown on the Communists and other radicals. Hoover responded by directing raids,

known as the Palmer Raids, resulting in the arrest of more than ten thousand suspected radicals.[2] Civil liberties were ignored, and the arrested suspects were denied legal counsel and beaten in many cases. Legal experts such as future Supreme Court Justices Felix Frankfurter, Harlan F. Stone, and Supreme Court Justice Oliver Wendell Holmes opposed the violations of civil liberties that included free speech. The mood of the country changed from one of anger directed against the radicals to criticism of the actions of the GID. The Red Scare ran its course in 1920, only to raise its head again in different form during the McCarthy era of the 1950s. Hoover's knowledge of Communism and its threat to the nation was gained during the Red Scare, but he managed to avoid criticism during that period.

The FBI benefited from the relationship of President Herbert Hoover and Jesuit priest Edmund A. Walsh, a staunch anticommunist, who was an expert on Russian affairs. Walsh was the founder of the Foreign Service School of Georgetown University in 1919, six years before the US Foreign Service itself existed, and he headed the Papal Relief Mission to Russia in 1922. He forecast with amazing accuracy the rise in military power of both Germany and Russia. Walsh taught classes in the Foreign Service School at Georgetown that attracted officers of the US Army and members of the diplomatic service. His testimony in 1932 before the Fish Committee (headed by Representative Hamilton Fish Jr.) to investigate Communist activity in the United States brought him to the attention of the FBI. Walsh contributed to the FBI long after the conclusion of World War II by lecturing at the FBI and at war colleges during the Cold War.[3]

In February 1950, Republican senator Joseph McCarthy of Wisconsin became involved in one of the most controversial issues in American history by charging Secretary of State Dean Acheson with knowingly hiring Communists in the State Department. McCarthy demanded a congressional investigation. His charges created a maelstrom in Congress and the nation, and the Senate began holding hearings within a month of his accusations. McCarthy became well-known but was also highly criticized for creating another Red Scare. Fearing the effect of the furor on his ability to get reelected,

he called on his closest advisors to seek suggestions regarding how he could retain his seat in the Senate. During that meeting in May, Walsh suggested he continue his campaign to rid the government of Communists employed in the Democratic administration.

One of McCarthy's closest allies in securing information was FBI director Hoover. William C. Sullivan, one of Hoover's agents and perhaps the most knowledgeable agent on Communism, later admitted that "we were the ones who made the McCarthy hearings possible. We fed McCarthy all the material he was using."[4] Sullivan would go on to say that "the FBI kept Joe McCarthy in business."[5] Hoover denied charges that the FBI leaked information to McCarthy. Although McCarthy was unable to prove his charges, McCarthyism, as it was called, continued to run rampant in the country, and his tactics, for which the Senate censored him in December 1954, destroyed the careers of many citizens.

To the surprise of no one, Clegg's reaction to the controversy was pro-Bureau, reminding others that the FBI was just a fact-finding agency and that decisions regarding prosecution were made at the level of the attorney general in the Justice Department. He pointed out, for example, that the FBI could discover the membership in the Communist Party in New Jersey and the membership list might be given to the Justice Department, the military authorities, and the secretary of state because of their direct or indirect interest. The FBI did not determine what was done with this information nor did it have any influence in what was done with it. The FBI could not tap telephone lines unless the attorney general gave the Bureau the authority to do so. Clegg further pointed out that soon after the bombing of Pearl Harbor and during World War II, the FBI investigated hundreds and hundreds of German sympathizers, whether they were activists or were just friendly toward Germany. The FBI ranked the subversives into A, B, and C lists, but President Roosevelt had all suspects arrested in order to avoid taking chances.[6] Clegg also recalled the mood of the country and of Washington during the 1940s and 1950s, saying that official Washington was upset that the Russians joined in the war against Japan just as Japan was preparing to surrender. The fear was that Russia would take over countries as steps toward communizing the world.[7]

Perhaps the best example of Clegg's role in investigating intelligence and espionage cases during the Cold War period involved Emil Julius Klaus Fuchs, a KGB spy who had stolen A-bomb secrets and given them to the Russians. Fuchs was a German-born physicist who received his doctorate from Bristol University in England and studied at Edinburgh University in Scotland. When Great Britain placed all Germans in internment camps at the outbreak of World War II, Fuchs was taken to Canada but released soon thereafter and returned to Edinburgh. He was later transferred to Columbia University in New York to work on the atomic bomb program known as the Manhattan Project. He worked on the project in Los Alamos, New Mexico, and became involved in spying for Russia, transferring his notes to a Soviet courier named "Raymond." Fuchs eventually was named head of the Theoretical Physics Division at the Harwell Atomic Energy Research Establishment in England, where he was arrested and charged with espionage. Under intense, repeated interviews, led by British MI5 intelligence special branch officer William "Jim" Skardon, Fuchs confessed, on January 23, 1950, that he had provided the Soviet Union with information regarding the atom bomb. Skardon had noted that Fuchs was under considerable mental stress and suggested to him that he clear his conscience and confess. After a brief period, Fuchs admitted that he had indeed been engaged in espionage for the Soviets from 1942 until 1949. He also admitted that he had joined the Communist Party in Germany and had gladly participated in providing secrets about the atomic bomb to Russia. After a speedy trial, Fuchs on March 1, 1940, was found guilty of passing military secrets to "a friendly nation" and the next day was given a light sentence, compared to the death sentences imposed upon Ethel and Julius Rosenberg, of fourteen years in prison. He was released after serving only nine years and settled in East Germany.

The FBI concentrated on learning the identity of Fuchs's contact in America, known as Raymond.[8] Under intense questioning Fuchs either refused or could not provide names of any other members of his spy ring.[9]

In May 1950, after lengthy negotiations between the British Home Office and the US State Department, the FBI was allowed to send agents to interview Fuchs. It was suggested to Hoover that he send Associate Director Clyde Tolson to England to handle protocol with the British, but Hoover, who agreed with the concept, was unwilling to send Tolson. However, he thought Clegg was capable of handling the potentially delicate relations with the British. On May 16, 1950, a request was made for a passport to be issued to Clegg.[10] Although the reason for the request was not mentioned, one can assume that the trip was related to the Fuchs case. The relationship of the FBI with British intelligence group MI5 was not based on total trust. In fact, the British were developing their own atom bomb and wished to keep its development a secret from the FBI and America. As a result, the British were reluctant to allow the FBI to have access to the Fuchs investigation and were also reluctant to allow the FBI to interview Fuchs. The main FBI interrogator selected by Hoover to extract from Fuchs the identity of "Raymond" was counterintelligence expert Robert Lamphere. Thus, Clegg and Lamphere were sent to England to talk to Fuchs, with Clegg handling relations with the British and Lamphere interviewing Fuchs.[11]

Lamphere was an obvious choice for Hoover, since he had been involved in high profile Soviet spy cases, including that of Gerhart Eisler, covert leader of the American Communist Party, and of Hede Massing, an actress and a Soviet intelligence operative. Lamphere was also involved in deciphering the Soviet intelligence codes that would lead to the capture of Julius and Ethel Rosenberg. Lamphere was placed in charge of counterintelligence against the Soviet bloc in 1947. He had found information that could only have come from within the top secret Manhattan Atomic Bomb Project based in Los Alamos. From the decoded messages, the FBI identified Klaus Fuchs as the spy who managed to supply the Soviet Union with US secrets and put MI5 onto him. The British arrested Fuchs, but an unanswered question remained regarding the identity of the US contact Fuchs had used—"Raymond." Although the identity of "Raymond" was not resolved at the time Clegg and Lamphere departed for England, the FBI had zeroed in on a Philadelphia laboratory chemist, Harry Gold. Gold, born Heinrich Golodnitsky, was the son of poor Russian immigrants who migrated to the United States from the Ukraine in 1914. He was a reluctant recruit to the Communists who had been recruited by the Soviets to spy on their behalf in 1935. Gold had a long history of stealing secrets that included formulas from the Philadelphia sugar manufacturer for which he worked. The FBI hunt for Harry Gold had intensified at the time of the Clegg-Lamphere visit to London, and the agency was convinced that he was the "Raymond" they had been seeking. The FBI clandestinely filmed Gold, so Clegg and Lamphere would have the latest photos of him when they met with Fuchs.

Hoover was unaware that Lamphere had a strong dislike for Clegg, and Lamphere was upset when he learned that Clegg had been assigned to accompany him on the trip to London.[12] Referring to Clegg by his nickname Troutmouth, Lamphere complained that Clegg had no experience in day-to-day field investigations and because Clegg was in charge of the dreaded Inspection Division of the Bureau, he was not well-liked by those agents who were involved in Bureau investigations. Many Bureau street agents had an us against them attitude against administrators and other high FBI officials. Lamphere felt that sending Clegg along was a bad idea because he also knew that Clegg had not endeared himself to British intelligence when he went to London in 1940. In addition, Lamphere felt that Clegg would be looking over his shoulder and would get involved in interrogation work in which he had little experience. When he discussed his concerns with D. M. "Mickey" Ladd, the Bureau's assistant director of the Domestic Intelligence Division, Ladd advised him to put his fears aside and concentrate on conducting the most thorough interview of Fuchs, but to also try to prevent Clegg from damaging the relationship of the FBI with British intelligence.[13]

The trip to London did not get off to a smooth start. On the train from Washington to New York, where Lamphere and Clegg were to board the plane for the trip overseas, Clegg broke his eyeglasses. With his glasses his vision was correctable to 20/20, but without them it was 20/70. When the train arrived in Baltimore, Clegg called his wife, Ruby Kathryn, and told her it was urgent for her to get his prescription from his ophthalmologist and telephone that information ahead to New York, where he could get a replacement. The FBI had obtained photographs and motion picture film of Harry Gold, shot without his knowledge from the window of a car, as he left his house the same morning Clegg and Lamphere were departing for London. They gave the developed photos to Clegg and Lamphere as they passed through Philadelphia on their way to New York.[14]

With the new eyeglasses in hand, Clegg and Lamphere boarded the plane for the thirteen-hour flight to London. Lamphere was detached or cool to Clegg during the flight as Clegg concentrated on reading the Fuchs comprehensive summary brief Lamphere had prepared. Based upon the questions Clegg asked him, Lamphere was stunned by his seeming lack of knowledge about espionage and counterintelligence operations and his anxiety about not wanting to incur the wrath of Director Hoover. But Lamphere relaxed when Clegg told him that while he would be present during the interviews with Fuchs, Lamphere was to handle the actual interrogation.

John Cimperman, the Bureau's liaison with British intelligence, met them at the airport, and they reviewed their strategy to conduct the Fuchs interrogation. Lamphere was surprised when Clegg told him of Hoover's reluctance to provide British intelligence with any information regarding their progress in obtaining the identification of "Raymond," since Jim Skardon was scheduled to sit in on the interviews and it would be impossible to keep him from learning that Harry Gold was the FBI's chief suspect. Clegg was opposed to telling Skardon anything. Nevertheless, the next day, Saturday, May 20, Clegg, Lamphere, and Cimperman met Skardon at MI5 headquarters, and the group went to Wormwood Scrubs, a British prison, in West London for the interview.

Heeding Mickey Ladd's earlier advice, Lamphere overcame the

mutual distrust between him and Clegg and the American interrogation proceeded. Fuchs was hesitant at first to talk with the FBI and was primarily concerned about the safety of his sister, Kristel Heinemann. Lamphere indicated that Fuchs had furnished information about "Raymond" to Skardon and that the prime purpose of this FBI visit was to identify "Raymond." Lamphere showed a dozen photos to Fuchs; he rejected most and said the three latest photos of Harry Gold were not clear enough for him to identify Gold as "Raymond." Fuchs said while he could not reject them, he could not positively identify the photos as being "Raymond." The session ended with little progress, and the FBI contingent went to Cimperman's office in the US Embassy, where Clegg prepared a detailed report that was sent via cable to Hoover.

Fuchs was more cooperative when the interview continued the following Monday and the film taken of Harry Gold was projected. He admitted that although he could not be absolutely positive, the film photos of Harry Gold taken in Philadelphia just as Lamphere and Clegg were headed to New York were likely those of "Raymond." Clegg immediately cabled Washington and Gold was confronted that day. On May 22, Harry Gold, when challenged by the FBI, admitted that he was "the man to whom Fuchs gave the information." Two days later, not knowing that Gold had already admitted being "Raymond," Fuchs was shown new photos of Harry Gold and he said, "Yes, that is my American contact." At last "Raymond" had been conclusively identified. The twenty or so interrogations Clegg and Lamphere had with Fuchs paid off handsomely. Fuchs would go on to identify more than one hundred Communist agents (including Americans, Britons, and Canadians) in the moving pictures the FBI sent to England for him to review.

According to Lamphere, Clegg gloated that the FBI had succeeded in identifying "Raymond" when MI5 had not.[15] American scientists had hoped that the Fuchs interrogation would reveal the extent of the information he gave to the Soviets. The Atomic Energy Commission listed some questions for Lamphere and Clegg that they hoped Fuchs would answer. But the two FBI agents concentrated on approaching the interview from the viewpoint of a police interrogation and did not feel qualified to ask follow-up questions regarding nuclear science.

Before Lamphere and Clegg returned to the United States, they, along with Cimperman, paid a courtesy call to Scotland Yard and had a meeting with Sir Percy Sillitoe, the director general of MI5. Sillitoe expressed his unhappiness with the way Director Hoover and the FBI handled the Fuchs case. He was affronted by the publicity generated by the arrest of Harry Gold and the implication that the FBI had succeeded where MI5 had failed. Lamphere was surprised by Clegg's strong response, expressing disappointment that the FBI had to wait many months before being allowed to interview Fuchs. He then reminded Sillitoe that neither the FBI nor MI5 could control the press. Clegg later indicated that he would favor the FBI breaking off relations with MI5 and deal only with the Special Branch of Scotland Yard, MI6; he drafted a memo to that effect to Hoover. However, relations between the FBI and MI5 would continue.[16]

Under interrogation, Gold admitted that he had been involved in espionage since 1934 and had helped Fuchs pass information about the Manhattan Project to the Soviet Union by way of Soviet general consul Anatoli Yakovlev. He admitted to carrying a crude drawing of the atomic bomb from the secret laboratory at Los Alamos to his Soviet handlers in New York. Gold's confession led to the arrest of David Greenglass, who had spied for the Soviet Union while working on the Manhattan Project. Greenglass's sister was Ethel Rosenberg, and his brother-in-law was Julius Rosenberg. Greenglass's testimony resulted in the arrest, trial, and execution of the Rosenbergs in 1953. In later trials, however, Greenglass was revealed to be a somewhat unreliable witness.[17] Lamphere did not think Ethel Rosenberg should have been executed since she had acted under the directions of her husband. He also feared that executing the mother of two children would be controversial and draw sympathy to her. On the other hand, he felt Julius Rosenberg deserved the death sentence.[18] Harry Gold was convicted and sentenced in 1951 to a thirty-year prison term but was paroled after serving only fourteen years.[19]

Hoover congratulated Clegg for the "effective manner" in which he conducted the interviews of Fuchs that resulted in the apprehension of Harry Gold, or "Raymond," and thanked him for a well-executed mission.[20] Letters of commendation were requested for Clegg and Special Agents Lamphere, Ernest J. van Loon, J. R. Kochenderfer, William Welte, Robert G. Jensen, and Norris Harzenstein. Raises were recommended for Special Agents T. Scott Miller and Richard E. Brennan. One of the more successful investigations in FBI history had ended. But this success was not without embarrassment to the FBI. Hoover would later learn that the FBI had overlooked its own records on Fuchs for at least four years. The agency was in possession of English translations of German documents captured during the war and had had these documents in its possession since soon after the war's end, at a time when Fuchs was actively spying for Russia. These documents indicated that Fuchs was a somewhat important Communist, but he remained undiscovered until after Fuchs confessed to the British.[21]

In his autobiography, Lamphere extracts some measure of satisfaction from his dealings with Clegg: "An article appeared in a London paper that reported the involvement of American intelligence indicating that Lamphere was conducting the interviews while Assistant Director Clegg was taking notes." Lamphere notes that "Clegg wasn't too happy about this but, because we weren't talking to the press, couldn't do much about it."[22]

Chapter Nine

The Relationship with Hoover

Justice is incidental to law and order.—Edgar Hoover

CLEGG'S UNABASHED LOYALTY TO DIRECTOR HOOVER was an accepted fact in the Bureau. Clegg was well aware that the reputation of the Bureau had deteriorated during the Warren Harding administration under the direction of William J. Burns from 1921 to 1924.[1] Burns earned the nickname "America's Sherlock Holmes" because of his work as a private investigator. He earned a reputation for success when he served in the Secret Service and for operating a detective agency, but he was also notoriously known for appointing anyone a senator or congressman wanted appointed to the Bureau of Investigation, regardless of qualifications. Burns was a close friend of Attorney General Henry Daugherty, who knew Burns continued to run his private investigator firm while serving as Bureau director. The investigation by Daugherty and Burns into the affairs of Montana senator Thomas J. Walsh resulted in what has been called the Daugherty-Burns scandal. The Bureau gained the image of being a scandal-ridden agency.

Burns was forced to resign by Attorney General Harlan Stone for misusing his official position and because of his role in the Daugherty-Burns scandal. J. Edgar Hoover was named interim and then permanent director. Under Burns, the Bureau had dwindled from over 1,100 agents to fewer than 650 when Hoover was appointed. Burns would later also be indirectly involved in the Teapot Dome scandal.

When Hoover served as head of the General Intelligence Division (GID) of the Bureau of Investigation (BOI) in the Justice Department and as assistant director of the BOI during the Daugherty-Burns era, he managed to avoid any taint of corruption or abusive conduct, just as he had avoided criticism for his role in dealing with the Red Scare. When Hoover was offered the job as director by Attorney General Harlan F. Stone, he accepted the promotion only on the condition that appointments to the Bureau were to be made free from all political influence. Stone and Hoover were committed to reforming the Bureau's operations and restoring public support without generating fears of developing a federal police force. Stone abolished the GID, limited Bureau investigations to violations of federal law, and prohibited any investigation of the political beliefs of US citizens. (Hoover obviously later circumvented the new directive). Stone also directed Hoover to remove incompetent agents and abolish the patronage appointment system.[2] Hoover's reputation was a prime motivation for Clegg's decision to join the Bureau instead of taking the bar examination.

Hoover received criticism for being ruthless and dictatorial, but his actions were necessary to remove the political hacks who did nothing. Clegg complained, "There was one fellow that I knew, he was still in when I was there, that would come into the New York office which had fifty or sixty men in it, that was a big office in those days, and he would come in every payday and get his check but he didn't do any of the work."[3] Not all political appointees were incompetent, and Hoover kept the competent and qualified while getting rid of the deadwood, which was enough to make many politicians angry. He raised the qualifications for becoming a Bureau agent by accepting only law school and accounting school graduates (accountants needed three years of experience). He would not approve any exceptions to the new requirements. Cronyism, prevalent under Burns, was no longer acceptable.

Clegg admired Hoover for standing up to powerful politicians, despite the risks, and recalled an incident in which an influential congressman came to Hoover's office, shook a finger in Hoover's face, and told him he wanted his two nephews who held somewhat high positions in the Bureau to get an increase in their salaries and rank. Hoover refused, saying, "My friend, they will rise or fall on their own merit and no political aid can assist them." The congressman responded, "Well, you're vulnerable and I'll get you for that."[4]

Hoover demanded loyalty, not just to himself but also to the Bureau. Within the agency, there was a loyalty that often developed into a personal attachment to Hoover. He turned an agency with an unsavory reputation into one envied by other federal agencies. In the beginning, Hoover approved all appointments himself and was rewarded by faithful service and hard work by successful applicants.

The director made a serious effort to sell the Bureau to the American people by publicizing its efforts and successes. Much of this publicity was centered on Hoover himself, and Clegg was an unabashed supporter. Clegg recalled a visit from a newspaperman who was a personal friend and also one of his fraternity brothers. His friend said, "Hugh, the FBI is getting too much publicity. All of this publicity is going to hurt you with the American people. It's going to hurt you with the Congress in due course." Clegg made no response other than to thank him.[5]

Clegg praised Hoover, saying, "He was the standard bearer. He was the flag. He was the escutcheon. He was the symbol that means FBI. We focused around him." By the building up of Hoover, the entire FBI was built up. "So he was a hero to all of us. He was Mr. It. He was Mr. FBI."[6] Clegg went so far as to say "he was my king."[7]

Hoover devoted his life to the Bureau and never married. Clegg considered him to be 100 percent patriotic and totally committed to America. He had no affiliation with any political party. Being a native of Washington, DC, Hoover had no political power base and could not even vote in federal elections. Yet Congress came to support him, admiring his disciplined approach to leadership. Once, Clegg proposed that Hoover enhance his image even further by going to New York to make a speech about law enforcement as a business and to Chicago to give a speech about law enforcement from a different angle, such as the importance of law enforcement to the economy in the form of recovered property, money, and automobiles. Over a five-month period, Clegg "had him" make eight speeches across the United States—even suggesting the month he would give the speech. Hoover once said, "Clegg here was trying to get me to run for president." Clegg was indeed convinced that he would have made the greatest president the country ever had. "He had the best memory, the best mind I've nearly ever seen."[8]

When Clegg was in the field, he heard complaints about such things as the lack of telephones and air conditioning and the presence of poorly trained clerks, but criticism was never directed toward Hoover himself. Despite disliking Hoover's nitpicking regulations, most agents praised him for imbuing the Bureau with a spirit of elitism, a feeling that the Bureau was a cut above other agencies.

Clegg recalled a story one former agent, Joseph Schott, told in a book of his that derided Hoover.[9] The title of the book, *No Left Turns* (1975), was based on a supposed incident in California when a car in which Hoover was a passenger was struck from the rear while making a left turn. Hoover, as the story goes, was sitting in the left rear seat behind his chauffeur. Hoover was shook up and thereafter refused to sit in the left rear seat. He would not permit his driver to make left turns. Despites reports from other agents that left turns when Hoover was a passenger were indeed prohibited, Clegg regarded that story as ridiculous and silly, claiming that in order for Hoover to leave the Justice Department building to go home, a left turn out of the basement to get to Constitution Avenue was required. "Otherwise, he'd be going toward Maryland and he didn't live in Maryland."[10]

Clegg's loyalty to Hoover extended to deliberately avoiding any discussion of a possible homosexual relationship between Hoover and Clyde Tolson, rumors of which circulated throughout the nation's capital. Tolson began government service as a clerk in the War Department and from 1919 to 1928 served as confidential secretary for the secretary of war in three different administrations before joining the Bureau in 1928. He had attempted to join the Bureau the year before but was rejected. Once he was finally accepted, he became chief clerk and was responsible for handling personnel and budgetary matters. He was promoted to assistant director in 1930 and associate director three years later. He became Hoover's right-hand man. The two worked together for over forty years.

Their relationship was the subject of much media suspicion, suggesting there was evidence of homosexuality. Tolson and Hoover, neither of whom ever married, ate together, socialized together, rode to work together, sometimes dressed in matching clothes, vacationed together, went to racetracks together on weekends, and worked so closely as to arouse suspicion. Despite the rumors, others suggested theirs was only a fraternal relationship. The pair would take lunch at noon at the Mayflower Hotel when they were in town and would dine at Harvey's Restaurant five nights a week if and when both were in Washington. Some agents smirked and referred to Hoover and Tolson as "J. Edna and Mother Tolson."[11] Since reporters hinted at a homosexual relationship, they often found themselves being investigated by the FBI. When Hoover died, Tolson inherited Hoover's estate, moved into his house, and accepted the flag from Hoover's coffin.

While many agents held Hoover in high regard, they considered Tolson a conniver. But Clegg, loyal to Hoover as always, praised Tolson as possessing a great deal of ability and as "a highly qualified man in many respects."[12] He also noted that since both men were single, they were free to travel together, whereas many assistants were married and had families and responsibilities.

As loyal as Clegg was to Hoover, the director's relationship with Clegg seemed to run hot and cold. Hoover was a classic micromanager. Many examples can be found in FBI files. In 1933, Hoover sent a memo to Tolson complaining about the performance of the assistant directors and their failure to give more attention to the intelligence operations of the Bureau. He also complained that when he returned to the office following a noon recess of a court proceeding, none of the assistant directors were at their desks. Hoover declared, "Henceforth, the officials of the Bureau who are to go to lunch at twelve o'clock should leave promptly at that time, and those who go at quarter to one are not to go until those return who have gone at twelve."[13]

Two years later, Hoover wrote Clegg complaining that during gymnasium training, someone kicked a medicine ball through the window of the locker room in the Bureau's roof gymnasium and that the ball fell several floors, causing damage to an automobile owned by a department employee. Hoover said that he had earlier issued instructions to Clegg and Tolson that medicine balls should not be used in connection with training on the roof. He went on to say

> I do not know how I can make myself any more clear on this point. I do not want the medicine balls used in the physical training on the roof or in the Locker Room because of possible danger if the balls fall to the building courts. I think that you should personally check the physical training which is being given, because I am satisfied that it is not being properly and efficiently conducted.[14]

A month earlier, Hoover had written to Tolson and Clegg expressing concern over training procedures. There were two cases in which employees complained of acquiring athlete's foot in the gymnasium. Hoover wrote,

> There is nothing which plagues athletic clubs and gymnasiums in this country more than athlete's foot and I am informed that it can be prevented if diligent and sometimes extreme methods are taken to establish the proper sanitary conditions. . . . Consequently I want immediate attention to be given to see that the proper disinfectants are used.

He also expressed displeasure with boxing matches being conducted during regular hours of training because some members of the staff were not fit to participate. However, he had no objection to conducting these matches after regular office hours.[15]

Hoover must have expressed his displeasure to Special Agent L. P. Oliver for borrowing money from other agents because Oliver wrote Hoover indicating that he would repay Special Agent J. H. Baldridge thirty dollars, Special Agent J. A. Robey twenty-four dollars, and Clegg fifty dollars. On April 6, 1936, Hoover wrote J. M. Keith, special agent in charge of the Washington DC, field office, and inquired whether Oliver had indeed made these payments on April 1. Hoover wrote again on May 26, 1936, to check if Oliver was continuing to make payments to Baldridge, Robey, and Clegg. On June 5, 1936, Keith wrote Hoover informing him that Oliver had been requested on several occasions to liquidate his debts and Oliver had promised to do so. However, as of June 5 he had made no further payments. On June 9, 1936, Hoover ordered Keith to instruct Oliver to advise his office at once as to when the next remittance will be made.[16]

Hoover wrote Clegg noting that the Bureau-owned truck used in conjunction with firearms training at Camp Ritchie, Maryland, was found to be in poor mechanical condition. He admonished Clegg, stating "It is absolutely necessary that more care be given to bureau automotive equipment in the future and it is my desire that this matter be made the subject of a discussion by you at the next supervisors' conference."[17]

Hoover's micromanaging continued into the 1940s. He wrote Clegg, Tolson, and Hince complaining about certain equipment purchased for the Training Center at Quantico. He was concerned in particular about the furnishings in the individual rooms reserved for visiting instructors. "The overstuffed chairs and couches which were procured are certainly impractical, and entirely too expensive," Hoover remarked. He ordered the furniture removed and returned to the Procurement Division in exchange for more practical furniture. He also complained that the type of floor lamps that were purchased were of a "most expensive and certainly impractical type." He objected to the purchase of rugs or floor coverings when "we had such substantial and adequate linoleum on the floor." He was concerned that dust and dirt were bound to be brought into the building and would be tracked on these rugs: "Individual small rugs beside the beds would be adequate." He then ordered the removal of all such floor coverings.[18]

Later, Hoover sent a memo to Clegg stating,

It is desired that you submit an immediate explanation as to the reason why the doors to Rooms 5256 and 5258, your Reception Room and Office, and Rooms 5262, 5244 and 5242, occupied by clerical employees in your division, were unlocked at 12:20 A.M., June 12, 1940.[19]

There is no evidence of a response from Clegg.

As Clegg was approaching retirement, Hoover continued to chastise and praise him. On one occasion, several special agent trainees were returning to Quantico after traveling to Washington for evaluation to determine if their performances had shown improvement. On the return trip to Quantico, the counselor conducted a quiz on the Manual of Rules and Regulations. When he learned of this, Hoover criticized Clegg, saying "I think it is patently dangerous for a driver of an automobile on such densely traveled highway as the one existing between Washington, DC, and Quantico, Virginia, to engage in extraneous conversations and particularly conduct a quiz course while endeavoring to properly operate the automobile equipment." Hoover wanted instructions issued to the effect "that drivers of automotive equipment are to devote their entire time and attention to their driving duties."

Hoover also admonished Clegg that it "was entirely inexcusable and inhuman for you to schedule appointments for five Special Agent Trainees in your office at 5:00 p.m. and then keep these men waiting an interminable length of time before commencing the interviews." He told Clegg that he would not tolerate a repetition of such incidents and ordered him to conduct all interviews promptly. Hoover also suggested that rather than "herding" these trainees in an automobile to be interviewed, Clegg should have gone to Quantico to interview them there. Hoover went on to criticize Clegg for forming a board of three agents, including Clegg himself, to interview trainees, thus wasting the time of the two additional agents. Hoover thought Clegg alone should have been able to arrive at a decision regarding applicant qualifications and make a recommendation. Hoover concluded, "I want you to know that I am extremely displeased with the entire handling of the training program by the Training and Inspection Division. . . . I will not tolerate further instances of inhuman and improper handling of the Special Agents Training program."[20]

Hoover was informed of these matters by Assistant Director J. P. Mohr, who had sent a memo to Hoover reminding him that a special agent had written him complaining about the way his separation from service in the Bureau was handled. The dismissed agent was told that a final interview had been set up prior to his dismissal and that he had to wait three hours for the interview to be conducted. Five trainees, including the agent who faced dismissal, were to be interviewed at 5:00 p.m., but Clegg was tied up and did not initiate the interviews until 6:00 p.m. The interviews continued until 7:30, and the dismissed agent was the last to be interviewed. He then complained to Hoover about his treatment. Hoover made a handwritten notation on Mohr's memo indicating that the entire matter was "atrociously handled by Clegg." Clegg provided an extensive response to the complaints of the agent but still received censure for his actions.[21] An inspection of the Training and Inspection Division had been conducted two weeks earlier by Inspector Harbo, who informed Clegg that "conditions found during the inspection reflected that he [Clegg] has continued to do an outstanding job."[22]

As often as Hoover criticized Clegg, he turned around and praised his work and continued to promote and rely on his assistant director. On the twenty-fifth anniversary of Clegg's service with the Bureau, Hoover congratulated him and went on to write,

> In the extremely important and responsible capacity which has characterized most of your FBI career, you have played a large part in helping to shape and perfect many of the Bureau's present day policies and standards, not the least of which has been the heavy responsibility for training Agent personnel. . . .
> I deeply appreciate the zealous, devoted and loyal manner in which you have discharged your responsibilities.[23]

Still, however, Hoover could not resist criticizing him. Just prior to Clegg's retirement, he ordered that a letter of censure be sent to Clegg for errors appearing in a letter he had written.[24]

During the many years Clegg and Hoover worked together and lived just eight to ten blocks apart, Hugh and Ruby Kathryn rarely socialized with Hoover. Ruby Kathryn once took some chicken soup to Hoover when he was ill with a cold or flu. Clegg said that he and Ruby visited Hoover's home and had dinner with him and his mother before she died and with him several times after her death but said both he and Hoover were not inclined to socialize much because they worked so hard.[25]

Clegg's loyalty to Hoover was never in doubt, despite the charges made by Special Agent Angus W. Taylor in 1938. After his retirement, Clegg appeared before the Mississippi chapter of the FBI National Academy Associates and proposed a resolution to name the new FBI building in Washington the J. Edgar Hoover Building for the FBI.[26] Indeed, the question of Clegg's loyalty was addressed in a 1954 letter from George E. Harding (whom Hoover regarded as "a good friend of the Bureau") to Hoover. Harding wrote,

> Now that Hugh Clegg has retired I feel that I should drop you
> a note and state that never in my business, government or any
> other affairs have I met a man who showed such great loyalty to
> his chief as Hugh Clegg did to you. His extreme devotion to you
> as Director was certainly noticeable in his talks and his con-
> tacts at all the law enforcement meetings that I have attended
> with him. He certainly was your emissary of good will in the
> Bureau also.[27]

Clegg consistently denied that he had any interest in pursuing the director's job, claiming "I wouldn't have had it with a twenty-foot pole. No sir. No sir."[28]

Hoover passed away in his home of an apparent heart attack on May 2, 1972, at the age of seventy-seven. No autopsy was performed, leading some to suspect that his death involved foul play. Even his death was not without controversy. His secretary for fifty-four years, Helen Gandy, loyal to Hoover to the last, destroyed all private and confidential files Hoover kept on everyone of importance in politics and in particular on those who were involved in the civil rights movement. Although she was criticized for her actions, Clegg defended her, stating that people often destroy personal files and that the files the secretary destroyed did not relate to official Bureau business.[29]

While Hoover was praised during his life for personifying integrity, courage, discipline, and honor, many of his faults came to light after his death and today he is perceived by many as a despot who abused his power and trampled upon the rights of thousands of famous and less-than-famous individuals. Clegg would never have agreed with these critics. Tolson died three years after his friend and was buried just a few yards from Hoover's grave.

Chapter Ten

Leaving the FBI
and Joining Ole Miss

Mr. Clegg will seek effective means of increasing the university endowment and will explore new sources of income. He will also
represent the university at meetings with civic and similar groups.
We feel most fortunate in obtaining his services for Ole Miss.
—Chancellor J. D. Williams

O N MARCH 14, 1952, FBI assistant director J. P. Mohr sent a
memo to Clyde Tolson regarding the possibility that Clegg
was contemplating retirement after twenty-six years of service to the Bureau. Mohr had met with Clegg earlier in the day and
told him there were rumors afloat that he was considering retirement. Mohr said he told Clegg that Hoover was anxious to know if
the rumors were true, since arrangements would have to be made
to replace him. Clegg emphatically stated that while he would like
to consider retirement at some point in the future, he had not con-
templated any plans at present and further stated that he had not recently discussed any such plans with anyone. He recalled that he did
discuss the matter of retirement with Hoover in November 1950 but
had not considered the matter since that time. Clegg emphasized
to Mohr that if indeed he did consider retirement, Hoover would
be the first to know. When Mohr asked Clegg if he knew how these
rumors got started, Clegg said that he had recently been experienc-
ing health problems with his feet and his susceptibility to the flu. In
fact, Clegg said, his wife and daughter were also having a tough time
handling the flu. Mohr ended the memo by stating that "although

Mr. Clegg looked in good health today, his voice was poor" and that the flu had left him in a weakened condition. In fact, following his conversation with Mohr, Clegg went home early.[1] In fact, Clegg was thinking of retiring.

One month following his communication with Mohr, Tolson was informed that Clegg had called indicating that on the way to Richmond to give a speech, he had experienced car trouble. Clegg's wife, Ruby, had just gotten out of bed with the flu and was very tired. Clegg said that, on his doctor's advice, he was taking his daughter out of town "to get her to a less changeable weather." Clegg wanted to drive his family to Mississippi when he finished his speech in Richmond. He felt that his wife was in no condition to drive such a long distance and decided that he would drive them to Mississippi and then take a train back to Washington. He took a leave of absence to deal with the latest health issue involving his daughter, Ruby Kathryn.[2] Her health problems related to her allergies continued throughout that summer. Agent Ed Mason informed Tolson that he had received a telephone call from Clegg, who was vacationing in New England. Clegg informed Mason that the hot days and cool nights there had reactivated his daughter's allergy problems and that she was now running a fever. Clegg did not allow his daughter's health problems to interfere with his Bureau obligations and informed Mason that he would drive his own car and arrive in Washington on Saturday. He would then turn around and take a train on Sunday to Lake Placid and then to Utica, New York, where he was scheduled to make several speeches.[3]

Eighteen months later, when Clegg submitted a formal application for retirement effective January 31, 1954, the main reason he gave Hoover was Ruby Kathryn's health problems. Clegg said that "the most unhappy day of my life to date" was the day of communicating this information to Hoover. True to his word that he would notify Hoover first should he decide to retire, Clegg had approached the director with his intentions to retire in October 1953. He told Hoover that the reasons he was retiring included "the necessity for the past five years of my young daughter going South each winter because of health conditions, the necessity of his wife accompanying her and remaining with her for most of the time of this necessary absence, and the various economic conditions involved."[4] Clegg was faced with a decision of either moving to the South or seeking the compensation necessary for him to maintain two homes.

His daughter was sensitive to changes in temperature and developed serious allergies before she was ten years old. Her pediatrician feared she would develop asthma. When her sinus problems would appear, she would have to miss school. In addition, Clegg and his wife were concerned that their daughter was too thin. The doctor advised Hugh and Ruby Kathryn to take their daughter to Florida before her condition worsened. Following his advice, they took her to Delway Beach, Florida, where their friends Ray and Peggy Whitley had moved, and Ruby Kathryn reacted favorably to the more constant temperatures. Clegg thought that the best approach for supporting his daughter's health would be to retire and find a more lucrative job. He had handsome offers to go elsewhere, such as New York state or Indiana, but their physician warned them not to do that because of the cold northern temperatures.[5]

Then Ole Miss came calling for the Cleggs. Hugh was about to make the transition from fighting criminals, gangsters, and Communist spies to being immersed in the battles of integration in a state that had a reputation as being perhaps the most racist in the country. The Civil War did not end at Appomattox. Mississippi inherited the role, willingly or by default, of being the last bastion of the Confederacy, and the Civil War was now being fought in the state's red clay hills and river delta, and to the dismay of the university, in the Lyceum of the state's flagship university.

Calling it "the most unhappy day of his life," Clegg submitted his formal application for retirement on January 7, 1954, effective at the end of January.[6] Clegg expressed his appreciation to Hoover for his leadership and friendship and personal considerations and noted that Hoover's accomplishments in his official and personal life "have made an enviable and unimpeachable record of service to your nation." He also praised "the unquestioned patriotism, devotion, sincerity, loyalty, fidelity, bravery and integrity of the Director." Clegg went on to laud Hoover for his "genius in selecting capable assistants" such as Tolson and others. On January 12, Hoover responded that he was aware of Clegg's personal situation requiring him to return to Mississippi. Hoover then stated that he

> cannot let this opportunity pass without reiterating what I have
> already told you of how deeply I have appreciated your loyal
> and untiring efforts on behalf of the Bureau during your entire
> career. You can take great satisfaction in knowing that you have
> made real and lasting contributions in the building of the Fed-
> eral Bureau of Investigation.

Hoover finished by extending to Clegg's wife and daughter his best wishes.[7] Hoover gave the Cleggs an autographed photograph of him, Hugh, and Kat. He signed it "To Ruby and Hugh Clegg—In appreciation of valued friendship."

Clegg's retirement generated much interest as word of his decision spread rapidly. Agent L. B. Nichols wrote Tolson indicating that Jack Carley, a reporter for the *Commercial Appeal* newspaper in Memphis, Tennessee, had asked him to confirm that Clegg was retiring to assume a position with the University of Mississippi. Nichols confirmed Clegg's retirement but made no comment about Clegg taking a position at the university.[8] Armed with this information, Carley published a story regarding Clegg's retirement and subsequent employment at Ole Miss. Also, that same day Carley printed an editorial regarding Clegg's move to Mississippi and led the editorial off by declaring that the University of Mississippi had "chosen well."[9] Carley published a subsequent article in which he quoted University of Mississippi chancellor J. D. Williams as saying "Mr. Clegg will seek effective means of increasing the university endowment and will explore new sources of income. He will also represent the university at meetings with civic and similar groups. We feel most fortunate in obtaining his services for Ole Miss."[10] A week later Carley's story was picked up by the *Washington Star*, which added the information that

Clegg's new title at the University of Mississippi would be director of university development.[11]

Clegg's retirement represented a major milestone in the history of the FBI. He received letters of commendation from Attorney General Herbert Brownell Jr. and Deputy Attorney General William P. Rogers. The South Carolina chapter of the National Academy Associates adopted a resolution praising him. Many law enforcement associations sent letters of appreciation. Hoover approved mounting Bureau Badge #7—the low number indicating a high ranking—and presented it to Clegg. The employees of the Training Division planned a reception for Clegg on January 27 at the Mayflower Hotel. A group of newspapermen representing the Press Club, including the newspapers in Jackson, Mississippi, and other southern papers, scheduled a smoker for Clegg on January 28. All US representatives and senators from Mississippi were invited, as well as Hoover, Tolson, and Nichols. Clegg received hundreds of letters from graduates of the FBI National Academy, the academy he had started in 1935.

When he first joined the Bureau, Clegg planned to work there for thirty months or so before practicing law. However, the practice of law did not appeal to him, whereas with the Bureau he felt he was making a contribution to the welfare of his country. With regard to the time he spent at the FBI, he said, "I loved it. I loved every aspect of it."[12]

Hugh and Ruby began planning their move from Washington to Oxford, Mississippi, but with many regrets. They had enjoyed the atmosphere of the nation's capital. Counting his time in law school, Clegg spent thirty-one years living in DC, and it was difficult to leave.[13] Since he spent much time away from home because of his traveling for the Bureau, it is not surprising that Hugh and Ruby's closest friends in Washington were FBI people. His closest personal friend was Ray Whitley, a fellow southerner from Jonesboro, Arkansas, and a Washington and Lee alumnus and law school graduate. Whitley was in charge of the New York field office, the FBI's largest. The Cleggs and Whitleys lived four blocks from each other. Ray's wife, Peggy, was one of the wealthiest women in the United States and was thought to own more US Steel stock than any other female. She was a Blair, a Cannon towel heir. Ray and Peggy moved to Del Ray Beach, Florida, but moved back to Washington when Ray, a heavy smoker, contracted lung cancer. As Ray's health deteriorated and death was approaching, Peggy had a sudden heart attack and died before her husband. Other close friends of the Cleggs were FBI people from Arkansas, Louisiana, Alabama, and Arizona. Ruby's closest friend was Mrs. Robert E. May, wife of an attorney. Their daughter attended Ole Miss while the Cleggs were there.[14]

Clegg was tempted with several job offers in New York and Texas more lucrative than the Ole Miss position. He had developed a close relationship with minister and author Dr. Norman Vincent Peale when Clegg interviewed directors of the Christian Civic League, who included Peale. Clegg was investigating charges made by the Christian Civic League superintendent, O. R. Miller, that one of Clegg's colleagues (Clegg did not name him) had violated the White Slave Traffic Act—charges that proved to be false.[15] Clegg sought guidance from Dr. Peale regarding whether or not to accept the Ole Miss position in view of having received the other offers. Clegg said he and Dr. Peale discussed the advantages and disadvantages of the move to Ole Miss; then both got down on their knees and prayed together. Clegg decided to return to Mississippi.[16]

It was no coincidence that Ruby was an alumna of Ole Miss, and Clegg often referred to himself as an "alumnus-in-law" of the university. He later enjoyed telling a story about how, in 1962, eight years after he joined Ole Miss, he was awarded an honorary lifetime membership in the University of Mississippi Alumni Association, only the eleventh person in the history of the university to receive that designation. When Hoover was sent a copy of an article that appeared in the *Jackson Daily News* reporting this honor and citing a resolution of praise for Clegg, he noted that "no letter necessary— honor strictly concerns Univ. of Mississippi and, in view of Meredith situation, letter not warranted."[17] Hoover was disappointed about the riots that resulted from the integration of Ole Miss by James Meredith the previous September of 1962.

Clegg officially retired from the Bureau on January 29, 1954, and arrived in Oxford on February 3. Almost at once he realized that he could not completely sever his ties with the FBI. On February 4, Colonel F. D. Kirby sent a telegram to agent Francis Crosby of the FBI indicating that his client, the William F. Broidy Company, desired to launch a new television program depicting the role of the FBI in the war on crime titled "Wanted by the FBI." The telegram indicated that Academy Award-winning actor Broderick Crawford would be featured and that Clegg "has agreed to serve as technical advisor" provided the proposal meets with the satisfaction of the Bureau. Kirby then asked for an appointment for Broidy and Crawford to meet with Hoover.[18] The next day L. B. Nichols, FBI assistant to the director, sent a memo to Clyde Tolson regarding the proposal. Agent Crosby became involved and told Kirby that nothing would be accomplished by this meeting and that no commitment could be made by the Bureau. Kirby told Crosby that he understood and felt bad about Clegg and the misrepresentation made about his participation. According to Kirby, his connection to Clegg was the friendship between Clegg and Kirby's father-in-law.

The Bureau's reaction to the proposal could not have been colder.[19] Nichols sent another memo to Tolson indicating that he had spoken with Clegg about the claims the Broidy Company had made to the effect that the television program would be under the supervision of Clegg. Clegg stated that this was absolutely not true and that he had turned down the offer as set forth in a memo Clegg had prepared prior to leaving Washington. Nichols directed Crosby to call Colonel Kirby denying Clegg's involvement and insisted that the Broidy Company stop making such representations and also insisted that the company not use the name of the FBI in any titles. Hoover made a handwritten notation at the bottom of the memo: "This is a cheap outfit. They are certainly presumptive in seeking a conference now after falsely trying to sell the FBI."[20] Without hesitation, Clegg wrote Nichols indicating his contacts with Kirby were few and favorable and that he had written Colonel Kirby that he had "absolutely no intention of participating in any program of any type relating to FBI work."[21]

The decision to accept the position at Ole Miss had not been easy, but he accepted the job at a much lower salary than he could have gotten elsewhere and at less than the salary he had been making at the FBI. He received an offer for a job in Atlanta soon after arriving at Ole Miss. The offer was attractive because temperatures there were generally similar to Oxford—and thus favorable for his daughter—and paid double the Ole Miss salary in addition to having other advantages. Clegg, perhaps being overly self-conscious, was not satisfied with his performance at the university and submitted a letter of resignation. He recalled that Chancellor J. D. Williams had contacted every dean of every college, including the medical center, and they urged Clegg to stay. The Chamber of Commerce also got involved in persuading him to remain at the university. Chancellor Williams doubled his salary, enhanced his title, and gave him a faculty house to live in, so he stayed at Ole Miss. Clegg recalled being surprised by the generosity of the chancellor: "I still don't know why. I hadn't done anything of any grandiose value to justify that, in my opinion."[22] Hugh and Kat moved into Faculty House Number 5, where his neighbors included history professors James Silver and Clare Marquette, both of whom both would figure prominently in the Meredith integration saga.

Clegg, however, could not resist continuing to explore other offers, and the FBI became aware of some of his efforts. Six months after Clegg had moved to Ole Miss, Agent Nichols sent a memo to Tolson indicating that Agent Clarence Kelley of the Houston office claimed he heard from two sources that Clegg was due to arrive in Houston that night for the express purpose of meeting with Mayor Roy Hofheinz to discuss the position of commissioner of public safety at Houston. Hofheinz himself later advised Kelley that Clegg was considering taking the job. Former agent A. F. Lorton claimed that James Ellis Clegg, Hugh's brother, had informed him of Hugh's intentions and supported the story. Kelley was instructed to keep the

Bureau informed and reminded Hofheinz that the director did not know of anyone to recommend for this position and that the FBI had no suggestions to offer.[23] Why certain agents in the FBI continued to maintain interest in Clegg's career moves was never made clear. Nichols later informed Tolson that the Houston office had received word that Clegg declined the position because of his Mississippi commitments. Hoover noted, "We want to now keep completely out of this."[24] Less than two weeks later, a newspaper story appeared in the *Houston Post* indicating that the Houston City Council had defeated the proposal of Mayor Hofheinz to establish the position of commissioner of police, making the entire matter moot.[25]

Williams's doubling of Clegg's salary was extremely unpopular with the faculty and other staff members, but academic jealousies have no birthday since they have existed since the beginnings of the education process. Salaries were quite low in higher education in Mississippi at the time—and, relatively speaking, remain so today. The state auditor at the time, who was considering running for state treasurer, published the salaries of higher-level administrators in the university system. When he published Clegg's salary as director of development and assistant to the chancellor, Clegg expected his pay to be a major issue among the faculty. However, Chancellor Williams told the faculty that the effort to keep Clegg was the first step in trying to get increased salaries for everyone, and the controversy abated. Nevertheless, Clegg was embarrassed by the publicity his salary generated.[26] It became obvious that Williams was determined to keep Clegg at Ole Miss. To the outsider, the pair had little in common. Charles Eagles, a history professor at the university, described Clegg as "the tough, bald, roly-poly bureaucrat" who complemented "the tall, academic, urbane chancellor."[27]

In spite of the salary controversy, Clegg's experience, his intimate knowledge of the federal government, his patriotism as evidenced by his service with the FBI, his knowledge of the realities of the Communist threat, his ability to work with conservative elements of government and society, and his friendships with many national figures meant his appointment was favorably received by the majority of the university community.[28] These assets, however, would soon place him in the middle of many controversial academic and political battles.

Clegg was ready for the challenges laid out to him by Chancellor Williams because Kat was happy. She made many friends on her return to Oxford and Ole Miss and became involved in local groups—such as a book club, the Garden Society, and University Dames—as well as becoming active in her church.

Clegg was not eager to sever his relationship with the Bureau and explored several ways of maintaining contact with Hoover and the FBI. Around the time that Clegg explored the Houston position, the special agent in charge of the FBI's Memphis office wrote Hoover suggesting that Clegg could, from time to time, be able to render unusual service to the FBI, more so than the normal professional contact, and be of future service to the Bureau. He recommended that Clegg be designated as a "Special Service Contact."[29] A week later Hoover responded, denying that designation for Clegg but suggesting that Clegg might be utilized as a special agent in charge contact or source of information.[30]

Nevertheless, Clegg was eager to continue collaborating with the Bureau in any way he could be effective. Hoover requested input from the Retirement Division of the US Civil Service Commission regarding the feasibility of employing Clegg in the capacity of an expert or consultant in which he would present lectures two or three times a year at law enforcement schools. Hoover urged the Memphis office to invite Clegg to attend general social functions of the field office and law enforcement meetings.[31]

Clegg also continued to maintain a strong interest in the FBI National Academy, the establishment of which was one of his major accomplishments at the FBI. A year after his retirement, he was invited to present a lecture to the FBI National Academy on Public Relations in Law Enforcement. He was paid ten dollars per diem and transportation expenses in addition to a one-hundred-dollar speakers fee.[32] Several other invitations followed, and then Hoover extended an invitation to Clegg to become a member of the Visiting Faculty of the FBI National Academy. Hoover specifically invited him to present a lecture titled "Obtaining Public Support for Law Enforcement" to the Academy on May 19, 1955. Clegg was paid first-class transportation costs and a fee of $150 (in lieu of a per diem; the extra $50 would defray the cost of meals and lodging).[33] Clegg sent a telegram to Hoover accepting the invitation and indicated that an honorarium would not be necessary if the process of providing the honorarium was too cumbersome.[34] Clegg presented a similar lecture to the academy the following October. His presentations to the National Academy became an almost annual event. As late as 1975, Clegg was invited by then-FBI director Clarence Kelley to speak at the one hundredth graduation exercise of the FBI National Academy. Kelley had earlier graciously invited Clegg to spend a week at the new multimillion dollar FBI Academy complex near Quantico, Virginia.[35]

As humble as Clegg had been over the years, he seemed to brag about other employment opportunities that continued to surface such as executive secretary the National Association of Chiropodists and staff director of the newly formed Commission on Government Security. Perhaps the most appealing offers were positions he considered taking at Indiana University. In January 1958, Special Agent H. G. Foster of the Indianapolis field office informed Hoover that Clegg had called him two days earlier to let him know that he had visited with Indiana University president Herman Wells to discuss the possibility of taking the position of chairman of the School of Police Administration. Clegg did not express great interest in the position but indicated he would keep Foster advised.[36] Two months later, Hoover was informed by agent R. D. Auerbach that Clegg had received an offer to become dean of men at Indiana University at a salary $2,000 higher than the current $14,000 he was earning at Ole Miss. Clegg told Auerbach that he would refuse the offer. Clegg then quietly let it be known that he might be interested in heading to Mississippi State University, the archrival of Ole Miss. Despite these temptations, Clegg remained at Ole Miss.

Hoover wrote Clegg expressing his appreciation of news items that appeared in Jackson, Mississippi, newspapers that reported generous comments which Clegg had made regarding the FBI and Hoover. Hoover also mentioned a newspaper clipping indicating that Clegg was being considered as a potential successor to the president at Mississippi State University. On February 24, 1960, *Jackson Daily News* columnist Jimmy Ward wrote about the Board of Trustees seeking a successor for the outgoing president, Ben Hilbun. Ward stated that quiet consideration was being given to Hugh Clegg, although Clegg had publicly denied interest in the position. Ward supported Clegg and wrote that his "conservative Mississippi attitude and alert mind add to his qualifications as a potential university president."[37] Dean W. Colvard succeeded Hilbun, and there is no evidence that Clegg formally applied for that position.

Clegg said he did not experience any transitional problems moving from the FBI to an academic community because he had served as president of the George Washington University Alumni Association for three years and had developed a close relationship with the GWU president, Dr. Cloyd Heck Marvin.[38] Marvin served as president of GWU for thirty-two years, from 1927 to 1959, and his administration was controversial and still considered scandalous by students fifty years later.[39]

Clegg said that as president of the GWU Alumni Association, he met often with the official alumni group and various committees. For three years, he served as chairman of the homecoming committee, so he felt as if he was in an academic community. He also felt that he was involved in educational processes when he was in charge of the Training and Inspection Division of the FBI and organizing the FBI National Academy and also spending time on university campuses recruiting new FBI agents. So even though he had spent time on campus primarily as a student, he felt involved with the academic community.

Clegg was impressed with many Ole Miss traditions and recalled listening to the 1953 Sugar Bowl game on the radio as Georgia Tech played Ole Miss. Clegg remembered hearing of how the Ole Miss band came on the field and marched into a formation that spelled out "Dixie." Then the largest Rebel flag—the Confederate battle flag—was carried over the band and the band would change formations under the flag and spell "Ole Miss" as the flag was carried off the field.[40] But when Ole Miss played the University of Texas in the 1958 Sugar Bowl, the flag was a source of criticism and embarrassment for Ole Miss. An editorial appeared in the Allentown, Pennsylvania, *Chronicle* on January 3, 1958, criticizing the Ole Miss band for unfurling a large Confederate flag and performing under it at halftime. Clegg was bothered by the criticism and retorted that "the flag had been made with loving hands by ladies on the university campus and from the city of Oxford. . . . It was the rebel flag of Ole Miss." Chancellor Williams wrote a letter to the editor of the *Chronicle* and defended the university and the university band.[41]

The Ole Miss band, under the directorship of Lyle Babcock, was embarrassed following that 1958 Sugar Bowl game when the ninety-foot-long, sixty-foot-wide, four-hundred-pound Confederate battle flag disappeared after it was displayed during the bowl game halftime. The flag was found that night in Hattiesburg, Mississippi—the home of Mississippi Southern College (renamed the University of Southern Mississippi in 1962). Some Mississippi Southern band members, who also performed at the game, tricked a porter into putting the flag on the Mississippi Southern band bus rather than the Ole Miss bus![42] The Ole Miss band would later somewhat redeem itself at the 1958 World Music Festival in Holland by winning first place in both the marching and concert competitions.

Clegg also had personal knowledge of Ole Miss before arriving that went beyond experiences related to him by his wife about the time when she was a student there. He was invited in the 1930s to speak at one of the regular weekly chapel meetings in Fulton Chapel and then years later to speak at an O.D.K. Mortar Board Forum. On several occasions he recruited potential FBI agents from the Ole Miss Law School. He also knew Mississippi governor Fielding Wright. They had a four-hour meeting in Clegg's Washington, DC, office where Wright told Clegg of his education plans for the state, which included the securing of funds from the legislature for building campus facilities for black students.

While vacationing in Mississippi in 1949, Clegg received a call from Governor Wright asking him to come to a meeting in Jackson but neglecting to reveal the meeting's purpose. Wright took him to meet with members of the General Joint Legislative Investigating Committee, chaired by John Junkin of Natchez, and including Curtis M. Swango (who would later preside over the trial of the accused murderers of Emmett Till) and Stanton A. Hall. Junkin told Clegg the committee was investigating Communism in Mississippi. Clegg told them there was much information in FBI files but that the files were confidential. He was then asked about two people in particular: Hodding Carter, a newspaper editor and publisher, and James Silver, a faculty member at Ole Miss who was on sabbatical leave in Aberdeen, Scotland, after receiving a Fulbright Scholarship.[43] Clegg informed the committee that Director Hoover had made public in a news magazine article the number of Communists in each state and that Mississippi ranked the lowest, having only one known Communist. Clegg then told the committee that he knew the name of that one Communist, and he was neither the editor nor the faculty member that the committee suspected. Clegg then pointed out the error of labeling sincere liberals as Communists and the gross mistake of labeling those people who disagreed "with us or our point of view" as Communists.[44]

One of Clegg's major responsibilities at Ole Miss was to sell education, particularly higher education, with special emphasis on Ole Miss, to the people of Mississippi. But he always put higher education first and Ole Miss second. His vast experience in making presentations to various groups for the FBI was an advantage when he traveled across the state selling education to civic clubs, women's groups, youth groups, and anyone who would listen. Clegg liked to tell the following story:

I was accused by one professor of selling Ole Miss and higher education as if it were soap. History professor James Silver suggested that "the administration became more and more appeasement minded, more and more involved . . . with presenting the Ole Miss story to the state as if it were a bar of soap."[45] In answer to that I can say "I tried." [Ironically] I remember one time one newspaper reporter told me, and I talked to Mr. Hoover and told him, that Mr. Hoover was "selling" the FBI "as if it were a soap or detergent." Whenever the FBI achieved success it made headlines. Hoover said, "Well, we're getting annually increased appropriations and I use that to increase salaries. The first time any member of the organization turns down the salary increase due to the fact that this publicity is distasteful to him, I'll listen to him." Rev. Billy Graham was accused of selling religion as if it were a soap.[46]

Other universities were doing the same thing—selling higher education to try to increase funding.

In addition to his duties as director of development and assistant to the chancellor, Clegg was also in charge of the university information news service and thus in a position to ensure maximum favorable publicity for the university. He was involved in what was called The Rebel Record—a project that had the news service department of the university prepare "brief, staccato-like statements" of university accomplishments every quarter. These reports were circulated to newspapers in every major city in the country and generated considerable national interest. Several students who enrolled at Ole Miss from distant sections of the country indicated they first heard of Ole Miss from these reports, which were published in their local papers—even when they were used simply as space fillers.[47]

Clegg was also assigned by Chancellor Williams to increase enrollment in more direct ways. When Clegg arrived, Ole Miss was third in enrollment among Mississippi institutions of higher education behind Mississippi State University and Mississippi Southern College. By October 1, 1962, Ole Miss had moved ahead of Mississippi State and Mississippi Southern, although the difference among the three institutions was only about two hundred students.

When Clegg arrived at Ole Miss, he received a copy of the university budget and thought that the appropriation of $9.6 million would be sufficient to run the university—until he learned that the budget was a biennial appropriation. Then, upon further reading of the budget, he was stunned to learn that this appropriation was for all eight institutions of higher learning in the state. It was around this time when Ole Miss and the other institutions began the campaign to vigorously sell higher education to the state.[48] About this same time, the economy of the state began to improve, and because of the combined efforts of the major universities to sell education, the legislature began to increase appropriations and salaries for higher education.

While Clegg had gotten off to a good start at Ole Miss, racism was always rearing its ugly head. Clegg began to find himself immersed in issues of race, segregation, tradition, integration, and so-called liberal faculty members rather than dealing with issues related to the economic growth of the university.

Chapter Eleven

Clennon King
and Ole Miss "Liberals"

But the closed society—bolstered by a general apathy, a lethargic
federal government, a widespread agricultural distress, an emigration
of the most dissatisfied, and the burgeoning power of the modern Ku
Klux Klan—was barely challenged.—James W. Silver

H UGH AND RUBY KATHRYN RETURNED to Mississippi and
to what Ole Miss history professor James W. Silver would
later call "the closed society."[1] They arrived at a time when
society and education in the country, and particularly Mississippi
and the Deep South, were undergoing dramatic changes that would
affect racial attitudes for decades to come. Always a bastion of segregation, Mississippi was at war with the concepts of integration and
racial equality, issues that were brought to a head at the time Clegg
arrived at Ole Miss. Emmett Till would be lynched some eighteen
months later near Money, Mississippi. When Clegg arrived at Ole
Miss on February 2, 1954, the US Supreme Court, headed by Chief
Justice Earl Warren, was about to release its landmark decision in
the famous *Brown v. Board of Education of Topeka* civil suit. On
May 17, 1954, the Court overturned the *Plessy v. Ferguson* "separate
but equal" decision of 1896 that permitted states to maintain segregation and ruled that laws allowing racial segregation violated the
Equal Protection Clause of the Fourteenth Amendment to the US
Constitution. Mississippi, like much of the South, was ill prepared
to meet the obligations imposed by this ruling. In the 1960s, the actions of the civil rights movement led to the integration of all public

places, including educational institutions. Clegg had experienced not only racial unrest in the nation's capital, but integration of the local transportation system and the beginning of the move to integrate its schools, so he felt prepared to return home and deal with racial issues in Mississippi.[2] On racial and all other issues, Clegg firmly believed that the Constitution is the cornerstone of our system of laws.[3]

Clegg was on the front lines when the seeds of integration at Ole Miss were planted; when charges of Communist infiltration of the faculty, begun in 1950, persisted into his tenure; and when the integration of Ole Miss by James Meredith was imminent. He had stepped into a firestorm. While he did not covet being put in that position, Clegg later looked back on that tumultuous period and said, "We came out all right."[4]

One of Clegg's first assignments was based on the knowledge and experience he had gained at the FBI in fighting the Communist threat to the country. In 1950, Ole Miss and other Mississippi universities were put on the defensive when Mississippi state representative Hamer McKenzie from Benton County, who was also an Ole Miss law student, charged that Ole Miss, Mississippi State, and other higher education institutions harbored liberal professors who taught Communism—liberalism and Communism often being conflated in the state. Among these liberal professors was Ole Miss history professor James W. Silver, who would become a central figure in the struggle against alleged Communists. The leaders of Ole Miss and Mississippi State denied these charges. Several key Ole Miss supporters, including William Winter, future governor of the state and one of McKenzie's law school classmates, also came to the defense of Silver and other liberals alleged to be Communists.[5]

Although support for McKenzie quickly vanished, the Mississippi legislature adopted an antisubversive law that required all university faculty and state employees to sign a loyalty oath as a condition for employment. This act broadened the definition of a subversive organization to one that engages in or advocates, abets, advises, or teaches, or a purpose of which is to engage in or advocate, abet, advise, or teach activities intended to overthrow, destroy, or alter, or to assist in the overthrow, destruction, or alteration of the constitutional form of government of the United States, or of the State of Mississippi . . . but does not and shall not be construed to mean an organization the bona fide purpose of which is to promote peace by alliances or unions with other governments or world federations, unions, or governments to be effected through constitutional means.

It also describes a subversive as a person who belongs to a subversive organization. Under this definition, no person belonging to a subversive organization could hold public office or be hired by the state of Mississippi, including Mississippi institutions of higher education, its junior colleges, and its public elementary and high schools. The act also required state agencies, including state-supported educational institutions, to conduct loyalty checks to ensure their employees were not subversives.[6]

Nevertheless, many Mississippians were convinced that most liberal faculty members at the state universities were Communists or leaned toward the Communist philosophy. Ole Miss was singled out as a center for liberals because some members of its faculty and staff expressed views that were opposed by a majority of Mississippians. In 1954, Chancellor Williams appeared before a Mississippi legislative committee to discuss the faculty hiring process at Ole Miss. He informed the committee that he relied on Clegg to make sure the applicant was neither a member of the Communist Party nor another kind of subversive. Clegg was surprised when Williams made this announcement, since he had not been made aware of his new responsibility.[7]

On February 17, 1955, the IHL Board of Trustees unanimously adopted a regulation that all speakers invited to the campus of any of the state institutions of higher learning must first be investigated and approved by the chancellor or president of the institution involved. The names of any invited speaker had to be filed with the executive secretary of the IHL Board of Trustees. Clegg was assigned the duty of carrying out invited speaker investigations for Ole Miss, but only Chancellor Williams could approve or disapprove a potential speaker. After Clegg would conduct an investigation, he would mark the application "OK" followed by his initials if no derogatory information surfaced during his investigation. If derogatory information was discovered, Clegg would take it to the university provost who would, in all probability, recommend to the chancellor that the potential speaker not be invited to campus.[8]

The issue of outside speakers became a two-edged sword, with speakers on both sides of the issue capable of generating controversy. Chancellor Williams and Clegg were in New York on university business and were unaware of any problem until Governor Hugh L. White called Clegg, criticized the two professors by name, and threatened to reduce the university's appropriation if the professors remained on the faculty. Clegg would later boast, "They did, and the legislature didn't."[9]

The conservative power structure in Mississippi, supported by the average white citizen, was strongly committed to segregation in the state in the 1950s. The overwhelming majority of the white population was for total segregation, opposing integration in any form. Some Mississippians went so far as to say they were in favor of slavery, whether they actually meant it or not. These anti-integration, total segregation sentiments were not restricted to Mississippi but were, rather, the rule of the day in the Deep South and many other parts of the country. Just after arriving at Ole Miss, Clegg heard complaints about some of the Ole Miss faculty being "too liberal." Those complaining said that some members of the faculty were "actually for integration." Groups such as the Citizens' Council, irritated with the apparent liberal views emanating from Ole Miss, wanted Chancellor Williams to meet with them so they could air their complaints. These invitations for a meeting were rejected.[10]

In June 1955 William J. Simmons, leader of the Jackson Citizens' Council movement, charged Ole Miss and Millsaps with hiring liberal professors who subverted Mississippi's policy of segregation. Simmons, who attended Millsaps College, graduated from Mississippi College, and studied French at the Institut de Touraine in Tours, France, returned to Mississippi and devoted full-time service to Citizens' Council activities. Chancellor Williams continued to vigorously defend the university and refute charges that there was Communist faculty at the university.[11]

Later that same month, Robert B. Patterson, the leader and founder of the first Citizens' Council, formed on July 11, 1954, rejected Williams's denials. He repeated Simmons's charge, claiming that textbooks were being used to promote ideas contrary to the best interests of the people of the state, in particular those of the white race. When Patterson made his charges public, Clegg was assigned the task of responding. After carefully examining the complaints, Clegg concluded that they had no basis in fact. Clegg defended the hiring practices of deans, which often involved hiring faculty with northern backgrounds; backed the independent status of the student newspaper; and attacked any form of censorship. His defense was widely appreciated in university circles.[12]

Morton B. King, a native of Shelbyville, Tennessee, joined the Ole Miss faculty in 1939 as an assistant professor of sociology and was instrumental in initiating a program of campuswide forums, lectures, and discussion groups called Religious Emphasis Week (REW). Will Davis Campbell, a civil rights activist, Baptist minister, and author, was born in rural Amite County, where his ancestors had settled in 1816. He was ordained at the age of seventeen and then attended Wake Forest College, Tulane University, and Yale Divinity School and held a pastorate in Louisiana. Because of his background and education, Campbell was offered and accepted the position of director of religious life at Ole Miss in August 1954. His first year at the university was uneventful, but he became involved in racial controversies in 1955 and 1956. One of Campbell's responsibilities involved coordinating and program planning for REW. He felt that the topics for the 1956 program should involve racial justice. Campbell specifically became embroiled in a couple of controversial issues. One involved his visit to Providence Farm, an experimental biracial community in Holmes County, whose activities were investigated by the local Citizens' Council. A second and more ominous controversy involved an invitation extended to the Reverend Alvin Kershaw to speak at the 1956 Religious Emphasis Week on "Jazz, Music and Religion."[13]

Kershaw had been active in civil rights issues in Ohio, where he taught philosophy at Miami University. He was a member of the National Association for the Advancement of Colored People (NAACP) and helped raise funds for the NAACP Legal Defense Fund. Kershaw had appeared on the CBS television quiz show, *The $64,000 Question*, won $32,000, and implied that he would donate his winnings to NAACP legal causes. The invitation of this controversial speaker ignited vigorous protests that involved the IHL Board of Trustees. Jackson newspapers published stories about Kershaw coming to speak at Ole Miss side by side with a story about Kershaw's intention to donate his quiz show winnings to the NAACP.[14] A member of the press contacted Kershaw, who confirmed that he was, indeed, coming to Ole Miss despite the protests and would discuss the evils of segregation.

Clegg was upset, feeling that Kershaw was out of line because this was not the topic he had been invited to address. The special committee that had been set up to handle the REW project met late one evening and at two o'clock in the morning. Chancellor Williams postponed Kershaw's visit and withdrew the invitation on the basis that he had been invited without the proper application being filled out by the director of religious life—Will Campbell.[15] Clegg was not invited to this meeting nor was he involved in the decision, although he supported the chancellor. While the majority of the faculty appeared to be placated by the chancellor's decision and assertion that this "was not the ditch to die in," Morton King, chairman of the Department of Sociology, resigned his administrative position and his faculty professorship in protest.[16] The application for Kershaw's invitation finally reached Clegg's desk, but only after the decision to withdraw the invitation had been made.[17]

Campbell's reputation as a liberal on issues involving racial justice led to two events in 1956 that contributed to Campbell's ultimate resignation from the university. One involved a party put on by Campbell's staff at the start of summer school. Someone had placed a piece of human feces powdered with sugar in the punch bowl. Campbell complained to Clegg but was told that it would be impossible to identify the culprit. The message sent to Campbell was obvious.[18] A second issue involved Campbell's encouragement of a young black minister, John E. Cameron, to enroll in a university correspondence course as a means of breaking the racial barrier. Campbell invited Cameron to his office in the Y Building to review the regulations regarding enrollment in correspondence courses and the two became engaged in a ping-pong game, after which Campbell gave Cameron a ride home. An acting summer school registrar, W. M. "Chubby" Ellis, observed the two playing ping-pong and complained to the dean of student personnel.[19] Campbell resigned from the university and assumed a position with the National Council of Churches in Nashville.

Clegg's involvement in the turmoil surrounding Campbell and the REW controversy and his decision to not become involved in the punch bowl issue appeared to be at odds with his willingness to take on other controversial issues. On the other hand, his experience with the FBI convinced him that identification of the punch bowl culprit would, indeed, be impossible. Clegg had limited interaction with Campbell and perhaps would not have recognized him if they passed each other. Still, Clegg helped quiet some of the controversies created by Campbell and defended him when necessary. Despite calls for the dismissal of Campbell because of his liberal viewpoint, Clegg claimed that Ole Miss never dismissed anyone during his time at the university because of his or her liberal or conservative philosophies.[20]

The university faced its first major integration crisis in 1958, when Georgia native Clennon W. King Jr. publicly announced his intention to enter Ole Miss. King attempted to enroll in the law school at the University of Georgia in the 1940s but was turned away. He was a minister and a history professor at all-black Alcorn State University and had gained the reputation of being a civil rights activist. He attempted to have one of his children integrate an all-white elementary public school in Mississippi. In May 1958, King contacted the executive secretary of the IHL Board of Trustees, E. R. Jobe, and informed him of his intention to pursue a PhD degree in history at Ole Miss. King had earned a master's degree in European history from Ohio State University and taught history at Alcorn A&M College (now Alcorn State University). Rather than using the normal application procedures and forms, King informed Jobe that he would personally apply for admission on the Oxford campus.[21] King first appeared on the public stage in 1957, when the *Jackson State Times* published a series of articles in which he presented his views on race relations, which favored segregation and criticized the NAACP.[22] His criticism of the NAACP resulted in a student boycott involving most of the Alcorn student body, during which students called King an Uncle Tom, accused him of demeaning women in his class, and demanded his removal. Sensitive to the student demands, the IHL Board removed President Jesse R. Otis, who was accused by the boycotting students of failing to address their complaints, and replaced him with J. D. Boyd. But Otis had already resigned effective April 1 for health reasons. The IHL board warned that students who did not comply with its orders to return to class would be expelled.[23]

The board later announced that King would be retained but would not be allowed to teach. He remained on the Alcorn faculty but chose not to return to the campus. In May 1958, Boyd and the IHL Board, satisfied that King's academic freedom had been protected, informed him that his contract would not be renewed. He then applied for admission to graduate school at Ole Miss. At that time, Ole Miss did not offer a doctoral degree in history, King's expressed area of interest.[24]

The Mississippi Board of Trustees of the IHL had given instructions that it was to be notified in the event a black applied for admission to any of the state's higher education institutions. The IHL and the office of the attorney general were notified that King had written

Ole Miss on May 11, 1958, regarding his intention to enroll but that he had not filled out the required application form. Detailed plans, including provisions of restroom facilities, that were approved by the IHL, the attorney general, the chancellor, and the division heads were made for his arrival. Meetings with faculty were held to disclose in detail the program of activities should King arrive. Chancellor Williams sought cooperation and asked the faculty to observe and report disturbances that might result. The suggestion applied only when professors were proceeding to classes or the library; they were assured they were not asked to be policemen. Plans were made to prevent violence and disorder and to protect King. Help was sought from the Mississippi Highway Patrol, the local sheriff, and police from the city of Oxford. All promised cooperation. Even the Ole Miss football team was involved, since a few years earlier the team had assisted the administration to help prevent a panty raid. While the faculty was divided on the issue, most appreciated being kept informed. Clegg was committed to the importance of informing faculty.[25] He recalled an amusing incident that occurred during a meeting with the faculty, helping add some levity to a serious situation. "I explained," Clegg said, "that the registrar, Mr. Robert Ellis, an assistant to the dean of student personnel, Mr. Tom Hines, and I would be the 'Registration Committee.' However, I said we would be the 'Reception Committee.' There was laughter." The entire plan then became widely known on campus as "Operation Reception Committee."[26]

Plans for King's arrival included having plainclothes Mississippi highway patrolmen accompany King on his bus ride from Gulfport to Oxford. Governor J. P. Coleman directed the plans with Attorney General Joe T. Patterson while staying twenty miles away in Batesville. Public Service Commissioner Tom Scarbrough directed fifty uniformed highway patrolmen and plainclothes policemen to take positions at the university's entrances and surround the Lyceum Building, the main administrative building on campus.[27]

At 9:00 a.m. on June 5, 1958, King arrived by taxi to register for summer school. Ellis met him at the education building and drove him to the Lyceum. Clegg met King at the front door and escorted him to the Registrar's Office. Ellis and Tom Hines arrived soon thereafter. Ellis informed King that the papers he presented did not constitute a complete application and pointed out several of its deficiencies. King was uninterested and wanted to start classes right away, but classes had not yet begun. King just sat in the office saying nothing for almost two hours. Word was sent by Coleman to remove King as a trespasser. Tom Scarborough, director of the Highway Patrol, came in and, rather than promptly removing him, sat down and tried to reason with King. He still would not move, so orders were sent to have him arrested. When King saw the patrol car coming, he ran up and down the aisles of the office hollering, "Help! Help! They are going to kill me." The press overheard the commotion, and Coleman told the highway patrol to take King and get him off campus.[28] He was arrested, taken to the university police department, and then hustled into a patrol car to be taken to Jackson for a lunacy test, as it was called at the time.

Later that same afternoon, officials in Lafayette County charged King with disturbing the peace and resisting arrest and secured a lunacy warrant against him. A lunacy hearing was held in Jackson with Hinds County chancery judge Stokes V. Robertson presiding. Robertson ordered King to be taken to the Mississippi State Hospital in Whitfield, Mississippi—the state's mental hospital—for observation and treatment.[29]

Clegg said that months later, King apologized to the governor and asked that his apology be extended to officials at Ole Miss. William P. Murphy, a member of the law school faculty and of the American Civil Liberties Union (ACLU), investigated the incident and informed the ACLU that King's rights had not been violated and that King had not been denied admission on the basis of race or denied due process.[30] Two weeks after being committed, no evidence of mental instability could be determined and King was released.

In 1960 King ran for the presidency of the United States as a candidate of the Independent Afro-American Party, becoming perhaps the first African American candidate for president. He ran for governor of Georgia in 1970, again for president in 1970, and then ran for mayor of Miami, Florida, in 1996 and for a seat in the Georgia legislature. King died after a battle with prostate cancer in 2000.

A year after returning to his home state, Clegg was given a difficult assignment. Segregationists in Mississippi were using all the means they could muster to fight the national civil rights movement. Education was the target of the *Brown v. Board of Education* Supreme Court decision and higher education became a focal point of the battle, as evidenced by the attempt of Clennon King to desegregate the University of Mississippi. Ole Miss had become the centerpiece of the desegregation battle in Mississippi. Clegg had refuted the charges lodged against Chancellor Williams and the university by Robert B. Patterson, the Citizens' Council leader, but the controversy would not go away.

Charges against several allegedly liberal faculty members at the university were led by "two very distinguished alumni": Edwin Wilburn Hooker Sr. and Hillery Edwin White, both of Lexington, Mississippi, in Holmes County, less than one hundred miles from Clegg's Mathiston birthplace. Clegg recalled that Hooker and White charged that thirty-one members of the faculty and staff possessed "liberal attitudes" contrary to the beliefs of a good many people in Mississippi.[31] Clegg allowed that Hooker and White were his friends, but he and they stood on the opposite side of this issue. He considered them to be "fine gentlemen, firm in their beliefs . . . who felt they were doing the State and University a favor by bringing the charges."[32]

Clegg opposed the efforts of Hooker and White.[33] Although Hooker and White lived next door to each other, they were not close friends or colleagues; Hooker was an outgoing businessman while White was a quiet lawyer. Both believed in segregation and both were members of the Citizens' Council. They worked to purge Ole Miss of those whom they considered to be undesirables and wanted to correct what they claimed was a threatening situation in which professors were teaching liberal and foreign ideas to students. Hooker and White also directed their anger against invitations to liberals to speak on the campus, including Supreme Court justice Felix Frankfurter, newspaperman Hodding Carter, and others with alleged Communist connections. Hooker in particular was incensed by the visit of the university's director of religious life, Will Campbell, to Providence Cooperative Farm, an experimental biracial community in Holmes County.[34] Hooker and White became self-appointed leaders of the effort to purify Ole Miss, and they generated support from alumni. They appointed a committee to address their concerns to the IHL Board of Trustees. When the board asked them to submit their concerns in writing, they presented a twenty-six-page complaint listing more than one hundred specific charges against university professors and organizations and included indictments of the administration. The views of Law School dean Robert J. Farley and law school faculty on racial issues were a major point of challenge. When the IHL Board informed the university of the complaint, Chancellor Williams assigned Clegg and Vice Chancellor W. Alton Bryant to answer the charges. Because of Clegg's FBI experience in the area of Communist activities and Bryant's academic teaching and administrative experience, the pair was well qualified to carry out the assignment.[35]

Clegg said the thirty-one faculty members involved in the formal complaint were the most outspoken members of the faculty, and he recalled several anecdotes about them. One professor, from a northern state, had gone into a doctor's office for treatment. There were two waiting rooms, one for whites and the other for blacks. The black waiting room was filled and when the professor saw some blacks standing and waiting, he brought one black into the white waiting room and introduced him to one of the southern ladies, even giving him a seat him next to her. This caused a great uproar among some local citizens, and the incident was included among the charges. Another professor made a commencement address at a high school in northwestern Mississippi and spoke on a subject about which he had been doing research and writing; namely, the way to integrate the institutions of learning in the community and the high school, including what steps to take to do it calmly and peacefully. That didn't rest well on the ears of his audience, and this incident was included in the charges.[36] Yet another faculty member, philosophy professor Quinter Marcellus Lyon,[37] whom Clegg regarded as a good friend, taught in his class that when the Israelites fled from Egypt and crossed the Red Sea, a high east wind came up and pushed the waters back. Lyon was accused of failing to suggest that the Lord caused an east wind to come and thus offending some in his class. Lyon's Christianity was not in doubt, since he held a position in the local Methodist Church as director of music and Sunday school teacher and published a book, *The Great Religions* (1957).[38] Nevertheless, he left the university after being accused of apostasy.[39]

A significant number of people in the state supported these charges, and many went to Lexington and urged Hooker and White to move forward with their attacks. Clegg recalled that five people signed the charges in addition to Hooker and White. He also felt that while some of the charges may have had a basis in fact, it was the point of view of the Ole Miss administration, of which he was a part, that academic freedom was a necessity. Each of the faculty and staff members accused had the opportunity to answer each charge and present their responses to the Board of Trustees. Chancellor Williams conducted an intense internal review while conducting an external public relations campaign to garner support for the university. Williams wanted the university response to the IHL to offer a rebuttal to each and every charge.

Along with Alton Bryant, Clegg took on a leadership role in defending the university and held meetings throughout the state to familiarize the alumni with the charges and the university responses to these charges. Clegg warned alumni of the possibility of legislative hearings leading to more damage to the university in the form of smears and phony allegations. He also stressed the importance of academic freedom in a university environment. He also cited the possibility of losing university accreditation and emphasized the disastrous consequences that such a loss would bring. On one occasion, Clegg met with a group of alumni at the Walthall Hotel in

Jackson. However, the president and executive secretary of the Citizens' Council, who were not alumni, attended the meeting in violation of Clegg's imposed conditions of the invitation being extended to "alumni only." Hooker and White were among the alumni who attended the meeting. White spoke up, pledging to give his life to prevent integration of any school in Mississippi. After the meeting, about one-third of those present came to Clegg to renew their support of Ole Miss. Clegg was invited to join the Citizens' Council, but he declined because he was aware of the racial basis on which the group was founded and because he was advised before he left Washington, DC, not to join the radical group.[40]

One hundred alumni from all sections of the state met twice in Jackson at the Heidelberg Hotel and, after Clegg presented the university's response to the Hooker and White charges, those alumni expressed unanimous support of the university. A steering committee, all but one of the members being lawyers, was formed to advise and counsel the chancellor and the staff. More meetings were scheduled in Jackson. The committee consisted of well-known citizens in the state and included Chester Curtis as chairman, Harvey Lee Morrison, George Payne Cossar, Thomas N. Turner, William Barbour, Judge Curtis Swango, and William S. Griffin.[41] The chancellor appointed Clegg coordinator of the committee. A distinguished auxiliary group was also formed and was called when Clegg needed to discuss a particular issue. Its members were Dr. Lamar S. Bailey, Fred Smith, Frank Everett, Orma Smith, Otho Smith, Lyle Bates, Judge Taylor McElroy, Baxter Wilson, S. M. Carter, James T. Singley, Martin V. B. Miller, Jack Doty, and Mitchell Salloum, many of them professionals and alumni who had a common bond of love and concern for the university.[42] Clegg later claimed that on more than one occasion, the committee saved the university from being closed. Clegg kept the university faculty informed by holding various meetings on campus.

Clegg and Bryant also met with each of the accused faculty to provide them an opportunity to respond. Several faculty members assumed a combative tone in their responses, and Clegg and Bryant worked to soften their attitudes. In its official response to these charges to the IHL board, the university rejected each and every charge and deemed all allegations to be baseless. The board backed the administration after investigating the charges and commended the chancellor, expressing full confidence in him, the institution, and the faculty and staff. The board also reiterated its commitment to academic freedom in higher education. Ole Miss survived the attacks and it became Clegg's role, as assistant to the chancellor, to lead the public relations response in every crisis faced by the university. When Clegg traveled the state on university business, the majority of alums supported the university; even the critics remained loyal to Ole Miss.[43]

Clegg became involved in another controversy that involved a magazine called *PayDay*. Clegg agreed to serve on the board of directors of a conservative organization called Patriotic American Youth—an organization whose only purpose, Clegg thought, was to promote Americanism and fight Communism. The chairman of the advisory board was Mississippi Supreme Court presiding justice Henry Lee Rodgers. The presidents of Mississippi State and Southern Mississippi served as vice-chairmen. The advisory board also included four former agents of the FBI among its twenty-six members. Months passed before Clegg received his first copy of the magazine. The first issue listed proposed programs that included showing films such as *Operation Abolition* and *Communism on the Map*. (*Operation Abolition* purported to show that opponents of the House Un-American Activities Committee were led by Communists, but a follow-up film titled *Operation Correction* used the same visuals but with voiceovers citing many major errors of fact.) It also presented a list of suggested conservative speakers that included US senator Barry Goldwater and news commentator Paul Harvey.[44] Clegg discovered that without his knowledge, he had been promoted to vice chairman of the advisory board. In addition to including many university administrators on its original board, *PayDay* included members of the Mississippi State Sovereignty Commission, a state-supported organization that defended and promoted segregation.

Clegg distanced himself from the organization and claimed that the magazine had begun to publish articles inconsistent with its avowed purposes. For this reason, he stated, he was resigning his membership and his advisory board position.[45]

Clegg was fully aware of the racial problems in the state. In 1957, he wrote Director Hoover expressing his concern about attitudes in the state regarding racial integration of public places and public education and offering to help Mississippi in its transition. He wrote, "I am, however, anxious to know what to do and how to serve in the real crisis we have in the South at this time. I suppose there is no easy answer, but certainly the right answers are not being used on many occasions at present."[46]

Clegg's acquaintances with prominent individuals cultivated during his time at the FBI had its advantages and disadvantages. In 1961, the law school invited US Supreme Court justice Tom C. Clark to be the featured speaker at a banquet honoring the Mississippi Supreme Court—perhaps with Clegg's encouragement. "Liberal" Ole Miss Law School dean Farley served as his host. Clark, whose father graduated from Ole Miss before he moved to Texas, was nominated to the Court in 1949 despite being criticized by liberals who thought he was too conservative. Once again the university was caught in the middle of controversy. To the surprise of no one, the university invitation drew the ire of state politicians such as Governor Ross Barnett and Mississippi house speaker Walter Sillers, since Clark was supportive of the *Brown v. Board of Education of Topeka* decision. They tried to block the invitation but failed. Clark's visit proved to be uneventful.[47]

Clegg did not realize that he would soon become embroiled in a defining event in the history of civil rights in America. As damaging as was the way the university and state handled the attempted integration of Ole Miss by Clennon King, the crisis and resulting riot resulting from the integration of Ole Miss by James Meredith in 1962 were even more devastating. Once again, Clegg found himself playing a major role in attempting to salvage the reputation of the university.

Chapter Twelve

Meredith Applies to Ole Miss

We speak now against the day when our Southern people who will
resist to the last these inevitable changes in social relations, will, when
they have been forced to accept what they at one time might have
accepted with dignity and goodwill. Will say "Why didn't someone tell
us this before? Tell us this in time?"—William Faulkner

WRITER WILLIE MORRIS, a native Mississippian and an
astute observer of life there, referred to the resistance of
the state of Mississippi to the integration of the University of Mississippi by James Meredith as "the last battle of the Civil
War, the last direct constitutional crisis between national and state
authority."[1] Clegg found himself immersed in this controversy.

In addition to Morris, several historians, including David Sansing,
Charles W. Eagles, Russell H. Barrett, James W. Silver, and William
Doyle, along with James Meredith himself, have written in eloquent
detail of the integration of Ole Miss and of the resulting riot that
caused the deaths of two individuals and caused almost irreparable
damage to the image of Ole Miss. But it is interesting to recall the
sequence of events as seen through the eyes of Hugh Clegg and to
read an account of the crisis written from his perspective. Clegg was
critical of the actions taken against his employer, by both the state of
Mississippi and the federal government. His criticism of the federal
marshals as well as his old bosses at the Department of Justice put
him in a difficult position, caught between the hammer and the an-
vil, between his loyalty to his former federal bosses and his loyalty to
his new employer, the University of Mississippi. It is not surprising
that his recollection of events is somewhat prejudiced.

On Friday, January 20, 1961, the country was energized by the inaugural address of President John F. Kennedy in which he exhorted his fellow countrymen to ask themselves what they can do for their country. Kennedy had been elected, in part, because of the strong civil rights platform adopted at the Democratic National Convention. Almost as if in response to this challenge, the next day James Meredith sent an undated letter to the University of Mississippi requesting an application form for admission. The university promptly responded, not realizing that the individual requesting the application form was black. Meredith returned his application to the university and included, as specified on the form, a photograph of himself. Viewing Meredith's photograph, the university registrar, Robert B. Ellis, realized the potential problems the application presented and notified Clegg, who had been designated by the chancellor to deal with any application for admission filed by a black person.[2]

Meredith was an African American native of Kosciusko, Mississippi, who had served in the US Air Force for two years before attending Jackson State University. Since the Ole Miss spring semester would start soon thereafter on February 6, 1961, Meredith requested immediate action on his application.[3] Under procedures established when Clennon King attempted to desegregate Ole Miss, the board of the IHL required the university to notify the board and the attorney general by telephone of the receipt of each communication from an African American. The attorney general's staff requested six photocopies of each communication. It was the responsibility of Clegg's office to handle these communications. Meredith was informed that the registrar had discontinued all applications for the spring semester received after January 25, 1961, one day before receiving Meredith's letter—quite a coincidence. Meredith was also notified that each institution of higher education, upon direction by the IHL Board of Trustees, required recommendations from five alumni. Meredith submitted recommendations from black citizens of Mississippi, none of whom were alumni. On February 20, Meredith expressed concern that his application for admission to the spring semester had been discontinued and requested admission to the upcoming June summer session. Clegg emphasized that the application was rejected because it lacked recommendations from five alumni.[4]

Delaying tactics continued, and in May 1961 the registrar informed Meredith that only forty-eight of the ninety credit hours submitted for transfer could be accepted. Regardless, Meredith asked that his application be given "pending" status. When word of Meredith's attempt to register at Ole Miss spread throughout the state, many white citizens became irate and threatened to try to close the university. On May 25, Meredith was told his application had been denied since Jackson State College was not an accredited member of the Southern Association of Colleges and Secondary Schools and the university permitted transfer of credits only from accredited schools. His application was considered closed by the university, but Meredith was not deterred.

One week later, attorneys in New York filed a complaint on behalf of Meredith and other blacks of the state and asked for a restraining order. US district judge Sidney C. Mize denied the request, but the US Court of Appeals suggested that the District Court hold a full trial on the matter. On June 29, a motion was filed in District Court on behalf of Meredith against the Board of Trustees of the IHL and its president, Charles D. Fair. Future US Supreme Court justice Thurgood Marshall was one of the attorneys filing on behalf of Meredith. On August 15, Ole Miss Registrar Robert Ellis testified that he would admit a Negro who met all admission requirements and that he had not been given instructions to the contrary. Once again, Judge Mize refused to grant a temporary injunction to admit Meredith and on February 5, 1962, dismissed the complaint. The case was appealed to the Fifth Circuit Court and a motion was filed to issue an injunction requiring admission. Yet again the motion was denied, and the Circuit Court proceeded to make a full review.[5]

On April 20, the US Fifth Circuit Court of Appeals heard Meredith's appeal but was in no apparent hurry to render a decision. On June 25, in a 2-1 decision, with Judges John Minor Wisdom and John R. Brown approving and Judge Dozier A. DeVane dissenting, the court reversed Judge Mize's ruling and found that Meredith had indeed been denied admission on the basis of race and ordered the district judge to issue the injunction for admission requested by Meredith's attorneys.[6] As the university's new academic year was approaching, actions on both sides of the issue picked up pace. On June 6, 1962, Meredith had been arrested for giving false information regarding his place of residence when he registered to vote in Hinds County,[7] but a week later the US Fifth Circuit Court of Appeals enjoined the state from proceeding with criminal charges against him. On September 4, 1962, the board unanimously approved registrar Ellis's denial of admission and withdrew from the university all authority regarding the admission and assumed that authority itself. On September 10, Associate Justice Hugo Black of the US Supreme Court vacated the four successive stays issued by Justice Ben F. Cameron of the US Fifth Circuit Court. Black polled the other members of the Supreme Court by telephone since court was not in session and issued an injunction against interference with the ruling of the Court of Appeals. Judge Mize then issued a sweeping injunction against the university on September 13, 1962.[8] Six days later, Meredith's attorney was informed that Meredith would be tried the next day in a justice of the peace court in Hinds County on false registration charges. Meredith did not appear and was found guilty in absentia. He was fined one hundred dollars and court costs and sentenced to a one-year term in the Hinds County Jail. On that same day, the Mississippi legislature passed a bill prohibiting any person convicted of a criminal charge and not pardoned or having a charge of moral turpitude pending from enrolling in any institution of higher learning. The bill also provided for a penalty against anyone aiding or abetting such enrollment.

The university, with Clegg taking a leadership role, made elaborate plans for Meredith's admission. All university plans were designed to comply with the order, avoid violence, and keep the university open. There was little outcry from students except for a cross set up early one morning on Fraternity Row. The University Police Department ordered the students not to set fire to the cross. Dean of

Students L. L. Love arrived and persuaded the crowd to remove the cross.[9]

The state of Mississippi would not yield to either common sense or the law. On September 13, Governor Ross Barnett directed all officers of the state to uphold the laws of Mississippi and interpose state sovereignty. On September 19, Jones County chancery judge L. B. Porter, a Barnett appointee, acting on behalf of the parents of forty-six students, issued an injunction that prohibited university officials or the board and various federal officials from taking any action to admit Meredith to Ole Miss.[10]

A day later, the Fifth Circuit Court of Appeals issued an injunction that prohibited the arrest of Meredith on false registration charges and restrained enforcement of Porter's injunction. That same day, the IHL Board notified Meredith to appear at the board's office in Jackson at 3:00 p.m. for registration, but the board was notified at noon that Meredith would instead appear at Ole Miss to register. Governor Barnett was on his way to Oxford after the Board of Trustees named him registrar of the university. Assuming that authority, Barnett refused to register Meredith. Meredith and the marshals left twenty-three minutes after they appeared before Barnett. That same day, Chancellor J. D. Williams, Dean of Liberal Arts A. B. Lewis, and Registrar Ellis were ordered to appear before US District Court judge Mize in Meridian to show cause why they should not be held in contempt. Since authority to register Meredith had been removed from the university, some saw this court action as persecution. Barnett met with the three university officials and urged them to go to jail if necessary. Ellis said he would not disobey a court order. The chancellor's attorney told Barnett that since the three were educators and not politicians, they were innocent and asked "why don't you act and not ask these innocent people to act for you." Barnett agreed. The three argued their noninvolvement before Judge Mize in view of the fact that the board had removed all their authority in the matter. Mize ruled in their favor.[11]

Clegg was caught between his loyalties to the Department of Justice that he served for so many years and to the state of Mississippi, his home state that he loved so much. In an attempt to resolve the situation, and with approval from the chancellor, he went to Memphis to call the US attorney general's office, fearing that a call in Mississippi would be somehow overheard. He telephoned Burke Marshall, the head of the Civil Rights Division of the Department of Justice, from a pay phone and then Attorney General Robert Kennedy came on the line. Clegg explained that jailing Barnett would only make him a martyr. He suggested that if any penalty was to be invoked against Barnett, it should be a fine. Both Marshall and Kennedy assured Clegg that they had no intention of sending Barnett to jail. Clegg then assured them that the university policy was to obey the Court's orders and both said they knew that.[12]

Clegg felt that the relationship between the University and the court could be "an *ex parte* relationship," not one of two opposing entities. Chancellor Williams agreed. Thus, the university attorney would make an appointment with the judge's clerk and arrange an appointment; then Clegg would accompany the attorney and be present for any disclosures or instructions given by the court. The court would be informed of any major disturbance. Thus, any actions of major significance by the administration would have prior or subsequent approval of a federal court judge.[13]

Chancellor Williams, Dean Lewis, Registrar Ellis, and the entire board were summoned to appear before the full panel of the Fifth Circuit Court of Appeals on September 24 to show cause why they should not be held in contempt. The group had met at the Roosevelt Hotel in New Orleans the previous day, along with the Mississippi attorney general, to make plans for the hearing. Clegg told this story about one board member, Ira L. "Shine" Morgan, who owned an appliance store in Oxford and was known as a great storyteller. Morgan said to the group,

> Let me ask you lawyers something. I have told the people of my city that I was going to stand firm. I told them that I had promised Ross Barnett, the governor of Mississippi, that I would stand firm until hell froze over. I would stand firm through fire

and water. I would not waiver in my position that we will not permit Meredith to register; and they were so appreciative of my position, that they even gave me going away presents when I came to New Orleans to face this court. Now I meant what I said when I told Ross that I would stand firm. I've been a friend of his through the years. I have supported him. I was supporting him still and till hell froze over and so on. But does this mean, this order of the court, that if I'm in the penitentiary of Atlanta that they're going to put Meredith in Ole Miss? I'll be over there and I can't do anything about it.

Shine was told, "That's exactly what it means." He asked two or three questions again, using different phraseology but meaning the same thing. And he said, "Well, it'd be no good in my going to the penitentiary if Meredith's going to Ole Miss, when I said 'I would go to the penitentiary to keep Meredith from registering.'" "That's right," he was told. Shine said, "Well, I'm just going to have to vote with the rest of you, that we'll just have to admit him. There's no other recourse." Someone said, "Well, what are you going to tell the governor?" "I'm going to say to him, 'Governor,' and to the people of Oxford who are friends of mine, 'Governor and friends, I have promised to stand by you to the bitter end, through fire and water, to the last ditch, till hell freezes over, but, Governor, you're just looking at the biggest damn liar in the State of Mississippi.'" The resulting laughter served to relax the tense group.[14] Shine's son, Ed, often told the story about the time, years later, when Governor Barnett and his father happened to share an elevator in the Woolfolk State Office Building in Jackson. As the elevator made its way up, Barnett asked Shine, "Shine, I remember you telling me that if anyone on the Board stood up for me that it would be you. You can count on me, Governor, to the bitter end, you said. What happened?" Not hesitating, Shine answered, "Ross, I told a damn lie!"[15]

While the group was meeting, Clegg remained in his room to receive messages. He got a call telling him that the university police chief, Burns Tatum, had received a request from Lafayette County sheriff Joe Ford to dig trenches and set up barricades at university entrances. Despite the temptation to reject the ridiculous suggestion, Clegg referred this message to the members of the Board of Trustees and the attorneys for the university who were present at the hotel. The board members responded that they would take "vigorous action against anybody who tried to block Meredith contrary to the orders of the court, anybody who dug up any part of the campus, or built barricades."[16] Clegg called Tatum back and informed him that the attorneys referred the matter to the board and that the board refused the request.

Eight of the nine Fifth Circuit judges were present at the hearing. (Judge Ben Cameron was absent.) After hearing the lawyers plead their case on behalf of the university, the court ruled that the three university officials were not in contempt. The court told the IHL Board of Trustees that if they did not devise an acceptable plan to register Meredith by that afternoon, the court would appoint anyone in the audience to act as registrar and Meredith would be registered in the courtroom. The Board decided to register Meredith in the state office building in Jackson on September 25 with Ellis and Dean Lewis being present. The court agreed. But when the Board met in Jackson and prepared to register Meredith, Barnett appeared and took control. Chief US Marshal James McShane, Justice Department attorney John Doar, one or two other marshals, and Meredith arrived soon afterwards. They appeared at the door of the offices of the board of trustees on the eleventh floor where Barnett blocked the entrance and asked the three, "Which one of you is James Meredith?" Barnett refused to register Meredith and the Meredith party departed.[17]

Mississippi lieutenant governor Paul Johnson attempted to separate the actions of the state and the university. Clegg states that he received a telephone call from the lieutenant governor asking that all university officials and employees refrain from contacting him, that he did not want the university, its employees, or students to become involved, that the issue was one between the federal government and the state. On September 26, Meredith and the marshals approached the campus via University Avenue at 10:55 a.m. Johnson blocked their entrance. After a little pushing, Meredith and the marshals left.[18]

Clegg had devised a plan that he was convinced would avoid violence. He sent word through his sources in the Justice Department urging Attorney General Robert Kennedy to call a meeting of people such as Judge Malcolm M. Montgomery (Governor Barnett's former law partner), Boyd Campbell (Barnett's former law partner, president of the US Chamber of Commerce, and Clegg's former high school teacher), federal judge Orma Smith (a Barnett supporter), Tom Watkins (Barnett's close legal advisor), Chester Curtis, Tommy Turner (a strong Barnett counselor), Fred Smith, and others from all sections of the state who would represent a cross section of recognized leaders from across Mississippi. The meeting could be held in Washington, Atlanta, Nashville, Memphis, Richmond, or anywhere. Kennedy could meet with the entire group and tell them,

> Gentlemen, it is the Constitutional requirement that the Department of Justice enforce the orders of the court. We're going to do it. Mr. Meredith is going to school at the University of Mississippi. He is going to be registered there. He is going to attend the school and nothing can stop us. We have the power of the federal government at our command. We're going to have it. Now then, your governor, because of conviction and because of political attitudes, has committed himself, has taken a strong stand, irrevocable, I would say but you can go back and tell the governor that you, a large group of Mississippians, lawyers, and advisors and friends, have talked to the attorney general, and they are going to put Meredith on the campus and nothing can stop them. They want to avoid bloodshed. Therefore you tell the governor that because his friends, his advisors, these distinguished Mississippians, these great lawyers, have counseled with him, "Governor, you've got to let him in. You mustn't stop him again." Then the governor will have an excuse to back

down and to say, "I have been advised, by my fellow Mississippians, as follows and there is nothing I can do".[19]

Clegg said this is where he tried to get a compromise with the federal government. His plan would allow the governor to save face and have an excuse to back down and give him a way out. Clegg continued, "But no, they (the Justice Department and the White House) wanted to exercise force." Clegg said his proposal would be better than the circus of the confrontations of Barnett and marshals that would follow. But the script had already been written by the time he presented his plan.

The negotiations that took place involved only the federal and state governments; the university was left completely out.[20] Clegg was later asked if, being a former law enforcement official, he would have done anything differently. Clegg referred to the solution he had proposed to no effect, and he was convinced that it would have worked to avoid the riot.[21] He reiterated, "All that ruckus, and sideshow, and juvenile tactics, could have been completely avoided."[22]

Clegg was then faced with another request. Governor Barnett wanted the university to provide dorm rooms for thirty-seven highway patrolmen. Clegg told him he would look into the matter. After talking with university officials, Clegg called back and informed Barnett that the university needed additional policemen on campus to prevent hooligans from coming on university grounds and that if the highway patrolmen could come on campus and work with university police chief Tatum and assure 100 percent cooperation, that the university could provide sleeping space in the gymnasium, since the officers would, in fact, be working for the university.[23]

Barnett and Robert Kennedy held a series of telephone conversations attempting to negotiate a plan that would result in the ultimate registration of Meredith. Barnett was seeking a way out whereby he would be able to save face. Clegg said that he had

received transcripts of forty-one telephone conversations between Mr. Barnett and Mr. Kennedy, including Tom Watkins, including Paul Johnson, and including some others. . . . They were going to arrange to permit the marshals to come in with guns and escort Meredith on campus. Barnett and his associates would stand in the gate and then the marshals would pull their pistols. In order to avoid bloodshed, they would back away and Meredith would come in. Childish! Juvenile![24]

Clegg presented these transcripts in his unpublished memoir, pointing out how childish and juvenile these negotiations were.[25] Clegg said that an examination of the content of these exchanges would lead many to consider them foolish as well as tragic.

These conversations between Governor Barnett, Attorney General Robert Kennedy, and Lieutenant Governor Johnson were held without the knowledge of the university or the board. Clegg was concerned that the university was being left out of these negotiations but would bear the final responsibility for the consequences of what was being planned.

As early as September 15, this exchange between Kennedy (RFK) and Barnett (RB) took place:

RFK: I think the first extremely important point that we are both interested in is that there be no violence; no disturbance: that he is protected. . . .
RB: I promise you, sir, there will be no violence. The people do not want to get involved in violence, strife; and I have urged them not to do so; and I do not anticipate any trouble.

Kennedy wanted to move Meredith onto the campus on Thursday, September 27, because the whole circuit court was going to consider the case on the next day in New Orleans, and he thought the problem would be greater once the court decided. Barnett wanted to stall Meredith's admission once again. Barnett told Kennedy that if Meredith were to come that afternoon, there would be problems since large crowds were gathering. Kennedy delayed Meredith's transfer from Memphis to the Ole Miss campus and then called it off. Prior to Kennedy's agreement to stall for more time, the following telephone conversation, as amazing in retrospect as it is, took place.

RFK: Hello

RB: Hello General, how are you?

RFK: Fine, Governor, how are you?

RB: I need a little sleep.

RFK: I just talked to Mr. Watkins and we are going to make this effort at 5 o'clock this afternoon your time.

RB: They will be here about 5 o'clock our time?

RFK: Is that satisfactory?

RB: Yes sir. That's all right.

RFK: I will send the Marshals I have available up there in Memphis and I expect there will be about 25 or 30 of them and they will come with Mr. Meredith and they will arrive wherever the gate is and I will have the head Marshal pull a gun and I will have the rest of them have their hands on their guns and their holsters. And then as I understand it he will go through and get in and you will make sure that law and order is preserved and that no harm will be done to Mr. McShane and Mr. Meredith.

RB: Oh, yes.

RFK: And then I think you will see that's accomplished?

RB: Yes [inaudible]. Hold just a minute, will you? Hello, General, I was under the impression that they were all going to pull their guns. This could be very embarrassing. We got a big crowd here and if one pulls his gun and we all turn it would be very embarrassing. Isn't it possible to have them all pull their guns?

RFK: I hate to have them all draw their guns as I think it could create harsh feelings. Isn't it sufficient if I have one man draw his gun and the others keep their hands on their holsters?

RB: They must all draw their guns. Then they should point their guns at us and then we could step aside. This could be very embarrassing down here for us. It is necessary. . .

RFK: If they all pull their guns is that all

RB: [Inaudible] I will have them put their sticks down before that happens. [Inaudible] There will be no shooting.

RFK: Then there will be no problem?

RB: [Inaudible] Everyone pull your guns and point them and we will stand aside and you will go right through.

RFK: You will make sure not the Marshals but the State Police will preserve law and order?

RB: There won't be any violence.

RFK: Then we can get the other people out as soon as possible.

RB: One second. General, we expect them all to draw their guns. Lt. Governor Johnson is sitting here with me [inaudible]. Will you talk to him?

JOHNSON: General.

RFK: How are you?

JOHNSON: It is absolutely necessary that they all draw their guns. There won't be any shooting.

RFK: Can you speak a little louder?

JOHNSON: We are telling them to lay their clubs aside and to leave their guns in their automobiles. But it is necessary to have all your people draw their guns, not just one [inaudible] and anyone who shoots at all to leave. We appreciate what they have done so far and go back home and that there would be no shooting under any circumstances.

RFK: The one problem—when we come down there representing the Federal Government and draw guns it's going to disturb your people, understandably.

JOHNSON: As much as it would bother them if they just drew one gun and 350 highway patrolmen . . .

RFK: If they all draw their guns and they go into the university, there after, law and order will be preserved by your people?

JOHNSON: We are going to attempt to preserve it.

RFK: They won't leave, will they? What I want to be sure is that it won't be left up to our people.

The issue of whether one marshal or all should draw their weapons continued to dominate the conversation. Kennedy confronted Governor Barnett and Lieutenant Governor Johnson to make sure there was no misunderstanding about the fact that the state would take responsibility and there would be no violence. Again, later in the same conversation, the issue of drawing guns would be a central point of the negotiations.

> RFK: Just as long as it is left at the local level. They will be there
> at 5 o'clock and draw their guns.
> RB: We are going to step aside if they do that.

After the decision to delay Meredith's admission until after the circuit court met in New Orleans and issued the inevitable order to admit Meredith, Kennedy and Barnett had the following telephone conversation on September 29, during which Kennedy had doubts about the entire gun-drawing discussion.

> RB: When you draw the guns, I will tell the people. In other
> words, we will step aside and you can walk in.
> RFK: I think it is silly going through this whole façade of your
> standing there; our people drawing guns; your stepping aside;
> to me it is dangerous and I think this has gone beyond the stage
> of politics.

When Barnett called Kennedy on Sunday morning, September 30, and reiterated his plan, Kennedy told Barnett he would not go along with the idea.[26] Clegg recalled that "this was silly . . . . It is ridiculous and asinine, like children playing. Doing everything but saying 'Bang-Bang.'"[27] Clegg was highly critical of the way Robert Kennedy handled this situation:

> I knew some Attorneys General, and know of others, who
> would have handled the matter in quite a different manner,

with no bloodshed, with no street, carnival-like confrontations—which served to inflame the populace and give them false hopes, with no conversations by phone of "silly," "juvenile," and "childish" suggestions for playacting.[28]

The university community was left out of the plans to register Meredith, but some spoke out. The elected editor of the student newspaper, Sidna Brower—considered a moderate—published an editorial on September 20 criticizing the way the press was sensationalizing the situation.[29] She wrote several editorials before and after the anti-integration riot critical of segregationists, deploring violence, and urging the student body not to become involved in the violence. Within hours after the riot, the student newspaper published a special edition featuring Brower's editorial, "The Violence Will Not Help," stating that student participation in the riot brought "dishonor and shame to the University and the State of Mississippi." Brower placed blame for the violence on the students and outsiders with no official connection with the university: "When students hurled rocks, bottles and eggs, the federal marshals were forced to resort to tear gas to back off the crowds."[30]

Her editorials brought mixed reactions. The national press praised her and the university faculty senate commended her. But she had several critics as well, including Citizens' Councils and some fellow students. A resolution was introduced to the student senate urging that body to censure her for editorially opposing student opinion and failing to support the rights of the students. Perhaps the bottom line was that those students opposed to the integration of the university criticized her for coming down hard on them but not hard enough on the marshals. The student senate then passed a resolution to reprimand her—a resolution that was approved overwhelmingly. At the same time, however, the student senate also commended her for deploring violence and endorsed editorial freedom.[31] Prior to the fortieth anniversary of the riot, the Associated Student Body Senate voted to repeal the censure and commended her belatedly for her editorial stance.

The faculty as a body remained largely silent during this period, although several faculty members were involved in trying to help avoid the path to confrontation with the federal government and open the doors to all qualified students who applied for admission. In an effort to elicit a stance of the faculty senate, one member, Dr. Russell H. Barrett, professor of political science, drafted a resolution in which a representative group of the university faculty would affirm its support of academic principles. Included in Barrett's resolution was a statement reaffirming that the primary purpose of institutions of higher learning was education and that carrying out this purpose should not be compromised by controversies, in particular the present controversy of admitting students to the university. The resolution went further, stating that once a clear and final legal determination regarding this issue has been made, it should be accepted and implemented in a manner that did not interfere with the process of education. It also urged that the present matter be resolved in a manner that did not affect the accreditation of the University of Mississippi and all institutions of higher learning in the state. The resolution ended with a call for support of the university administration by everyone who believed in the value of education. The faculty senate did not meet to consider this resolution, thus remaining silent during the crisis.[32]

On September 28, the Southern Association of Colleges and Schools (SACS) announced that it would consider the accreditation of all public colleges in Mississippi at its November meeting. Fearing that a loss of accreditation for Ole Miss was imminent, Clegg telephoned US Representative Frank Smith. Smith had the reputation of quietly working for racial reconciliation, a factor that resulted in his losing his congressional seat when his moderation led him to support the presidential bid of John F. Kennedy.[33] Clegg asked Smith[34] to "pass along to the President and the Attorney General the threat that Ole Miss would have SACS on them for citing the University officials in a motion of contempt."[35]

The next day, Saturday, September 29, Chancellor Williams came to Clegg's office to discuss plans for Meredith's arrival. Just before noon, Clegg answered his phone and was surprised that Robert Kennedy had called him directly. Kennedy wanted the university to issue instructions to the student body that, under threat of expulsion, they were not to assemble or demonstrate when Meredith arrived. Clegg explained that the university would not threaten students or issue orders that it could not enforce. Clegg then told Kennedy that threatening students was not the way to get cooperation. Chancellor Williams overheard the conversation and agreed with what Clegg told the attorney general. Soon afterwards, Kennedy released a statement to a London correspondent calling the university weak.[36] Clegg would claim that university officials were put in an untenable position by both the state and the federal governments, "university officials who were served with injunctions by state judges not to admit Meredith, while the federal court issued an injunction to admit him!"[37]

Chapter Thirteen

The Riot and the Aftermath

Somebody jumped the gun.—Nicholas Katzenbach

S UNDAY, SEPTEMBER 30, would prove to be the darkest day in the history of Ole Miss. Events were spinning out of control and many feared the worst. Meredith would be coming to campus and would be registered. Segregation at institutions of higher learning in Mississippi would end. But many white citizens of the state could not accept the inevitable. That morning, Clegg sent word to Barnett to tape record a message urging the students not to resort to violence, but his request did not get through to the governor. The university made plans to use the radio and student newspaper to call on students to remain calm. University officials were expecting Meredith to arrive on the following Monday or even Tuesday. Clegg went to the chancellor's residence on Sunday afternoon at 3:00 p.m. with Dean of Students L. L. Love to review plans for the registration the next day, thinking the university was still in control of the situation. Chancellor Williams, Clegg, and Love thought they were planning for events to occur on Monday, but federal marshals had already left Memphis. They would be in Oxford in just an hour.[1] Immediately after Clegg arrived at the chancellor's residence, he received a telephone call from Burke Marshall, head of the Civil Rights Division of the Justice Department. Williams and Love were alongside Clegg, desperately trying to overhear the conversation. Marshall bluntly informed Clegg that Meredith would arrive within the hour.[2]

It is surprising that university administrators were unaware of the impending arrival of US marshals that Sunday afternoon. Ole Miss journalism professor Jere Hoar was at the University Oxford Airport to see if shipping could be arranged for an English Setter bird dog to an out-of-state buyer. Hoar saw a number of men rushing around with pistols visible on their hips. He took them to be out-of-county deputy sheriffs he'd seen on campus previously. The harried clerk inside the building told him US marshals had arrived. The few civilian cars on the airport property were blocked at the exit until military trucks, with their canvas covers rolled up and the marshals clearly visible inside, departed. Hoar followed them in his car to the campus. Cars pulled to the side of the road leading out of the airport as the military trucks passed. A thin row of civilians stood on the side of the road. Some of the marshals waved and some of the people waved back while a few softly booed.[3]

Clegg pleaded with Burke Marshall to delay Meredith's arrival, but Marshall refused. No one at Ole Miss was aware of the deal struck between Governor Barnett and Attorney General Robert Kennedy that morning.[4] Williams said Ole Miss would refuse to register Meredith on the Sabbath, and Marshall agreed to yield on the issue of a Sunday registration but insisted that Meredith be registered Monday morning. Just before 4:00 p.m., Attorney General Robert Kennedy called the chancellor and informed him that Meredith would indeed be arriving on the Ole Miss campus that afternoon. Williams was astounded and called Clegg to the phone to get him to try to convince Kennedy to change this plan. Clegg tried to explain to Kennedy, to no avail, that the university was closed for the weekend and that it would be impossible to get together those responsible for implementing the university's plans for Meredith's arrival to put the plan into operation. Clegg then tried another approach, explaining that since this was the Bible Belt, the people would be upset if the Sabbath were desecrated by registering Meredith on that day.

These arguments fell on deaf ears, since the agreement between Kennedy and Barnett had already been made and was being put into effect.[5] Clegg was then informed that the highway patrol had admitted the US marshals to the campus. In fact, they were driving past the chancellor's home at that moment. Chancellor Williams would later state that he lost control of the university at 4:00 p.m. on that

Sunday afternoon with the arrival of hundreds of armed US deputy marshals.[6]

Clegg and Love went to the Lyceum Building at 4:15 and met with Mississippi Highway patrol director Colonel T. B. Birdsong and university police chief Burns Tatum. Two truckloads of federal marshals were there when Clegg and Love arrived. They conferred with Deputy US Attorney General Nicholas Katzenbach, US Attorney John Doar and Chief US Marshal James McShane. Clegg opened the Lyceum and the group went to Clegg's office, where the university officials agreed, despite their objections, that federal officials would take over the offices of Dean Love and the dean of women.[7] While with the FBI, Clegg had enjoyed having the weight of the federal government behind him, but now he felt that the federal government was overstepping its bounds by taking over the university. Other marshals surrounded the Lyceum for reasons that still seem unclear— Meredith would not appear at the Lyceum that evening. To no avail, Clegg tried calling IHL Board president T. J. Tubb; Charles Fair, the immediate past president of the board; and Governor Barnett. Barnett's secretary told Clegg that the governor had gone fishing and would not be back until Monday morning.[8]

Crowds gathered around the Lyceum and the Lyceum Circle and began to get rowdy. At 7:15 p.m., state senator George Yarborough, president pro tempore of the Mississippi Senate, and Senator John McLaurin arrived at Clegg's office. Yarborough had a proclamation from Governor Barnett authorizing him to act on behalf of the governor. Yarborough told Katzenbach it was obvious that the Justice Department had taken over the campus, so the highway patrol was rendered unnecessary. The maintenance of law and order would be in the hands of the marshals. Yarborough wanted the patrol withdrawn at 8:00 p.m., the Justice Department wanted him to wait until 9:00 p.m., and Yarborough settled on 8:30. The governor was called and the patrol remained. Accounts vary somewhat, but about 556 deputized US marshals arrived on Sunday: 336 border patrolmen, 97 penitentiary guards, and 123 deputy US marshals.[9] As the crowd got more and more out of control, the marshals fired tear gas. Clegg says he was not present when the gas was fired. Katzenbach later said, "We are sorry. Somebody jumped the gun," even given the abuse to which the marshals had been subjected. He was told, "You have just started a riot."[10] The events that took place during the riot have been well documented and do not need to be recounted in detail here.

Clegg arrived at home at 9:25 that Sunday night, rushed straight to the telephone, and made calls to the Highway Patrol, the University Clinic, the local hospital, and the chancellor's residence. He learned that several people had been injured in the riot and that Paul Guihard, a French journalist, had been killed. Another death was reported—Walter Ray Gunter from Abbeville, Mississippi, a bystander, not a participant in the riot. Both men were fatally struck by .38 caliber bullets.[11] No one was ever charged in their deaths.

Clegg called the university attorney, members of the alumni steering committee, and the governor. This time the governor took his call and expressed concern over the violence and condemned the marshals for instigating the riot. The call turned into a speech by the governor. As he was ranting, Clegg's wife told him that the provost, Dr. Charles Haywood, and a faculty member had been in the house but that they grew impatient and left. Clegg then went to the chancellor's residence before midnight. He and other members of the administration sat on the porch of the chancellor's residence located adjacent to a wooded area called the Grove, next to the Lyceum Circle, and watched the riot take place. Present with Clegg at the chancellor's residence were three IHL Board members: T. J. Tubb, Charles Fair, and S. R. Evans, along with the chancellor, Provost Haywood; the assistant director of development, George Street; and the director of the physical plant, John White. Others drifted in and out. There was widespread fear that the Lyceum Building would be burned, but the first of the federalized National Guard arrived with one of William Faulkner's nephews, Captain Murry "Chooky" Falkner [sic], in charge. Clegg would later remember, "We almost shouted with joy."[12] The situation finally quieted down around 2:00 a.m.

On Monday, two individuals from the Department of Justice

came to Clegg's office and told him that of all those who were part of the mob, only sixty-five to seventy-five people in the crowd of twelve to fifteen hundred were seriously misbehaving. Clegg said he was told at 10:30 or 11:00 or so on Sunday night that "practically all students had gone to their dormitories." Despite an agreement reached on October 1 between Clegg, Dean Love, and Katzenbach that the university would handle the discipline of the students apprehended, on October 11 the Department of Justice submitted charges against eleven students. Shortly after bringing these charges, two of the eleven were found to be nonstudents and charges were not brought against a third because of an incorrect identification. Then the Justice Department withdrew charges against five of the remaining eight students with the admission that it did not have sufficient evidence to convict. Of the remaining three students, one was found completely innocent and the remaining two were found guilty of minor charges, none of which involved firearms or other dangerous weapons.

Nevertheless, the university felt that all eight should be tried by the Student Judicial Council for violations of University regulations and all eight were found guilty. Sentences imposed varied from disciplinary probation to dismissal from the university with the sentence suspended. As soon as Governor Barnett learned of the university's actions, he appointed nine prominent lawyers to represent them. The lawyers met in Oxford and were prepared to seek an injunction to prevent the university from following normal disciplinary procedures. However, the university administration stoutly defended its actions and normal disciplinary procedures were followed to the letter.

Therefore, Clegg thought the mob consisted primarily of outsiders. At least thirteen students from other colleges were involved. Crowds from Memphis and surrounding areas poured onto the campus. Among the crowd were "weird looking" people who wore long hair before long hair had become a fad, and it was obvious to Clegg that these "weirdos" did not appear to be in the student age bracket. Clegg was told by an unidentified "high ranking official of a business in Jackson" that someone, also unidentified, had come to his office two days after the riot and told him that his son was on top of the Y building on the Lyceum Circle with a rifle and fired into the crowd and the marshals.[13]

Clegg and Chancellor Williams drove to Jackson a few days after the riot and reviewed the tragic situation. Both were convinced that the prime responsibility for initiating the riot lay with the marshals. Williams asked Clegg to make notes so their observations could be brought to the attention of a congressional investigation that had been requested and promised but was later cancelled. Clegg recalled that he was leaving from the western exit of the Lyceum sometime after 9:00 p.m. on that Sunday night. A policeman from Greenwood offered to get the car Clegg had driven onto the campus earlier that afternoon, but he brought the wrong car. Clegg was standing and waiting when three young boys, appearing to be freshmen, came walking by. Clegg heard a tear gun blast—a marshal to his right had fired a gas shell at the youths. Clegg recounted, "There was no excuse or reason to fire the gas shell at them." Several additional gas shells were fired as the boys tried to avoid being hit. Clegg said, "They, the marshals, were exhibiting the characteristics of wild, trigger-happy exhibitionists on a safari."[14]

Tubb wanted Chancellor Williams to contact the Mississippi congressional delegation and request a meeting on the whole affair but probably with an emphasis on the marshals. Clegg was asked to call Senator John Stennis; he tried but could not establish contact. Then he tried to call Senator Jim Eastland, who was chairman of the Senate Judiciary Committee, but his number was unlisted. Clegg called Eastland's administrative assistant, Courtney Pace, and gave him an account of what had happened so he could report to both Stennis and Eastland. Pace arranged for the entire Mississippi delegation to assemble in Eastland's office,[15] and at 6:00 a.m. Clegg received a telephone call from the meeting. Stennis assumed the role as principal spokesman and asked Clegg to dictate his report to a stenographer, who was also present. All members of the delegation were on extensions and could hear Clegg's report. Clegg, not so modestly, said that Stennis complimented him on presenting the most unbiased, objective, fair, and unemotional report he had ever heard.[16]

Eastland promised to initiate an investigation, but Barnett requested that a congressional investigation not be conducted. Members of the Mississippi congressional delegation stood on the floor of Congress to defend Governor Barnett and entered into the *Congressional Record* the report given to them by Clegg. Eastland read before the Senate the following:

> Influenced by ex-FBI official Hugh Clegg, the report called the firing of tear gas "unnecessary and illogical" and alleged the federal actions to be "clear indications of amateurism by untrained marshals who had poor leadership with bad judgment." The Justice Department's "incompetency and unjustified action . . . led to and provoked" the riot.[17]

The entire congressional delegation—with the sole exception of Representative Frank Smith—placed direct blame for the riot on the federal courts, the marshals, and the Kennedy administration.[18]

The sun rose Monday morning to reveal the extensive damage from the riot—hundreds of gas shells in front of the Lyceum, broken bottles, burned automobiles, nine bullets embedded in the columns and frame around the main entrance to the Lyceum, and three additional bullets inside. (Some of the bullet holes remained visible on the columns fifty years after the riot.) Clegg, as did many alumni, considered the Lyceum Building to be the "heart of the university."[19] If so, then that heart now appeared to be broken. As soldiers marched around the campus, many with fixed bayonets, James Meredith registered Monday morning before 8:00 a.m. He enrolled in courses in history, French, Spanish, political science, mathematics, and English[20] and went to his first class[21]—a 9:00 a.m. American history class taught by Professor Clare Marquette.[22]

Black reporters were prevented from covering Meredith's registration. While denying that the reason had anything to do with race, Clegg told Larry Still, associate editor of *Jet*, a magazine marketed mostly to blacks, that

> with tensions as high as they are, any colored reporter might create a problem . . . we believe it might be in the best interest not to invite such reporters . . . and not admit them on campus. We're not discriminating against your publication . . . we feel it would be better if they sent a reporter of another race.[23]

Investigations aimed at placing blame for the riot continued. A report from the Mississippi legislative committee investigating the riot stated that the marshals spit upon and cursed students. As many as eighty-five students (the Justice Department indicated sixty-five students misbehaved) were taken into custody and jammed into a seventeen-by-forty-feet basement room with no tear gas masks although tear gas lingered in the air. According to this report, several students were struck on the shins and jabbed in the back with nightsticks, and some students were badly beaten and given no medical treatment. Others were beaten when they asked to use the toilet or call a lawyer. This situation was corrected upon the demand of university authorities. Several incidents of violence by the marshals were cited in the report. The committee report also claimed that the next day, some students were stopped and searched at gunpoint while on their way to class, but these claims could not be fully substantiated. Clegg spoke up for the legislative committee, noting that some of the members were lawyers and that two outstanding attorneys were listed as counsel for the committee: one a former FBI agent and the other a past president of the American Bar Association. In preparing its findings, the committee reported that it did not feel it was desirable or necessary to interview faculty who were not conducting administrative duties on the day of the riot.

When the matter was taken up by a Lafayette County grand jury, it is not surprising that the panel concluded that the marshals were inexperienced and improperly trained, that the leadership of the marshals was of the poorest sort, and that hasty action by Chief Marshal James P. McShane actually precipitated the riot. When Clegg arrived home, he telephoned the State Highway Patrol headquarters on campus and an Officer Olin Flynn recounted atrocities by "trigger-happy marshals." Clegg later called the headquarters again and was told by Patrolman George Hendricks how "trigger-happy marshals" were firing gas shells at uniformed patrolmen.[24]

Chancellor Williams called a meeting of all available student leaders and even invited Deputy US Attorney General Nicholas Katzenbach. Katzenbach took over the meeting and urged cooperation between the university and its students and the federal contingent. Associated Student Body president Richard Wilson and the editor of the student newspaper, Sidna Brower, objected to Katzenbach's attempt to take over the meeting. Clegg cited evidence that the federal government interfered with the operational details involved in running the university, claiming Defense Secretary Robert McNamara and Secretary of the Army Cyrus Vance ordered that the homecoming football game against the University of Houston on October 6 not be played in Oxford but rather in Jackson or Houston. Ole Miss athletic director C. M. "Tad" Smith and Chancellor Williams chose, under the circumstances, to play the game in Jackson.[25] Ole Miss won the game 40-7 and finished the season undefeated, a remarkable achievement considering the turmoil on campus.

Clegg felt that he might have overstepped his bounds during the crisis, that he had usurped the functions of other major staffers and division heads—even the chancellor—every administrator, in fact, except the provost. He had spent his early years at Ole Miss carefully avoiding getting involved in academic issues. At a meeting of division heads four months after the riot, Clegg was concerned about what they would say about his involvement. Although he had been designated by the chancellor to coordinate all matters relating to Meredith's registration, he went to the meeting intending to apologize. At the meeting, however, he was flabbergasted when Chancellor Williams told Clegg, "You were magnificent," and the division heads agreed. Even the chancellor's wife would later express her gratitude to Clegg.[26]

Based on Clegg's experience in training FBI agents, Chancellor Williams suggested to him two years later that he request the FBI to consider giving training to college and university security officials on how to deal with differing right- and left-wing student political groups, as well as conservative and liberal professors on college campuses. Such additional training, Clegg thought, would be beneficial, and he passed the suggestion on to the special agent in charge of the Jackson FBI field office, Roy Moore, who passed it on to Director Hoover. Hoover denied the request. Clegg referenced one incident that occurred on the Ole Miss campus during its recent Spring Festival. Some "radicals from the Memphis area" incited a "mixed group" from Tougaloo College in Jackson to demonstrate. The demonstration resulted in the destruction of a privately owned automobile and other property. The Ole Miss chief security officer felt inadequately trained and educated to properly handle this and similar potential situations, prompting Clegg's suggestion. The FBI assistant director, J. J. Casper, expressed the opinion that there were unfavorable aspects to a campus police training program as described by Clegg, and the program was not initiated.[27] Casper expressed concern that although campus police enjoyed the status of law enforcement officers in some states, they were under the control of the administering body of the college or university and were guided more by the mandates of that body than by either municipal or state laws and had to follow policies and instructions of those administrators. He also felt that such a training program could not be confined to state colleges and universities without offending the private schools, which would not receive such help. Casper, however, did not object to the head of Ole Miss security attending police training schools in that area, including those schools devoted to mob and riot control.

Clegg's involvement in the Meredith desegregation crisis damaged his relationship with the Bureau. Prior to the riot, Clegg had accepted an invitation to present a lecture at the seventieth session of the FBI National Academy. However, following the riot, it was felt that Clegg's appearance might prove to be an embarrassment to the Bureau. In a memorandum from agent John F. Malone to Memphis Special Agent in Charge Roy Mohr, Malone referred to a telephone call received by Special Agent in Charge Karl Dissly of the FBI Memphis field office from Clegg on October 20, 1962, inquiring into the Bureau's attitude as to whether he should attend the session and present his lecture. In relating this conversation to Malone, Dissly acknowledged that while Clegg's loyalty to the Bureau was unquestioned, "Mr. Clegg has undergone quite a bit of emotional strain during the University of Mississippi integration crisis" and further noted that he noticed "indications of possible instability on the part of Mr. Clegg during the problem." Dissly recommended that it would be better if Clegg did not appear. Not wanting to bother the director or Clyde Tolson, Dissly had asked for Mohr's views concerning Clegg's appearance. Dissly was instructed to advise Clegg that the Bureau would leave the decision as to whether he should appear or not up to him.[28] Agent Mohr recommended that the Bureau take no action because he was certain Clegg would not appear if doing so would embarrass the Bureau. Hoover agreed, and Clegg did not appear.

Considering that every individual involved in the Meredith desegregation crisis must have experienced emotional strain to one degree or another, it is interesting that the Bureau sought to use this fact as the basis for canceling Clegg's appearance. There is no evidence that Clegg ever showed any indication of "possible instability" before, during, or after the crisis—an observation confirmed by Clegg's daughter. Instead of making a decision on this issue, the Bureau relied on Clegg's loyalty to the Bureau to be the deciding factor.

Twelve years after the riot, Clegg interviewed former Governor Ross Barnett. Barnett could not succeed himself, but four years later he ran again for governor, losing in the first round of the Democratic primary, finishing fourth behind eventual winner John Bell Williams. In the interview, Barnett defended his actions in handling the desegregation of Ole Miss and indicated he would be vindicated in the future. When asked by Clegg if the arrangement made between Barnett and Robert Kennedy was juvenile or childish, the former governor said the idea did not originate with him but with Lieutenant Governor Paul B. Johnson. Barnett said he always insisted that there be no violence. Later, Clegg interviewed former governor Paul B. Johnson. Johnson denied Barnett's recollection regarding the origin of the idea for marshals to pull their guns in order to get Meredith registered and agreed that this plan was juvenile and childish.[29] Clegg would later write friends, "Two groups of idiots met on our campus and defamed our sacred soil,"[30] probably referring to federal and state ineptness.

An issue that still provokes controversy fifty years later is the question of who actually started the riot. Clegg was adamant about what caused the marshals to fire the tear gas. There can be no question that the marshals were ill prepared for the task at hand or that they were harassed unmercifully. For nearly two hours, the marshals had been pelted with obscenities, lighted cigarette butts, stones, bottles, lead pipes, and even acid.[31] On the other hand, Clegg claimed that marshals spat upon the students and cursed them repeatedly.[32] (Interestingly, President Kennedy addressed the nation on national television at 8:00 p.m. CST urging cooperation and moderation—at almost the precise time that Chief Marshal McShane gave the order to fire the tear gas.)

Although Clegg claimed that "Federal stupidity and state demagoguery were responsible for what happened,"[33] it has been asserted by other observers that if any Ole Miss or state official had taken a leadership role and stepped forward to try to control the crowd agitated by former general Edwin Walker, violence could have been avoided. Walker fought in both World War II and the Korean conflict but had gained more fame for his ultraconservative political views. While Chancellor Williams and some faculty members did mingle with the crowd urging peace and calm, they failed to exert any authority and instead relinquished control.[34]

In his autobiography, Frank Smith, former Democratic US representative from Mississippi and an anomaly in Mississippi politics by being a liberal in racial matters, wrote "university officials fought the order of admission down to the last step."[35] He further asserted,

> The reaction of many otherwise intelligent Mississippians was hard to fathom. Hugh Clegg, a special assistant to the university chancellor and a former FBI official, called me to ask that I pass along to the President and the Attorney General the threat that Ole Miss would have the Southern Association of Colleges and Schools on them for citing the university officials in a motion for contempt. On the Saturday night before the fateful Sunday, he called me again, asking that the President agree to some mediation with friends of the governor. There seemed to be no realization that the admission of Meredith was beyond negotiation.[36]

Clegg responded by saying he had never read Smith's autobiography.[37] Also, Clegg's claim that the marshals were trigger happy and fired tear gas prematurely was countered by a public statement, signed by sixty-five members of the Ole Miss faculty, blaming the rioters and exonerating the marshals.[38]

Ole Miss history professor James Silver's account of the action of the marshals differs markedly from the observations of Clegg as relayed to the congressional delegation. In an October 10 letter he wrote to Arthur Schlesinger Jr., special assistant to President Kennedy, Silver stated that he was an eyewitness to the events that occurred on that Sunday night from 5:30 p.m. that afternoon until 3:00 a.m. the following Monday morning. He further stated that there was no blunder on the part of the marshals, but rather that they had taken considerable abuse from the crowd for at least two hours. He also suggested that there was a conspiracy by Mississippi politicians in Jackson and Washington to shift the blame to the marshals for starting the riot.[39]

During the entire affair, faculty members of the university, with a few exceptions, remained silent and issued no public statements reflecting their concerns. However, the Academic Council, consisting of the provost and the deans of the various schools and colleges, adopted and made public two statements. One congratulated and commended the chancellor and the faculty, staff, and students for the rapid way that normal operations of the university had been restored. The second statement suggested that the actions of students against faculty members by verbal and sometimes physical harassment—several faculty members having attempted to instill student discipline using grading as a penalty against those who harassed Meredith—had constituted students exercising their academic freedom.[40]

A voice of the faculty was finally heard. On October 3, Richard S. Stewart, an assistant professor of ancient history, introduced a resolution at a meeting of the university chapter of the American Association of University Professors (AAUP) to place the chapter on record regarding issues surrounding the riot. Acknowledging errors of judgment made by those who had assumed authority for operating the university, the resolution was critical of attempts by "men in prominent positions" at the university to place blame for the riot totally on the marshals and claimed that such attempts were almost completely false. The resolution ended by urging every patriotic citizen to refrain from publishing inflammatory statements and to obey the law while encouraging others to do the same. It further stated that riots, weapons, and agitators have no place at a university. The resolution was overwhelmingly adopted and signed by forty-five members of the chapter as well as nineteen faculty members who were not members of the chapter but who had expressed a desire to sign the statement. The response to this action was popular among other national AAUP chapters as well as with President Kennedy. A two-to-one majority of individuals responding voiced their support of the resolution. As expected, however, groups such as the Greenwood Citizens' Council published a list of the signers of the resolution and encouraged harassment of them.[41]

There was enough blame to be placed on everyone involved, including the university administration, in which Clegg played a major role, for failure to develop an alternate plan when its original plan became moot. And although the university was kept out of the agreement between Barnett and Robert Kennedy and was not informed of the decision to bring Meredith to campus on Sunday rather than on Monday, the day for which the university had prepared, still the administration can be blamed for making little effort to control the crowds.[42]

Clegg was indeed caught in the middle of the battle. Deputy Attorney General Nicholas Katzenbach was quoted by FBI agent Karl Dissly as saying that during the crisis, Clegg was "carrying water on both shoulders."[43] Several years after the riot, Clegg would say, "Both sides were terribly wrong" and regardless of how bad the actions of the marshals were, "I maintain that the mobsters were worse because there can never be a justification for a mob with violence, as we had it there. It's just an unfortunate thing."[44] While it remains unclear exactly who was responsible for initiating the riot—despite overwhelming evidence that the marshals fired tear gas only after being harassed and abused for from one to two hours before the order to fire the gas was given—it is clear that at the time, Clegg chose to side with Mississippi and Ole Miss.

There is no evidence in either Clegg's oral history or his unpublished manuscript that he had any direct contact with Meredith (although Clegg's daughter, Ruby Kathryn, attended a political science summer school course with Meredith.) Clegg admired the courage displayed by Meredith in desegregating the university, the better so since he had worked with courageous men during his days with the FBI. So it is curious that there is no evidence of a meeting between the two ever having occurred. In a private conversation during November 2013 Meredith, wearing an Ole Miss cap and an Ole Miss sweatshirt, did not recall ever meeting Clegg face-to-face, but he was well aware of the role Clegg had played in the crisis. Meredith thought Clegg, relying on his FBI experiences, actually "ran the university" during those turbulent days.[45]

There were many heroes who emerged from the riot, the most obvious being James Meredith himself. The bravery of those charged with protecting Meredith's safety, however, should not go unnoticed. However, much blame is attributable to those who could have averted the crisis but failed to do so. Yet if the finger of blame was to be pointed at any one person, it would have to be Governor Ross Barnett, a race-baiter, demagogue, and politician who almost single-handedly destroyed the academic reputation of the University of Mississippi and projected a backwards image of its people to the nation. Those who encouraged him to take his reprehensible actions and spurred him on must also share the blame.

Many students participated in the constant harassment of Meredith, but there was a small group of students whose actions placed the interests of the university above any personal feelings. The 1962 Ole Miss football team, under legendary coach Johnny Vaught, managed to isolate itself from the campus unrest and focus on its mission. Vaught was convinced that "successful football kept Ole Miss from closing its doors that year."[46] The fact that the team was able to complete an undefeated season, including a victory in the Sugar Bowl, under these circumstances is one of the more amazing stories in sports.

The 1962 riot cast a continuing stigma on the academic credibility of Ole Miss, but the university has taken encouraging and controversial steps to restore and enhance its national image. A life-size, bronze statue of James Meredith commemorating his courage and perseverance was dedicated on campus in October 2006 and stands between the Lyceum Building and the J. D. Williams Library. In 2011, a pond on campus was dedicated to the memory of "liberal" Ole Miss history professor James W. Silver, who was deeply involved in the crisis and who fought with courage for racial equality in Mississippi and the South generally. Among other progressive actions, the university has taken steps to dissociate itself from symbols considered racially offensive, such as banning the display of the Confederate battle flag at university events, prohibiting the university band from playing "Dixie," and replacing the Colonel Rebel mascot. The number of minority students enrolled has increased year by year, as has the number of minority faculty and staff members at the university.

Professor emeritus of history at Ole Miss, Dr. David Sansing, concluded his sesquicentennial history of the University of Mississippi on a high note by observing how significantly the public image and perception of Ole Miss has changed. He concluded that because of years of "dedication and service by its faculty, staff, students, and alumni, the University of Mississippi is at last free of those negative perceptions and is poised to fulfill its mission and destiny as it enters the new millennium."[47]

Chapter Fourteen

Ole Miss Accomplishments and Retirement

Moral leadership in a State and in a Nation is more important
than economic leadership. A moral depression is more harmful than
an economic depression. Both are bad. A spiritual depression is
disastrous. History produces the evidence of this fact.
—Hugh H. Clegg

W HEN HE ARRIVED AT OLE MISS, one of the first assignments Clegg was given related to university development. Chancellor Williams was concerned that Ole Miss and Oxford were not easy to access by common modes of transportation. While Oxford had bus service to Jackson and Memphis, there was no passenger train service in or out of town, nor was there bus service from Tupelo, Clarksdale, or the Delta area of the state. To worsen transportation matters, the highways that passed through Oxford were in poor shape. Because Oxford was located in the far northern region of Mississippi, Chancellor Williams told Clegg that the university and Oxford needed an airport and challenged him to secure one and establish air service to the university community, in particular, regular airline service to Memphis and the South in general. Williams told Clegg that the chances were ten thousand to one against Clegg getting funding for an airport but asked him to try. Clegg was faced with this daunting task, and even if successful in securing an airport, he would then be faced with the challenge of securing an airline to service Oxford and Ole Miss—and the odds would be ten thousand to one against that happening as well.

Clegg set out to answer the chancellor's challenge, and wasting no time, he put together a plan. Using contacts he had made over the years, he solicited the support of C. A. "Bud" Moore, the director of the State Aeronautics Commission; former governor Hugh White; Mississippi's entire congressional delegation; officials of the city of Oxford and of Lafayette County; alumni; friends; and the state legislature. University engineer and the superintendent of buildings and grounds Andrew B. Hargis found a location for the airport.[1] Wilburn Hooker Sr. was asked to serve as chairman of a committee to plan a new airport for the university.[2]

Despite the overwhelming odds, after only two years Clegg was successful in meeting both of the chancellor's challenges. Mississippi's state-owned airport, the University Oxford Airport (now also often referred to as the Airport at Ole Miss), was opened in 1956 with a 4,000-foot runway. The runway was lengthened to 4,700 feet in 1957, and the Oxford-University community began to reap the benefits of air travel. That year, E. O. Champion and his two sons, Dean and Elvis, began offering flight training programs and started an air charter service. In 1959, Southern Airlines initiated air carrier service into and out of Oxford offering two flights to Jackson and two flights to Memphis daily. The airport and airline service were secured despite the objections of an airline president and a group within the Federal Aviation Administration in Washington.

Shortly after his retirement in 1968, the Mississippi legislature adopted a joint resolution of thanks and commendation to recognize Clegg's important contributions to the state and nation. Subsequently, the University Oxford Airport was designated as Hugh H. Clegg Field (more commonly known as Clegg Field)—without a doubt one of Clegg's highest lifetime honors, and an honor that remains in effect to this day.[3]

Ole Miss needed favorable publicity and a boost in public relations during the periods of strife and racial tensions at the university starting in the 1950s. The 1958 Brussels World Fair provided that boost. The Ole Miss Marching Band had received much publicity (both favorable and unfavorable) resulting from appearances on television and at regular season and bowl football games. Part of the attention given to the band was due to the fact that its members wore Confederate uniforms and that a huge, football field–length Confederate flag was featured in the halftime performances.

The US commissioner general of the Brussels Universal and International Exhibition sent the band a special invitation to participate in the Brussels World Fair. Only three bands in the country were invited, and only two participated: the Ole Miss Band and the University of California–Berkeley Band. The US State Department approved and encouraged the trip but would not provide any funding; the band would have to pay its own way. The trip would prove to be expensive. Approximately $39,000 was needed for transportation and food to send the seventy-to-eighty band members; the band director, Lyle Babcock; baton twirlers, known as the Rebelettes; and chaperones to Brussels.

Clegg was asked to serve as chairman of the fund-raising campaign committee but turned the invitation down because of his heavy work schedule. Instead, he coordinated the trip and the necessary fund-raising from his office at the university. He nominated E. F. "Sleepy" Yerby to head the fund-raising effort and Yerby, who had his own dance band, did an outstanding job. Several years later, Yerby became an executive assistant to Chancellor Porter Fortune and, in time, the university continuing education center was named the E. F. Yerby Conference Center in his honor.

The campaign to raise funds generated statewide interest. Supporters from rival universities Mississippi State and Mississippi Southern, as well as Millsaps and Mississippi College, donated hundred-dollar checks, five-dollar checks, and one-dollar bills. Former governor Hugh L. White was eager to accept Clegg's invitation to become state chairman of the fund-raising effort since he and Clegg had developed a close personal relationship. When he was governor, White had set a state goal of balancing agricultural and industrial activities and created a Balance Agriculture with Industry program and an Agricultural and Industrial (AI) Board. Clegg convinced appropriate university administrators and the university band to advertise AI Board activities as part of the band's halftime shows. Clegg proposed that the band include small-size, painted, and cardboard or light plywood signs of the capital; various industries; the Mississippi River; a steamboat; and so on to advertise Mississippi. This approach gained the favor of the legislature and former governor White, who returned the favor to help raise funds to send the band to the Brussels.[4]

Communities throughout the state pitched in. Vicksburg and other towns went in together to make up a pool to donate money. The whole state seemed excited that a Mississippi school had been selected as one of only three bands invited to the Brussels World's Fair. The $39,000 goal was reached ten days before the date of scheduled departure, with a total amount of $40,778.46 being raised.[5]

It was later learned that a music competition called the World Band Festival was being held in Kerkrade, the Netherlands, before the start of the Brussels exhibition. The university decided to enter the Ole Miss Marching Band in this competition as well. On Sunday, August 24, 1958, the band and the accompanying delegation, which included the Ole Miss business manager, Yerby, and chaperones, took a train to New York City by way of St. Louis and then flew to Amsterdam and subsequently to Kerkrade. The band was an instant overseas success and earned the highest score and first prize during the Concert Competition, feats they duplicated in the Honors Competition and Marching Band Competition. They were given an award by the president of France for being named the outstanding band at the festival. At a time when Ole Miss and Mississippi needed favorable publicity, the Ole Miss Band came through. The band attracted favorable attention by visiting American, Dutch, Belgian, and French cemeteries to honor the war dead and represented the entire state of Mississippi, not just Ole Miss. The band then went on to Brussels and performed for six straight days at the World's Fair.

The University of California–Berkeley band experienced similar challenges in accepting the invitation but through a series of fundraisers that included a sparsely attended concert at the Greek Theater, a fiasco at a Hillsborough mansion, a ten-day playathon in San

Francisco, and an appearance on the television game show *Truth or Consequences*, the band met its challenges. The band's drum major would recall the success of the band in upstaging the Soviet exhibit featuring a replica of its *Sputnik* satellite through the band's twice-daily performances at the nearby US pavilion.[6] Both the Ole Miss and UC Berkeley bands were big hits at the fair, since European bands were primarily military bands and the audiences were not accustomed to the music and the tempo of the US marching bands.

Four years later, Ole Miss band director Lyle Babcock became embroiled in the Meredith crisis. Babcock proposed that the band change its uniform from the Confederate attire that had been adopted earlier. He felt that the Ole Miss Rebel concept had been overemphasized and that it was not in the best interests of the university to continue to push such southern traditionalism. Babcock's decision was overruled by Governor Ross Barnett.[7] However, the band did retire the Confederate uniforms after the 1963 football season and replaced them with uniforms featuring a Confederate flag panel on the chest. Then those uniforms were replaced in 1968 by black uniforms with a white overlay with blue and red lettering and trim.[8]

Ole Miss learned that the US Department of Agriculture had plans to develop a soil sedimentation laboratory in the Tallahatchie-Yazoo basin and decided to make a concerted effort to have the laboratory established in Oxford. Mississippi State University, with its rich heritage of research in agriculture, was a natural competitor for the lab. Ole Miss argued it was better positioned to have the facility since Oxford was located closer to the headwaters of the basin. The Department of Agriculture had been leaning toward Oxford, and although Clegg would not admit that there was a direct competition with Mississippi State, he boasted that because of his Washington contacts and many trips to Washington to support the department's decision, the US Department of Agriculture–Agricultural Research Service National Sedimentation Laboratory was established in Oxford at a site adjacent to the university airport. The first part of the present laboratory facility was built in 1958. Ole Miss benefited, and still benefits, from research collaborations afforded by the proximity of the laboratory. In fact, the first director of that lab became the coordinator of research at Ole Miss when he retired.[9]

During this time, Clegg experienced heart problems. His brother, James Ellis, notified Special Agent in Charge Julius Lopez in the FBI's Memphis office that Hugh had suffered a heart attack on April 12, 1957, and was hospitalized in Oxford. His physicians requested copies of the electrocardiograph reports taken of Clegg during his Bureau annual physical examinations. These reports were airmailed from the Bethesda US Naval Hospital.[10] Clegg indicated that he wanted his old friend, Dr. Norman Vincent Peale, to be notified and be requested to pray for him. However, Clegg's daughter claims there was no evidence of a heart attack; rather, she feels his problems were due to a panic attack.

Clegg recovered and was determined to meet his commitment to speak to the FBI National Academy on May 16. His wife urged the FBI not to mention anything to indicate he would not be able to meet that commitment—but she didn't want her husband to be made aware of her intervention at this time.[11] Director Hoover personally contacted Ruby Kathryn and telegraphed Clegg offering all possible assistance.[12] A Memphis heart specialist, Dr. Lyle Motley, found that Clegg had suffered acute coronary insufficiency without thrombosis and recommended three weeks of bed rest.[13]

A week following Clegg's hospitalization, Ruby Kathryn wrote Director Hoover thanking him for sending the telegram offering his assistance:

> For years I have wanted to tell you how thankful I am for Hugh's association with you. It has meant so much to us both to be able to call you a friend. To be part of the FBI team gives a man and his wife a sense of pride, dedication and integrity that I wish every American could feel. I have been truly sorry many times that Hugh saw fit, because of Ruby Kathryn's health, to retire. He will never be as happy as he was there. He has been doing a much needed job here in Mississippi but look what it did to him.[14]

He had not suffered any permanent injury to his heart, and Clegg returned home on May 2. Clegg missed his May 16 presentation, but Hoover invited him to lecture the FBI National Academy on the topic "Obtaining Public Support for Law Enforcement" on October 24.[15]

In July 1957, fully recovered from his heart attack, he became involved in urging members of the Mississippi congressional delegation, as well as his old friend Senator Everett Dirksen, to rectify the 1957 Supreme Court decision in the case of *Jencks v. United States* that would make FBI files open to defendants in legal actions.[16] Clegg argued that citizen cooperation in identifying criminals and criminal acts required a measure of confidentiality, and if the Supreme Court decision was to be the final word in this matter, fewer citizens would cooperate in the future. Clinton Jencks was a labor organizer and union president in New Mexico who was convicted for lying about his membership in the Communist Party. During the trial, crucial testimony against Jencks was presented by two paid undercover FBI agents who claimed to have regularly provided the FBI with reports on the matters on which they testified. Lawyers for Jencks moved that the reports on which the agents based their testimony be produced, but their motions were denied. Jencks appealed his case to the US Supreme Court, which ruled in his favor and reversed the previous decision of the Federal District Court.

Clegg's close friend, Justice Tom C. Clark, argued against the majority opinion, writing that unless Congress nullified the decision, intelligence agencies engaged in law enforcement might "as well close up shop." There is no indication that Clegg used his friendship to attempt to influence Clark. Due in part to Clegg's lobbying efforts, Congress adopted what became known as the Jencks Act, amending the US Code to require the prosecutor to produce a verbatim statement made by a witness but only after the witness had actually testified and not in pre-trial hearings.

A few weeks before he retired from Ole Miss, Clegg was surprised to learn that he had been appointed chairman of the Mississippi Crime Commission. Governor Paul Johnson sent a highway patrol airplane to take Clegg and Dr. Charles Fortenberry, the head of the Ole Miss political science department, to Johnson's office in Jackson. When they arrived, a Johnson aide told them to report to the law enforcement academy near Whitfield. The two had no real idea of what was going to take place, but graduation exercises for a large number of highway patrolmen were being held at the academy. The governor greeted them and Dr. Fortenberry was cited for his outstanding performance in the law enforcement program. Then Johnson announced that he was appointing Clegg as chairman of the state's Crime Commission, the first Clegg knew of his appointment. He served as chairman of the Mississippi Crime Commission on a part-time basis from 1966 to 1968.

Accepting this challenge in the same spirit in which he accepted all other challenges, Clegg led a group that formed the Crime Commission. Clegg pushed to have the commission integrated and proposed a list of potential black commission members to the governor for consideration. Clegg's list included Dr. Laurence Jones, founder and longtime head of Piney Woods Country Life School, but the governor selected three other black leaders to serve: Dr. John A. Peoples Jr., president of Jackson State from 1967 to 1984; Dr. Walter Washington, head of Utica Junior College for twelve years and later president of Alcorn State from 1969 to 1994—and the first African American to receive a doctorate in Mississippi (from Southern Mississippi)—and the principal of a black school in Meridian. At first Clegg thought he had broken ground in helping to appoint the first integrated commission or organization in the state, but Johnson informed him that there had previously been an integrated education board. Clegg served as chairman of the Crime Commission on a part-time basis from 1966 to 1968 while continuing to fulfill his Ole Miss commitments.[17]

Unfortunately, 1958 turned out to be a sad year for Clegg. His mother died in her sleep on January 23 and his father passed away from a heart attack while driving his automobile a few months later on May 7. His parents had celebrated their sixtieth wedding anniversary on October 17, 1957.

Clegg continued his interactions with the Bureau. In the early morning hours of April 25, 1959, Mack Charles Parker, a twenty-three-year-old black man, was kidnapped by a mob of hooded and masked men from his jail cell in the Pearl River County Courthouse, where he was waiting trial on charges that he had raped a pregnant white woman. Parker had been indicted by the grand jury of two counts of kidnapping and one count of rape. His kidnappers beat him, shot him twice, and killed him twenty miles west of Poplarville, Mississippi. His chained body was thrown from the Pearl River Bridge separating Mississippi and Louisiana. The sheriff notified the FBI and sixty agents came to Poplarville to investigate. Neither blacks nor whites were willing to talk about the lynching or provide any assistance to the FBI and their investigation. Many residents of the area resented the resulting media attention and the presence of the FBI.

Clegg, who knew the Mississippi political scene as well as anyone, called C. D. DeLoach of the FBI and alerted the Bureau that much of the criticism of the FBI was related to the upcoming Mississippi gubernatorial race between State Auditor E. Boyd Golding and Lieutenant Governor Carroll Gartin, who was supported by Governor James P. Coleman.[18] Golding was highly critical of comments made by Coleman praising the work of the FBI, and Clegg felt that the Bureau was being made a political football. Clegg then praised the courage of FBI agent Zack Van Landingham, who stood before a civic meeting and defended the Bureau. Several members of the mob were later identified by the FBI but no indictments or convictions were ever obtained, even though three of the suspects admitted their guilt.[19] The FBI reopened its investigation fifty years later, but all of the suspects identified by the FBI in 1959 had died before then.

Clegg spent his final years at Ole Miss dealing with issues much less controversial than the crises he was used to handling. He was able to devote his time and energy to doing the things that Chancellor Williams had originally hired him to do: university development, recruiting, fund-raising, and so on. He maintained his involvement with the FBI by presenting, on almost an annual basis, lectures at the

FBI National Academy, a task he truly enjoyed. He also gave many more media interviews than he had in the past, recounting his days at the FBI and at Ole Miss.[20]

Clegg announced his retirement from Ole Miss effective June 30, 1968, just prior to reaching the state-mandated retirement age of seventy. A dinner was scheduled on June 20 to honor his many accomplishments for the university. George Street, director of development, telephoned Director Hoover's office to notify him of the dinner and invited him to send a telegram to Clegg that could be read at the dinner. Hoover did not hesitate and sent a wire:

> It is indeed a pleasure to join your many friends who are honoring you tonight. You have contributed untiringly and unselfishly of your time and talents to every position you have held both in the FBI and at the University of Mississippi. Your achievements have been outstanding and I want to extend my sincerest best wishes to you for every happiness in your forthcoming retirement.[21]

Clegg's contributions to Ole Miss were perhaps best summed up in a citation presented upon his retirement. At the university's 1968 commencement exercise held on May 28, Chancellor Porter L. Fortune Jr.—who was named to head the university in February 1968 following the retirement of J. D. Williams in January—read and presented the following citation to Clegg:[22]

> The University of Mississippi extends to Hugh H. Clegg this citation as an acknowledgement of its debt and an expression of its gratitude for fourteen years of devoted and distinguished service to the University as Assistant to the Chancellor and Director of Development and later as Assistant to the Chancellor and Consultant in Development. With vigor and unflagging effort he built the development and public relations programs of the University. Keeping before him the goal of supporting the academic thrust of the institution, he played an important

role in securing funds for new buildings and in persuading do-
nors and legislators to support the university more adequately.
In a period of great difficulty his wise counsel and his persuasive genius were important factors in the successful struggle to
maintain the integrity of the University. His courage, his personal honesty, his capacity for working harmoniously with others, his broad and intimate knowledge of public affairs, and his
loyalty to the University qualified him as the University's chief
"trouble-shooter" at a time when such service was a paramount
need. The University of Mississippi will always be indebted to
him for the substantial contributions he made to its growth and
well-being.

Following the ceremonies, the University Outstanding Professor of the Year, Accountancy Professor Eugene Peery, said that
while highly laudatory, the "citation should have been fifty times
more expressive than it was." Two women staff retirees reminded
the chancellor how much Clegg would be missed. Former chancellor Williams said, "He is the most underpaid man on the campus."
A member of the board of trustees told Clegg that if he had been
twenty years younger, he would have urged Clegg's appointment as
president of his alma mater.

The university, the Bureau, and the state continued to honor Clegg
after his retirement. The Mississippi legislature adopted a resolution
commending Clegg on his service to the state.[23] He was named a
recipient of the 1969 First Federal Foundation Award given annually
by the University of Mississippi for outstanding achievement and
distinguished service to Mississippi.[24] Following his retirement, he
was invited to attend the FBI National Academy refresher course at
the new FBI Academy facility in Quantico, Virginia, where he was
presented a plaque recognizing the impact he had had on law enforcement training over the years.[25]

Clegg expressed his appreciation for the invitation and the plaque
to the newly appointed director of the FBI, Clarence M. Kelley. Following Hoover's death in 1972, L. Patrick Gray was named acting

director but resigned soon thereafter because of his involvement with the Watergate crisis of the Nixon administration. Kelley was then named director in 1973. At that time, pressure was being put on the Bureau to hire female agents, which Hoover had declined to do. Clegg recalled to Kelley his experience with FBI female agent Lenore Houston in 1927 and advised him that if he were to "get any flack about having women Special Agents, I can assure you this is not a new experience."[26]

The Cleggs moved to Anguilla, Ruby Kathryn's hometown, following his second retirement and spent his postretirement years there. He became involved with the Anguilla Methodist Church adult Sunday school classes and served on the administrative board of the Anguilla Methodist Church. He wrote an unpublished manuscript of his years at Ole Miss titled "Somebody Jumped the Gun" and worked on a second manuscript titled "Inside the FBI," which was not completed. He also sat for a lengthy interview in 1975 as part of the University of Southern Mississippi oral history project. His loyalty to the FBI surfaced at the end of the interview when he stated that "in reciting many incidents and cases I have said 'we' when I meant the FBI. The FBI is a 'We' organization and not an 'I' organization. Frequently in saying 'we' I was personally remote and not involved in the incident described herein."[27]

In one of the final interviews Clegg granted after his retirement,[28] Clegg's personal qualities of loyalty and modesty remained consistent. Clegg considered J. Edgar Hoover to be a genius in many respects and expressed the opinion that he thought Hoover should have been president of the United States. When reports surfaced that the FBI maintained surveillance of congressmen and journalists, Clegg simply said he did not believe them and remained convinced of the role that the FBI played in domestic intelligence gathering. He defended this role of the agency in bringing into custody German Americans, Italian Americans, and "some" Japanese Americans who had criticized US policies while supporting the policies of America's adversaries. The FBI had compiled lists of these people running into the thousands, and when the attack on Pearl Harbor thrust the country into World War II, picked up 90 percent of these on presidential orders. However, he claimed that the detention of thousands of Japanese Americans in Hawaii and on the West Coast was a military operation and did not involve the FBI.

He characteristically downplayed his role in the investigations of criminals such as Al Capone, John Dillinger, and Bonnie and Clyde while readily acknowledging his acquaintance with popular law enforcement officers such as Elliott Ness of *The Untouchables* fame, claiming Ness was a good investigator.[29] Clegg did not hesitate to demonstrate pride in establishing the FBI National Academy, a role for which he was honored at the Academy's one hundredth graduation exercises in 1975. Little mention was made in this interview regarding the experiences Clegg had while at Ole Miss, although the reporter mentioned that "Clegg's gentle personality probably fit in well on campus." The interview ended with the then-Greenville FBI chief, John Neelley, describing Clegg as "a tough cookie."

Adding to his numerous honors at the FBI and Ole Miss, in 1969 the official publication of the Society of Former Special Agents of the FBI recognized Clegg as "one of the legendary personalities of the FBI during his 27 1/2 years as a Special Agent, Special Agent in Charge, Inspector and Assistant Director."[30]

His history of heart problems surfaced again in October 1977, and he was admitted to the cardiac intensive care unit at the University of Mississippi Medical Center in Jackson. Hugh and Kat moved to Tupelo and stayed at their daughter's home. Kat's health history is not well-known, but she had suffered from rheumatic fever in her youth. Her daughter recalled that her mother had undergone gallbladder surgery later in life and during surgery her heart stopped beating. She claimed that to her recollection, her mother was the first person to undergo open heart massage to be revived by this method. Kat suffered a heart attack and was found in an upstairs bedroom by her daughter and taken to the hospital. Ruby Kathryn passed away on May 15, 1979.

Hugh returned alone to their home in Anguilla and later fell and broke his hip. He was taken to the hospital in Rolling Fork, and when he was released six weeks later, he decided to move to Tupelo rather than return to Anguilla. He chose to stay in a nursing home rather than at the home of his daughter's family so he would be less of a bother. One night, a male aide attempted to carry him to the bathroom and Hugh protested that it took two people to move him. The aide said he could carry him by himself and picked him up. But the aide dropped him and Hugh's hip was crushed once again. As Hugh lay on the floor, he called his daughter and told her to come get him and take him to the emergency room. Seven months after Kat passed away, he died in his sleep from apparent heart failure at the extended care facility of the North Mississippi Medical Center in Tupelo on December 12, 1979. He was buried next to his wife in the Golden Link Cemetery in Anguilla.

Clegg was always optimistic for the future of Ole Miss. Despite the image setback caused by the Meredith desegregation crisis, he predicted continued growth for the university:

> Ole Miss lives. It is a living, breathing, dynamic, progressive, and vital institution of higher learning. It does not just endure; it is vigorous, active, and is going forward in strength. . . . Its problems, far, far less in number than its successes, have contributed to making its students and its alumni clearer thinking, more logical, greater problem-solving people—many of whom attained great success in far-reaching areas of our globe. The University has a great tradition. Its influence on the life and history of the area is unequalled in the field of higher education. The University is planning courageously. It has a vital concept of its mission. Its prestige is assured. Quality, integrity, devotion and enthusiasm mark the spirit and achievements of Ole Miss. Each day finds it at the doorstep of destiny and the opportunity for greater service. With faith and vision, the foundation is being laid for a better tomorrow.[31]

Clegg's optimism is bearing fruit. As David Sansing noted in his sesquicentennial history of Ole Miss, the public perception of the university has changed dramatically.[32] The university recently marked the fiftieth anniversary of Meredith's desegregation of the university with a series of programs featuring nationally known speakers. During the academic year, the Ole Miss student body elected its first African American female student body president and its first African American Homecoming Queen. (In 2000, it had chosen an African American male as president of the student body.) Few would argue that the foundation for a better university has indeed been laid. In 2008, Ole Miss hosted the first presidential debate between John McCain and Barack Obama. CBS news reporter Bob Schieffer, who was on campus to report the 1962 riot, returned for the first time to cover the debate. On his national news program, *Face the Nation*, Schieffer noted how "black and white students were working together to welcome reporters and official visitors" and that the riot and resulting unrest "seemed long ago and far away." He ended his commentary saying, "we still have a long way to go in this country to insure that every American is treated fairly, but as I walked across the Ole Miss campus Friday, it helped me understand that in less than my lifetime, we have also come a very long way."[33]

Hugh Clegg made significant contributions to his nation and his home state during his two careers. Few men could serve both entities with the degree of loyalty he demonstrated while consistently striving to stay out of the spotlight.

Epilogue

The two careers of Hugh Clegg were characterized by perhaps his strongest quality: loyalty. He was loyal to his hometown of Mathiston, Mississippi, and to Webster County, returning there many times throughout his life after moving to Washington, DC, and Oxford, Mississippi. Clegg would return to present the high school commencement address to Mathiston High School on several occasions.[1] Since he had also served as president of Wood Junior College in Mathiston, he returned there to attend numerous functions. He maintained a strong interest in his birthplace and recognized the influence that having been raised there had on his two careers and his family life. In return, the citizens of Mathiston were proud of his accomplishments.

His days in the FBI were defined by his being "one of Hoover's favorite agents, much valued for his loyalty and his indiscriminately high opinion of Hoover's leadership. That loyalty, coupled with his unquestionable bravery, led to his promotion to assistant director in 1932, after only six years in the Bureau."[2] Also documented has been his loyalty to his fellow agent, Melvin Purvis, who was not one of Director Hoover's favorites and with whom Clegg shared the failed raid at Little Bohemia. Referring to Purvis, Clegg said,

> His loyalty is intense. . . . He has a feeling that as part of the Bureau it is his organization and he is willing to go to the limit for the organization and for anyone connected with it, from administrative officials down to the lowest salaried clerical employee; yet, if an employee gets off the reservation he is equally alert to protect the Bureau's interests.[3]

When Purvis came under intense criticism by Hoover for the way he responded to the death of fellow agent, Sam Cowley, Clegg once again came to his defense. When Clegg was charged with evaluating Purvis at a conference of agents in charge in April 1935 after Purvis had been on restricted duty since the previous November, Clegg noted that Purvis's major problem was being too protective of the agents under his supervision: "He has participated in a considerable number of raids and I believe is somewhat too much inclined to personally participate in some of the investigative activities of this character rather than to delegate the leadership to others." Despite Hoover essentially placing Purvis in administrative purgatory, Clegg told the conference, "I feel in all sincerity that he is intensely loyal to the Director and to the Bureau. His high personal regard for the Director continues unabated in spite of what he probably feels to be some sort of punitive administrative action which has been taken in his case." Unfortunately Hoover was not impressed with Clegg's evaluation and support for Purvis.[4]

Clegg was intensely loyal to Director Hoover, calling him "the standard bearer. He was the flag. He was the seal. He was the escutcheon that identified the FBI. He did not demand loyalty, he obtained it and commanded it after he acquired it."[5] Clegg resisted every opportunity to publicly criticize Hoover's professional and personal lives. Clegg had often been accused of seeking Hoover's job as director, charges he emphatically rejected out of hand. George E. Harding, whom Hoover regarded as a good friend of the Bureau, wrote Hoover shortly after Clegg retired:

> Now that Hugh Clegg has retired I feel that I should drop you a note and state that never in my business, government or any other affairs have I met a man who showed such great loyalty to his chief as High Clegg did to you. His extreme devotion to you as Director was certainly very noticeable in his talks and his contacts at all the law enforcement meetings which I have attended with him. He certainly was your emissary of good will in the Bureau also.[6]

He was loyal to his new boss, the University of Mississippi, choosing to take the side of the university in its conflict with his former boss, the federal government, during the Meredith crisis. That quality of loyalty he displayed at the FBI stood him in good stead during his career at Ole Miss as well. His loyalty to Chancellor J. D. Williams and the University of Mississippi is well documented. Surviving Ole Miss colleagues of Clegg had general impressions of Clegg but did not offer great insight into his personality. Common descriptions included terms and phrases such as tough but fair, efficient, loyal, effective, the chancellor's right-hand man. At his retirement, Chancellor Porter L. Fortune, when describing his contributions to Ole Miss said, "His loyalty to the University qualified him as the University's chief 'trouble-shooter.'"[7]

During his interviews with the University of Southern Mississippi, Clegg discussed the time that Governor Theodore Bilbo, an outspoken bigot, defeated Clegg's friend, incumbent Senator Hubert Stephens in a contest for a US Senate seat. Although Clegg was disappointed that Bilbo won the election, he admitted that he had "no special feeling against Bilbo. He was one of my senators. I have a penchant for being loyal to my crowd."[8]

Clegg was also a company man, consistently choosing in both of his careers to put himself second to his employers. He was rarely comfortable being in the public eye, and there are surprisingly very few photographs of him in the public domain. No photographs of Clegg could be found relating to his time at Ole Miss except for standard administrative photos that appeared in university yearbooks.

He never publicly upstaged his employers or his colleagues. He was comfortable in his role of supporting his bosses. He was a good family man and a good administrator, albeit not very efficient when it came to handling paperwork. Clegg reveled in public relations and establishing contacts with key national and state leaders, contacts that stood him in good stead throughout his two careers. Despite his involvement in political matters, he never considered going into politics himself.

When being interviewed for his oral history for the University of Southern Mississippi, the interviewer, Dr. Caudill, asked, "from your point now, retired from the FBI and the University of Mississippi and also writing and everything. Assume you were given the opportunity to make the trip again, through life, what would you druther repeat?" Clegg responded, "Both of them! . . . I couldn't afford to miss it."[9]

Hugh Clegg made significant contributions to his nation and his home state during his two careers. Few men could serve both entities with the degree of loyalty he demonstrated while consistently striving to stay out of the spotlight.

And, of course, there is Clegg Field.

Acknowledgments

This biography would not have been undertaken, much less completed, without the support, advice, encouragement, and inspiration provided by many individuals, especially Jere R. Hoar, professor emeritus of journalism, and David G. Sansing, professor emeritus of history, to whom this book is dedicated. Both were outstanding teachers, now retired, during their tenures at the University of Mississippi, and both are also distinguished writers. Jere Hoar was a member of the faculty during the Meredith crisis and provided several anecdotes about his observations of the crisis. David Sansing wrote the centennial history of the University of Mississippi, from which much in this biography was drawn. Both graciously read all or major parts of this manuscript and provided valuable suggestions and critiques. I am deeply appreciative to both of these outstanding educators, respected authors, and friends.

The constant encouragement of Deborah Freeland also contributed immeasurably to this endeavor and is deeply appreciated. Deborah, a videographer in the Division of Outreach and Continuing Education at Ole Miss, was invaluable in attempting to secure photographs of Hugh Clegg through the Library of Congress (LOC) and assembling high resolution copies of photographs in this book. She also designed the cover of this book. Jonathan Eaker of the Prints and Photographs division of the LOC was able to locate only one photograph of Clegg, which is surprising considering the important role Clegg played at the FBI but is consistent with Clegg's desire to remain out of the public eye.

Several individuals provided information, clarification, and insight into the life of Hugh Clegg and his wife, Ruby Kathryn "Kat" Clegg, and in particular their daughter, Ruby Kathryn Clegg Patterson. Clegg's daughter was especially helpful in providing anecdotal information during the several interviews I had with her. She and her husband, Aubrey, were particularly helpful in providing photographs of the family from their collections. Their assistance is much appreciated. Hugh Clegg did not seek publicity or the camera so there are surprisingly few photographs available of his days at either the FBI or at Ole Miss. Hugh's nephew, Gary Gardner, the son of Clegg's youngest sister, Kate Hardison, and James Gardner, still lives in Hugh Clegg's birthplace, Mathiston, Mississippi, and was particularly helpful in providing valuable information on the history of Clegg's family and his relationship with his uncle.

Lavelle McAlpin, the mayor pro tem of Mathiston, member of the Mathiston Board of Aldermen, teacher of history and local culture at East Webster High School, and is considered by many who live in Mathiston to be the town's unofficial historian. He was an invaluable source of information regarding the history of Hugh Clegg's birthplace. Lavelle is currently writing a definitive history of Mathiston and graciously shared several newspaper articles relating to Hugh Clegg and the Clegg family as well as several photographs from his private collection of photos of Mathiston in the early 1900s. He was especially helpful in providing information regarding the embezzlement at the banks of Mathiston, Weir, and Heidelberg as well as providing information regarding the 1906 Mathiston tornado that nearly destroyed the town.

Renowned artist and arts commentator, William "Bill" Dunlap, a native of Mathiston, provided information about Mathiston and connected me to valuable sources of information in Webster County. Bill, who still owns a home and a studio in Mathiston, also provided considerable encouragement for this biography. Belinda Stewart, proprietor of Belinda Stewart Architects, P.A., in Eupora, Mississippi, also served as an important source of information regarding the history of Webster County and the characteristics of its people. She also provided insight regarding the regional environment in which Hugh was raised. Longtime Mathiston resident Dempsey Blanton provided valuable background information regarding the railroads that came to Mathiston in its early days as well as the history of the town itself.

Gathering information on Clegg's days at the FBI was greatly facilitated by former agents of the FBI, particularly Ed Lee, who resides in Oxford. Ed contacted several former agents he knew regarding this project, and many responded to his request for information, namely Elston Hill, Burl E. Cloninger, Jim Blasingame, Dwight Garretson, Michael Morrell, Cartha D. DeLoach, Donnie Young, Harold Fabriz, Larry Sollars, Del Hahn, and Neil J. Welch. Ed also contacted Larry Wack, a retired FBI special agent who served the agency for thirty years and is the owner of the internet website that is very popular among former FBI agents, "Faded Glory: Dusty Roads of an FBI Era." Larry was a valuable source of information regarding the FBI and was very helpful in securing difficult-to-obtain information. Ed also provided insight into the makings of an FBI agent and the dress codes established by J. Edgar Hoover. Former FBI agent Dwight Ball graciously shared his knowledge of the agency and his recollections of Hugh Clegg. Over two thousand pages of files relating to Clegg's time at the FBI were obtained from the agency under the federal Freedom of Information Act.

James Meredith has spent considerable time at my tailgating tent at Ole Miss football games—usually wearing an Ole Miss cap and shirt. A true American hero, his unique personal viewpoint of the crisis that surrounded him during those turbulent days was invaluable in attempting to understand the mentality of those involved at the federal, state, and university levels.

Federal judge Neal B. Biggers of the Northern District of Mississippi provided helpful discussions of the historical and legal issues surrounding the desegregation of Ole Miss. Judge Biggers, a first-year law student during the Meredith crisis, also provided insightful information regarding the accompanying riot from the student perspective. His insight and friendship are much valued.

Arthur McIntosh, a student at Ole Miss in the early 1960s, provided a valuable perspective on the Meredith integration crisis from a student point of view. Arthur was a great traveling companion on several interview trips to Eupora, Mathiston, and Tupelo and asked pertinent questions of those interviewed. The encouragement this friend provided to complete this biography is deeply appreciated.

Jep Clemens, a friend and former student member of the Ole Miss Marching Band, was a valuable source for the history of the band and the band uniforms, as was Dr. William DeJournett, associate professor of music at the University of Mississippi.

Mrs. Betsy Murphy Dyke, who currently lives in Oxford, is the daughter of Margaret Elizabeth Turner Murphy, the woman who was Hugh's secretary for part of his time at the FBI. Betsy and her husband, David Dyke, provided pertinent information about meeting Clegg and his daughter when she arrived in Oxford to visit the university. They also provided additional information about Clegg's time at the FBI during which her mother served as Clegg's secretary. Mrs. Murphy, whom Hugh and others called Betty, still resides in Dallas.

Oxford residents John Morgan and Ed Morgan Jr., grandsons of former IHL Board of Trustees member Ira L. "Shine" Morgan, were helpful in providing background stories about their grandfather and their father, Ed Morgan, that took place during the Meredith desegregation crisis.

Several members of the University of Mississippi faculty and staff, along with former students, all of whom who knew Hugh Clegg during his time at Ole Miss, were helpful in providing information regarding his days at the university, particularly Ed Meek, former director of University Public Relations and benefactor of the Meek School of Journalism and New Media; Dr. Charles Taylor; professor emeritus of accountancy; and Ken Wooten. Also, a book by former university provost Dr. Gerald Walton, *The University of Mississippi: A Pictorial History* (2008), provided great insight into Ole Miss during the period in which Clegg served the university. Former student newspaper editor Sidna Brower Mitchell Cooks also provided insight into Hugh Clegg and the atmosphere surrounding the integration of Ole Miss. Journalism professor and author Joe Atkins provided important advice on the manuscript submission process for which I am grateful.

The daughter of Chancellor J. D. Williams, Harter Crutcher, and her son Robert Pepper Crutcher Jr. also provided valuable insight into Hugh's character. Pepper gave me a copy of the letter Hugh had written to him when he was born.

Lloyd McManus, manager of University Oxford Airport, and Jim Windham, director of procurement services at Ole Miss, were of great assistance in providing information regarding the history of the airport that Hugh Clegg helped get funded. The longtime airport manager, Jeff Meaders, compiled all of the historical records related to the airport and, before he passed away, gave them to Jim Windham. Jim in turn gave them to Lloyd McManus, who believed the records should be kept at the airport. Their assistance is greatly appreciated.

I would be remiss if I failed to acknowledge the valuable assistance provided by the staff of the University of Mississippi Department of Archives and Collections of the J. D. Williams Library, especially Jennifer Ford, head of Archives and Special Collections; Pamela Williamson, visual collections librarian; Sally Leigh McWhite, Political Papers archivist; and Kathryn Michaelis, Special Collections Digital Initiatives librarian. They provided access to the unpublished Hugh Clegg book manuscript as well as several collections archived by the university. Jessica Leming, Visual Collections librarian and assistant professor and selector for Studio Art and Art History was particularly helpful in searching for photographs of Clegg in the university archives during his days at Ole Miss, and her efforts are much appreciated.

This biography could not have been published without the competence and expertise of the staff of University Press of Mississippi, especially the efforts of Director Leila Salisbury, who guided this work on its publication path; Editorial Associate Valerie Jones, who coordinated the photographs; Managing Editor Anne Stascavage, who moved the manuscript into production; Marketing Assistant Courtney McCreary, who coordinated the catalog description; and

Art Director John Langston, who handled the cover design. I am especially indebted to copy editor Dr. Michael Levine whose brilliance, patience, meticulousness and knowledge made this manuscript readable. He must have been bemused and challenged by editing the work of a scientist schooled in writing only in the third person, past tense, and passive voice—but he did not flinch. I am indebted to them all.

Throughout my life, professionally and personally, I have been fortunate to have the support and love of my three children, Debra Price, Dr. Michael J. Borne, and MerriBeth Catalano, and my nine grandchildren, Rachael, Baker, Taylor, and Bess Borne; Mary Katherine Price; Jason Price; and Madison, Jordan, and Cole Catalano. I have also benefited over the years from the encouragement and support of my colleagues in the Department of Medicinal Chemistry and the School of Pharmacy of the University of Mississippi. I am deeply grateful to all.

Appendix

Clegg Family Tree

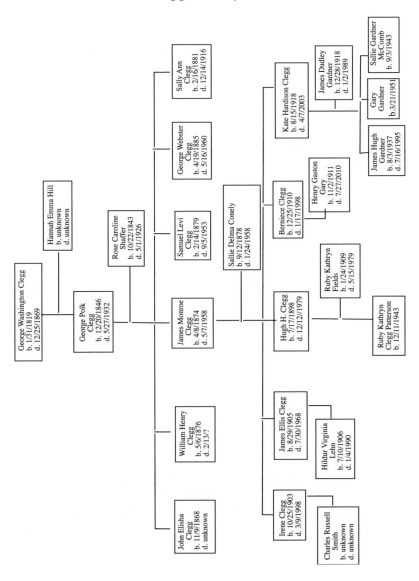

Notes

Abbreviations

USMOH   "Oral History with Mr. Hugh H. Clegg, Native Mississippian, Former Assistant Director of the FBI and Educator," University of Southern Mississippi Center for Oral History and Cultural Heritage, Hattiesburg, Mississippi, 1977.

HHCUM   "Somebody Jumped the Gun," Hugh H. Clegg, Unpublished Manuscript, Archives Department, J. D. Williams Library, University of Mississippi, Oxford.

FBIHHC   FBI Files on Hugh H. Clegg, File 67-HQ-6524 obtained under FOIPA Request No. 1137997-000.

Prologue

1. Bryan Burrough, *Public Enemies: America's Greatest Crime Wave and the Birth of the FBI, 1933-34*, Penguin Press, 2004, p. 11.

2. Demspey Blanton, face-to-face conversation with the author, Summer 2013.

3. Alston Purvis and Alex T. Tresniowski, *The Vendetta: FBI Hero Melvin Purvis's War against Crime, and J. Edgar Hoover's War against Him, Public-Affairs*, October 10, 2005, pp. 93–94.

4. Ibid., p. 43.

5. Ibid., pp. 268–269.

6. Ed Meek, face-to-face conversation with the author, Fall 2012.

7. Robert Pepper Crutcher Jr., Letter from Hugh Clegg, October 14, 1957, copy provided from Crutcher's personal collection.

8. USMOH, "Oral History with Mr. Hugh H. Clegg, Native Mississippian, Former Assistant Director of the FBI and Educator," University of Southern Mississippi Center for Oral History and Cultural Heritage, 1977.

9. HHCUM, "Somebody Jumped the Gun," Hugh H. Clegg, Unpublished

Manuscript, Archives Department, J. D. Williams Library, University of Mississippi, Oxford.

10. Purvis and Tresniowski, *The Vendetta*, p. 43.

11. Mrs. Ruby Kathryn Clegg Patterson Jr., several face-to-face conversations with the author, beginning Summer 2012.

Introduction

1. Robert J. Lamphere and Tom Shachtman, *The FBI-KGB War: A Special Agent's Story*, Mercer University Press, 1986.

2. M. Wesley Swearingen, *FBI Secrets: An Agent's Exposé*, South End Press, 1994.

1. Growing Up in Mathiston

1. Lavelle McAlpin, several face-to-face conversations with the author, beginning June 2013.

2. Ibid.; C. A. Lindbergh, *The Spirit of St. Louis*, Charles Scribner's Sons, 1953.

3. "History of Mathiston, MS," at http://www.rootsweb.ancestry .com/~mswebst1/mathistonhis.html.

4. The internet records of the Golden Link Cemetery in Anguilla, Mississippi, compiled by Larry Wheeler, list his date of birth as July 17, 1895. See http://files.usgwarchives.net/ms/sharkey/cemeteries/goldenlinks.txt, while the oral history interview given to the University of Southern Mississippi lists his date of birth as July 17, 1903. (USMOH, p. 1)

5. Ibid., p. 11.

6. Ibid., p. 12.

7. FBIHHC Letter from Special Agent R. C. Suran to Hoover, June 29, 1943

8. See http://www.rootsweb.ancestry.com/~mswebst1/2000obits.html.

9. USMOH, p. 13

10. Ibid., p. 126

11. Ibid., p. 13

12. "Seek Georgians for Bank Theft," *Atlanta Constitution*, February 1, 2014.

13. "Absconding Cashier Is Placed in Prison," *Atlanta Constitution*, June 1, 1914.

14. FBIHHC Files, October 30, 1957.

15. USMOH, p. 13.

16. USMOH, p. 10.

17. FBIHHC Files, October 30, 1957.

18. USMOH, p. 13.

19. Lavelle McAlpin, "2011 Tornado Mirrors That of 1906," *Webster Progress-Times*, June 27, 2013.

20. USMOH, p. 15.

21. J. B. Campbell, *For the Public Good: The Story of Boyd Campbell and the Mississippi School Supply Company*, Necomen Press, 1963.

22. USMOH, p. 18.

23. Ibid., p. 20.

24. Ibid., p. 21.

25. Ibid., p. 22.

26. "An Inventory to the Julian B. Fiebelman Papers," Manuscript Collection No. 94, American Jewish Archives, Cincinnati, Ohio; Marcie Cohen Ferris and Mark I. Greenberg, eds., *Jewish Roots in Southern Soil: A New History*, University Press of New England, 2006, p. 204.

27. USMOH, p. 24.

28. Ibid., p. 100.

29. Ibid., pp. 25–26.

2. A Move to Washington: The Early Days at the FBI

1. USMOH, p. 28.

2. Ibid., p. 102.

3. The Federal Bureau of Investigation did not receive this name until March 22, 1935. Prior to that time, the agency was called the Bureau of Investigation or the Division of Investigation.

4. USMOH, p. 31.

5. Athan G. Theoharis, ed., *The FBI: A Comprehensive Reference Guide*, Oryx Press, 1999.

6. USMOH, p. 66.

7. Ibid., p. 30.

8. FBIHHC Letter, Clegg to Director Hoover, June 15, 1926.

9. Ibid., Files, Memo from Agent Estopinal, July 16, 1926.

10. Ibid., Memo from Hoover to Agent Nathan, July 17, 1926.

11. Ibid., Letter from Hoover to Clegg, July 29, 1926.

12. Ibid., Letter from Clegg to Hoover, August 2, 1926.

13. Ibid., Letter, Director Hoover to Clegg, August 6, 1926.

14. Ibid., Letter from Clegg to Hoover, August 10, 1926.

15. Ibid., Letter from Agent Sisk to Hoover, August 11, 1926.

16. Ibid., Letter from Clegg to Hoover, August 12, 1926.

17. Ibid., Letter from Agent Sisk to Hoover, August 13, 1926.

18. Ibid., Letter Agent Baley to Director Hoover, August 13, 1926.

19. Ibid., Letter from Acting Director to Agent Baley, August 19, 1926.

20. USMOH, p. 32.

21. FBIHHC Efficiency Rating Sheet, completed by Agent Baley, September 30, 1926.

22. Ibid., Efficiency Rating Sheet, completed by Agent Baley, March 31, 1927.

23. Ibid., Letter to Agent Frank Cole from Acting Director, May 6, 1927.

24. USMOH, p. 33.

25. "A Byte Out of History: One African-American Special Agents' Story," at http://www.fbi.gov./news/stories/2005 February/Amos022805.

26. Philadelphia FBI Files, at http://philadelphia.fbi.gov/history.htm.

27. "Ms. Agents," *Time*, July 31, 1972.

28. *The FBI: A Centennial History, 1908–2008*, US Department of Justice, Office of Public Affairs, Federal Bureau of Investigation, 2009.

29. Hoover required all female employees to wear dresses or skirts, and while male employees were allowed the privilege of smoking at their desks, female employees were not permitted to do so.

30. Cody McFayden, *Abandoned*, Random House, 2009, p. 83.

31. Bryan Burrough, *Public Enemies: America's Greatest Crime Wave and the Birth of the FBI, 1933-34*, Penguin Press, 2004, p. 12.

32. FBIHHC Letter from J.H. Daly to Hoover, June 23, 1927.

33. Ibid., Letter from Herman J. Callaway for the Attorney General to Hoover, undated.

34. Ibid., Letter from Hoover to Clegg, August 17, 1927.

35. Ibid., Memo from Hoover to Clegg, March 27, 1927.

36. Ibid., Undated letter from Clegg to Hoover from a New York City address.

37. Ibid., Report filed by Inspector Egan, September 20, 1927.

38. Ibid., Memo from Hoover to Nathan, September 23, 1927.

39. Ibid., Memo from Hoover to Clegg, February 17, 1928.

40. Ibid., Report from inspector Keith to Hoover, October 6, 1928.

41. Ibid., Letter from Hoover to Clegg, October 18, 1928.

42. Ibid., Letter from US Attorney Thomas J. Hawkins to Hoover, December 6, 1928.

43. Ibid., Memo from Hoover to Clegg, December 11, 1928.

44. Ibid., Letter from Hoover to Clegg, January 10, 1929.

45. Ibid., Letter from Hoover to Appointment Clerk Sornberger, July 27, 1929.

46. Ibid., Memo from Hoover to Clegg, August 7, 1929.

47. USMOH, p. 34.

48. Ferdinand Lundberg, *Imperial Hearst—A Social Biography*, Equinox Cooperative Press, 1936.

49. "Army & Navy: Epic Lobby," *Time*, September 23, 1929.

50. *Sunday Spartanburg Herald-Journal*, May 27, 1934.

51. Carrie A. Foster, *The Women and the Warriors: The U.S. Section of the Women's International League for Peace and Freedom*, Syracuse University Press, 1995, p. 89.

52. Richard W. Fanning, *Peace and Disarmament: Naval Rivalry and Arms Control*, University Press of Kentucky, 1995, p. 103.

53. Foster, *The Women and the Warriors*, p. 89.

54. FBIHHC Letter from Hoover to Clegg, February 10, 1930.

55. Ibid., Letter from Clegg to Hoover, February 13, 1930.

56. Ibid., Letter from Hoover to Clegg, February 14, 1930.

57. Ibid., Letter from Clegg to Hoover, February 14, 1930.

58. Ibid., Letter from Hoover to Clegg, February 18, 1930.

59. Ibid., Letter from Hoover to Clegg, February 24, 1930.

60. Ibid., Letter from Hoover to Clegg, March 22, 1930.

61. Ibid., Letter from Clegg to Hoover, March 24, 1930.

62. Ibid., Efficiency Rating Sheet, March 31, 1930.

63. Ibid., Memo from Hoover to Clegg, April 22, 1930.

64. Ibid., Report from Inspector J.M. Keith, May 1, 1930.

65. Ibid., Memo from Keith to Hoover, May 5, 1930.

66. Ibid., Memo from Hoover to Clegg, November 12, 1930.

67. Ibid., Letter from Hoover to Clegg, November 20, 1930.

68. Ibid., Letter from Hoover to Clegg, January 9, 1931.

69. Theoharis, ed., *The FBI*, p. 175.

70. *FBI National Academy*, Turner Publishing, 2000.

71. "A Milestone in Police Training Seventy-Five Years Ago," at http://www.fbi.gov/news/stories/2010/july/national-academy/academy-turns-seventyfive.

72. Curt Gentry, *J. Edgar Hoover: The Man and the Secrets*, W. W. Norton, 1991.

73. Julie R. Linkins, "FBI Academy: 25 Years of Law Enforcement Leadership," *FBI Law Enforcement Bulletin*, May 1997.

74. Theoharis, ed., *The FBI*, p. 175.

75. USMOH, p. 107.

76. Ibid.

77. "The FBI Pledge for Law Enforcement Officers," *FBI Law Enforcement Bulletin*, December 1937, p. 2.

78. USMOH, p. 108.

79. Ibid., p. 115.

80. Ibid., p. 105.

81. FBIHHC Memo from Hoover to Clegg, September 20, 1941.

82. Ibid., Report of physical examination to Clegg, January 8, 1952.

83. Ibid., Letter from Hoover to Clegg, May 20, 1929.

84. Ibid., Memo from Hoover to Clegg, April 17, 1930.

Chapter 3. Making Important Contacts

1. FBIHHC Letter from Freiburg to Hoover, January 24, 1933.

2. Ibid., Letter from Bogert to Hoover, December 6, 1933.

3. Ibid., *Hartford Courant*, March 12, 1936.

4. Ibid., Letter from Scharf to Clegg, March 25, 1936.

5. Ibid., Letter from Maude to Hoover, March 31, 1942.

6. Ibid., Memo from Rogers to Clegg, July 13, 1952.

7. *The New Yorker*, October 4, 1930.

8. According to Washington social protocol, the vice president and his wife ranked second behind the president and first lady, then came the chief justice of the Supreme Court and his wife, then the Speaker of the House of Representatives and his wife (Alice Roosevelt Longworth), followed by the foreign ambassadors. The jealousy regarding who would assume the role of "second first lady" at social events reached major proportions. In February 1929, the Senate Ladies Luncheon Club decreed that an "official hostess" could be only the "wife of the official." Meanwhile, Curtis had notified the State Department that his sister would be his "official hostess." Outgoing secretary of state Frank Kellogg agreed with the Club and decided that "in State social functions Mrs. Edward (Dolly) Gann . . . is to be seated after the wives of the ambassadors." Curtis publicly requested Kellogg to reverse his decision, which meant that the wife of the chief justice, the wife of the Speaker of the House (Alice Longworth), as well as the wives of the ambassadors would all outrank Dolly Gann. The new secretary of state, Henry L. Stimson, inherited the problem and decided that the State Department would no longer dictate the official order of precedence in Washington society (*The New Yorker*, October 4, 1930). When the question of what to do with Dolly's husband arose, Alice replied, "I think Mr. Gann's place is in the home."

The issue became a congressional and international problem (the British diplomat supported Dolly). Alabama senator Tom "Cotton Tom" Heflin declared, "It is against the American principle to ask the official hostess of the vice-president to step down for any foreigner" ("Dolly Gann vs. Princess Alice," *Milwaukee Journal*, February 9, 1949). Stimson stated that "all world problems sink into insignificance . . . when compared with the great question as to where the vice-president's sister shall sit at the dinner table" (Stacy A. Cordery, *Alice: Alice Roosevelt Longworth, from White House Princess to Washington Power Broker*, Viking Penguin, 2007). But while Alice and Dolly claimed there was no feud, Alice enjoyed making a little mischief over the matter while Dolly referred to the feud as a "tempest in a teapot" (Dolly Curtis Gann, *Dolly Gann's Book*, Doubleday, Doran and Company, 1933). When Dolly Gann died at the age of eighty-seven, Alice

Longworth was distressed at the news and declared Dolly to be an old, old friend.

9. USMOH, p. 40.

10. Jennifer Rosenberg, "History of the Academy Awards: The 4th Academy Awards—1930/31," at http://history1900s.about.com./od/fadsfashion/a/1930awards.htm.

11. FBIHHC Letter from Hoover to Clegg, November 25, 1931.

12. USMOH, p. 41.

13. Timothy W. Bjorkmen, *Verne Sankey: America's First Public Enemy*, University of Oklahoma Press, 2007, p. 141.

14. S. O'Dea Schenken, *From Suffrage to the Senate: An Encyclopedia of American Women in Politics*, ABC-Clio, 1999, p. 74.

15. T. L. Hall, *Supreme Court Justices*, Facts on File, 2001, p. 308.

16. USMOH, p. 42.

17. Ibid. In relating this story, Clegg must have been mistaken. A search reveals that during this time, the only movie in which both Cagney and Sothern were cast was *Footlight Parade*. However, that movie was released in 1933 by Warner Brothers, a year before the Cummings group made its tour. And Sothern played only the minor role of a chorus girl in that film. The only other movie in which Cagney and Sothern appeared together, *You, John Jones*, was not released until 1943.

18. John Knobler, *Capone: The Life and World of Al Capone*, Da Capo Press, 1971.

19. Gregory L. Wellman, *History of Alcatraz Island, 1853–2008*, Arcadia Publishing, 2008.

20. Robert J. Schoenberg, *Mr. Capone*, William Morrow, 1992, p. 335.

21. "Alcatraz: The Warden Johnston Years, 1933–1948—Alcatraz Prisoners Numbers 1 to 50," at http://www.notfrisco2.com/alcatraz/inmates/data/alist01.html.

22. USMOH, p. 42.

23. Ibid., p. 43.

24. Ibid.

25. "New 'Devil's Isle' Planned by U.S.," *Pittsburgh Post-Gazette*, August 3, 1935.

26. "Attorney General Cummings to Pay Mining City a Visit," *Montana Standard*, August 15, 1934.

27. Everett McKinley Dirksen, *The Education of a Senator*, University of Illinois Press, 1998.

28. USMOH, pp. 115–116.

29. Ibid., p. 49.

30. Ibid., p. 51.

31. Merle Miller, *Plain Speaking: An Oral Biography of Harry Truman*, Berkley Publishing, 1974.

32. FBIHHC Letter from Clegg to Hoover, August 2, 1939.

33. "Crime: This Is Lepke," *Time*, September 4, 1939.

34. P. R. Kavieff, *The Life and Times of Lepke Buchalter: America's Most Ruthless Labor Racketeer*, Barricade Books, 2006.

35. FBIHHC Letter from Clegg to Hoover, August 2, 1939.

36. Mary M. Stolberg, *Fighting Organized Crime: Politics, Justice, and the Legacy of Thomas E. Dewey*, Northeastern University Press, 1995.

Chapter 4. The Tumultuous '30s: Kidnappers and Gangsters

1. "Former G-Man Recalls Crime-busting Experiences," *Delta Democrat Times*, November 11, 1976.

2. USMOH, p. 39.

3. Laurence Bergreen, *Capone: The Man and the Era*, Simon and Schuster, 1994.

4. Kobler, *Capone*, Da Capo Press, 1992.

5. USMOH, p. 54.

6. Ibid.

7. Ibid., p. 52.

8. MUM00191 and MUM00192, Percy E. Foxworth Collection, University of Mississippi Department of Archives and Special Collections, University, MS 38677, University, MS. During World War II, Foxworth directed double agent operations against the Germans and Japanese as chief of the FBI's Special Intelligence Service. In 1943, he was killed in a military airplane accident along with FBI agent Harold D. Haberfield and thirty-three others. Foxworth and Haberfield were on an undercover secret mission to

North Africa to investigate an American citizen, Charles Bedaux, a reported Nazi collaborator. Haberfield was a new agent in the Bureau and was selected because of his knowledge of North Africa and his ability to speak German, French, and Portuguese. Whether Bedaux was, in fact, a Nazi collaborator is open to debate since it has been suggested that he saved the lives of many Jews from Nazi persecution (Jim Cristy, *The Price of Power: A Biography of Charles Eugene Bedaux*, Doubleday, 1984). Although sabotage was the suspected cause of the crash that killed Foxworth and Haberfield, the accident was later determined to be due to mechanical problems. The US Navy launched a Liberty ship, named the SS *Percy E. Foxworth*, in his honor.

9. USMOH, p. 53.

10. Ibid.

11. Gentry, *J. Edgar Hoover*, 163.

12. USMOH, p. 53.

13. Ibid.

14. Burrough, *Public Enemies*, p. 331.

15. "Streets of St. Paul: The Edward Bremer Kidnapping," at http://www.streetsofsaintpaul.com/2011/12/edward-bremer-kidnapping.html.

16. USMOH, p. 54.

17. FBIHHC Files, Memo from Hoover to Tolson, Clegg, and eight other agents, February 16, 1934, and Memo from W. R. Glavin to Tolson, Clegg, and eighteen other agents, April 23, 1934.

18. Burrough, *Public Enemies*, p. 50.

19. Ibid., p. 47.

20. "Missouri Legends: Kansas City Massacre—Gangsters vs. the Law," at http://www.legendsofamerica.com/mo-kansascitymassacre.html.

21. Burrough, *Public Enemies*, pp. 52–53.

22. Ibid., p. 55.

23. Ibid., p. 58.

24. Larry McMurtry and Diana Ossana, *Pretty Boy Floyd*, Simon and Schuster, 1994; Robert Unger, *The Union Station Massacre: The Original Sin of Hoover's FBI*, Kansas City Star Books, 2005.

25. Burrough, *Public Enemies*, p. 219.

26. Ibid., p. 220.

27. Claire Bond Potter, *War on Crime: Bandits, G-Men, and the Politics of Mass Culture*, Rutgers University Press, 1998.

28. Steven Nickel and William J. Helmer, *Baby Face Nelson: A Portrait of a Public Enemy*, Cumberland House Publishing, 2002.

29. Purvis, *The Vendetta*, pp. 259–263.

30. Burrough, *Public Enemies*, p. 481.

31. Purvis, *The Vendetta*, pp. 259–263.

32. Ibid.

33. Burrough, *Public Enemies*, p. 481.

34. Purvis, *The Vendetta*, pp. 259–263.

35. "Crime: Two for One," *Time*, December 10, 1934.

36. Burrough, *Public Enemies*, p. 47.

37. USMOH, p. 55.

38. Burrough, *Public Enemies*, pp. 540–541.

39. "Karpis Rushed by Fast Plane to Old Haunts," *Southeast Missourian*, May 2, 1936.

40. FBI "New Orleans" Barker-Karpis File #7-15 FOIPA, #445856, in Richard Kudish, "Alvin Karpis: Pursuit of the Last Public Enemy," at http://www.crimelibrary.com/gangsters_outlaws/outlaws/karpis/7.html.

41. "Faded Glory: Dusty Roads of An FBI Era," at http://historicalgmen.squarespace.com/karpis-arrest-whose-necktie.

42. USMOH, p. 55.

Chapter 5. John Dillinger and Little Bohemia

1. Michael Mann, dir., *Public Enemies*, film, 2009.

2. From Alan May and Marilyn Bardsley, "John Dillinger," TruTV, at http://www.trutv.com/library/crime/gangsters_outlaws/outlaws/dillinger/1.html.

3. Burrough, *Public Enemies*, p. 138.

4. See http://www.parkbugle.org/index.php?option=com_content&view=article&id=1546:gangster&catid=13:articles.

5. G. Russell Girardin and William J. Helmer, *Dillinger: The Untold Story*, Indiana University Press, 1994, p. 296.

6. Nickel and Helmer, *Baby Face Nelson*.

7. Burrough, *Public Enemies*, pp. 276–278.

8. Clegg developed an interesting, friendly relationship with Bessie Skinner when she was being interrogated. Clegg spoke to her about the life of criminals and suggested to her that when she got out of jail, she should leave the area and go somewhere so she could establish a clean life and, he joked, marry the mayor of the town. She was subsequently found guilty of conspiracy to harbor a fugitive and received a fifteen-month sentence and a fine of one thousand dollars. She was sent to the Women's Penitentiary in Alderson, West Virginia, and mailed Clegg postcards nearly every month to thank him for all he had done for her. Clegg claimed that all he had done was treat her fairly.

9. Mann, dir. *Public Enemies*, film. In the movie, actor John Hoogenakker plays the role of Hugh Clegg.

10. FBIHHC Files, Memo from Hugh H. Clegg to Director J. Edgar Hoover, "Re: John Dillinger, with aliases, I.O. 1217, et al., HMVTA. Harboring Fug. From Justice, St. Paul File No. 25-2434, April 25, 1934."

11. FBIHHC Files, Report to Hoover prepared by Agent Harold Nathan, June 1, 1934, "Attempt to Apprehend John Dillinger, with aliases, Fugitive, et al., National Motor Vehicle Theft Act, at Little Bohemia Inn, Manitowish, Wisconsin."

12. Purvis, *The Vendetta*, p. 93.

13. In his report, Clegg spells this name as Wenetka.

14. The six men were Dillinger, Baby Face Nelson, Homer VanMeter, Tommy Carroll, John "Red" Hamilton, and Pat Reilly. The four women were Patricia Cherrington; Marie Comforti; Jean Delaney; and Nelson's wife, Helen Gillis.

15. Hoffman was the driver, Boisneau occupied the middle seat, and Morris sat on the passenger side.

16. Clegg's daughter recalls that Hugh told the story of going back to the site of the shootout the next day and seeing in a tree that he had stood behind as the raid unfolded a bullet hole right above where his head would have been.

17. FBIHHC Files, Memo from W. R. Glavin to Clyde Tolson, Clegg, and eighteen other agents, April 23, 1934.

18. FBIHHC Files, Memo from Hoover to Agents Edwards, April, Quinn,

Tolson, Clegg, Cowley, Bennington, Locke, Schilder, and Coffey, February 16, 1934.

19. An interesting sidelight to the raid relates to the unavailability of essential equipment, particularly automobiles, to the Bureau. After the raid, Purvis wrote Hoover and pointed out damage done to a Buick coupe that was abandoned by Dillinger at Little Bohemia and then confiscated by the FBI. Purvis had obtained a detailed estimate of costs that would be required to put the car in good condition so the Bureau could use it. The total cost of eight dollars was presumably approved.

20. FBIHHC Files, Copy of Memo, Unaddressed, Left Corner Designation "JEH:HCB(mtr)," May 8, 1934.

21. FBIHHC Files, Letter from Hoover to Clegg, July 5, 1934.

22. Ibid.

23. Ibid., Memo from Clegg to Hoover, July 9, 1934.

24. Ibid., Letter from Edward A. Tamm to Hoover, May 2, 1934.

25. Burrough, *Public Enemies*, pp. 340–341.

26. Purvis, *The Vendetta*, pp. 132–133.

27. Burrough, *Public Enemies*, p. 342.

28. Report, "Allegations and Rumors in Connection with the Conduct of an Expedition in an Attempt to Apprehend John Dillinger and Others at Little Bohemia Inn, Manitowish, Wisconsin, on April 22, 1934," by Agent H. Nathan, June 1, 1934, cited in "Faded Glory: Dusty Roads of an FBI Era," at http://historicaalgmen.squarespace.com/temporary-downloads-for -xgboys.

29. E-mail from Larry Wack to Ed Lee, January 17, 2013.

30. Purvis, *The Vendetta*, p. 135.

31. "Dillinger Slain in Chicago; Shot Dead by Federal Men in Front of Movie Theatre," *New York Times*, July 23, 1934.

32. NMissCommentor, "Odd Little Coincidences in History," at http:// nmisscommentor.com/2009/06/10

Chapter 6. Family Life

1. USMOH, p. 74.

2. FBIHHC Files, July 2, 1941.

3. USMOH, p. 75.

4. E-mail from Ms. Belinda Stewart, May 14, 2012, and Ms. Belinda Stewart, face-to-face conversation with the author, June 26, 1912.

5. Mrs. Betsy Murphy Dyke, face-to-face conversation with the author, August 13, 2012.

6. USMOH, p. 70.

7. Ibid., p. 76.

8. Ibid., p. 70.

9. Ibid., p. 71.

10. E-mail from Cartha D. DeLoach, April 17, 2010.

11. USMOH, p. 72.

12. Ibid., p. 76.

13. Ms. Belinda Stewart, face-to-face conversation with the author, November 13, 2013.

Chapter 7. The FBI and World War II

1. FBIHHC Files, Memo from Angus W. Taylor to Clyde Tolson, June 30, 1938.

2. FBIHHC Files, Letter from Clegg to Hoover, October 15, 1938.

3. FBIHHC Files, Letters from Clyde Tolson to Colonel F. H. Lincoln, May 7, 1935 and May 8, 1935.

4. See https://www.cia.gov/library/center-for-the-study-of-intelligence/csi-publications/books-and-monographs/oss/index.htm.

5. FBIHHC Files, Memo from Hoover to Tolson, Clegg, and Tamm, November 12, 1940.

6. Clegg told a story about the British experience in espionage. "One of the places I stopped when in England was just outside Oxford. I can't think of the name, but right across the street from the Bear Inn . . . were the homes of Oliver Goldsmith and Chaucer. Their homes were just one house between [sic], Chaucer, in the records they have found in England, had made several trips to the continent and submitted an expense account for intelligence operations. He was a spy for Britain! So, they had a great deal of experience, as you can see, since Chaucer himself was an agent of the British government in France, and Austria, and Italy, or wherever he went, as well as doing some writing on the side" (USMOH, p. 44).

7. FBIHHC Files, Memo from Clegg to Hoover, November 12, 1940.

8. Ibid., Memo from Tolson to Hoover, December 10, 1940.

9. Rhodri Jeffreys-Jones, *The FBI: A History*, Vail-Ballou Press, 2007, p. 108.

10. USMOH, p. 45.

11. Tim Weiner, *Enemies: A History of the FBI*, Random House, 2012, p. 99.

12. FBIHHC Files, Memo from Clegg and Hince to Hoover, January 20, 1941.

13. Robert J. Lamphere and Tom Shachtman, *The FBI-KGB War: A Special Agent's Story*, Mercer University Press, 1986.

14. Perhaps the most ridiculous instance of absurd criticism involved an incident in which Hoover had to come to his defense. On January 29, 1938, Dr. Harriet M. Doane of Pulaski, New York, wrote Hoover complaining about a photograph of one of his aides (Clegg) that appeared in the Syracuse, New York *Post-Standard* newspaper. "It seems to me to be an unfortunate pose for a man in his position to be standing with his foot on an upholstered chair. It certainly gives the wrong impression to those of the public who have regard for other people's property." Hoover had a good laugh over this. He wrote Dr. Doane acknowledging receipt of her letter of complaint. Three handwritten notations appear at the foot of the FBI's typewritten version of her handwritten letter of complaint, presumably made by Hoover that states, "Well! Well!," "Posed by the newspaper man— suggest the hotel be requested to sue," and "also standing with the open palm outstretched may give a wrong impression!" (FBIHHC Files, Letter from Hoover to Dr. Harriet Doane, February 4, 1938). In his response to Dr. Doane, Hoover defends Clegg by stating, "I desire to advise that Mr. Clegg was posed by the newspaper men at their request." I suspect that Clegg never put his foot on an upholstered chair ever again, no matter who would make such a request. The photo of Clegg and the chair appears in his FBI file.

15. USMOH, pp. 46–47.

16. "The Press: Official Censor," *Time*, December 29, 1941.

17. "Byron Price, Wartime Chief of U.S. Censorship, Is Dead," *New York Times*, August 8, 1981.

18. USMOH, pp. 46–47.

19. S. L. Vaughn, ed., *Encyclopedia of American Journalism*, Taylor and Francis Group, 2008, p. 372.

20. FBIHHC Files, Memo from Hoover to Clegg, January 20, 1942.

21. Ibid., Letter from Hoover to Clegg, March 5, 1942.

22. USMOH, p. 114.

23. FBIHHC Files, Memo from Clegg to Hoover, April 9, 1945.

Chapter 8. Postwar Communism and Espionage: Emil Julius Klaus Fuchs and Harry Gold

1. USMOH, pp. 66–67.

2. K. D. Ackerman, *Young J. Edgar Hoover: Hoover, the Red Scare, and the Assault on Civil Liberties*, Da Capo Press, 2007.

3. P. J. McNamara, *A Catholic Cold War: Edmund A. Walsh, S.J., and the Politics of American Anticommunism*, Fordham University Press, 2005. Walsh was instrumental in establishing diplomatic relations for the US government in Baghdad in 1931. Following World War II, he served as a consultant to Chief US Prosecutor Robert Jackson at the Nuremberg Trials.

4. M. Stanton Evans, *Blacklisted by History: The Untold Story of Senator Joe McCarthy and His Fight against America's Enemies*, Three Rivers Press, 2007.

5. David Kraken, "A Conspiracy to Expose Communist Subversion in the American Government," at http://www.writing.com/mai/view_item_id/605217-J-Edgar Hoover-and-McCarthyism.

6. USMOH, p. 68

7. Ibid., p. 69

8. R. C. Williams, *Klaus Fuchs, Atom Spy*, Harvard University Press, 1987.

9. Jonathan Kirsch, "Harry Gold: The Man Who Testified against the Rosenbergs," Jewish Journal.com, October 7, 2010.

10. FBIHHC Files, Memo from Hoover to Ruth Shipley, May 16, 1950.

11. John F. Fox Jr., "In the Enemy's House: Venona and the Maturation of American Counterintelligence," paper presented at the Symposium on Cryptologic History, Center for Cryptologic History, Baltimore, MD, October 27, 2005.

12. Jeffreys-Jones, *The FBI*, p. 152.

13. Lamphere and Shachtman, *FBI-KGB War*, pp. 144–159.

14. FBIHHC Files, June 8, 1950.

15. Lamphere and Shachtman, *FBI-KGB War*, pp. 144–159.

16. Ibid.

17. Kirsch, "Harry Gold."

18. Douglas Martin, "Robert J. Lamphere, 83, Spy Chaser for the F.B.I., Dies," *New York Times*, February 11, 2001.

19. A. M. Hornblum, *The Invisible Harry Gold: The Man Who gave the Soviets the Atom Bomb*, Yale University Press, 2010.

20. FBIHHC Files, June 8, 1950.

21. Weiner, *Enemies*, p. 167.

22. Lamphere and Shachtman, *FBI-KGB War*, pp. 144–159.

Chapter 9. The Relationship with Hoover

1. USMOH, p. 66.

2. Theoharis, ed., *The FBI*.

3. USMOH, p. 66.

4. Ibid., p. 110.

5. Ibid., p. 56.

6. Ibid.

7. Ibid., p. 63.

8. Ibid., p. 57.

9. Joseph L. Schott, *No Left Turns: The FBI in Peace and War*, Praeger, 1975.

10. USMOH, p. 58.

11. Larry Flynt and David Eisenbach, *One Nation Under Sex: How the Private Lives of Presidents, First Ladies and Their Lovers Changed the Course of American History*, Palgrave Macmillan, 2011, p. 144.

12. USMOH, p. 61.

13. FBIHHC Files, Memo from Hoover to Tolson, May 12, 1933.

14. Ibid., Memo from Hoover to Clegg, November 19, 1935.

15. Ibid., Memo from Hoover to Tolson and Clegg, October 12, 1935.

16. Ibid., Memo from L. P. Oliver to Hoover, March 6, 1936.

17. Ibid., Memo from Hoover to Clegg, July 6, 1938.

18. Ibid., Memo from Hoover to Clegg, Tolson, Hince, May 16, 1940.

19. Ibid., Memo from Hoover to Clegg, June 13, 1940.

20. Ibid., Memo in Clegg's Files, February 21, 1952.

21. Ibid.

22. Ibid., Memo from Inspector Harbo to Clegg, February 7, 1952.

23. Ibid., Memo from Hoover to Clegg, August 12, 1951.

24. Ibid., Memo from Hoover to Clegg, August 18, 1953.

25. USMOH, p. 63.

26. FBIHHC Files, Clegg's Notes, January 27, 1971.

27. Ibid., Letter from Harding to Hoover, February 11, 1954.

28. USMOH, p. 60.

29. Ibid., p. 104.

Chapter 10. Leaving the FBI and Joining Ole Miss

1. FBIHHC Files, Memo from J. P. Mohr to Clyde Tolson, March 14, 1952.

2. Ibid., Memo from L.C.B. to Tolson, April 16, 1952.

3. Ibid., Memo from E. D. Mason to Tolson, July 18, 1952.

4. Ibid., Letter from Clegg to Hoover, January 7, 1954.

5. USMOH, p. 70.

6. FBIHHC Files, Letter from Clegg to Hoover, January 7, 1954.

7. Ibid., Letter from Hoover to Clegg, January 12, 1954.

8. Ibid., Memo from Nichols to Tolson, January 14, 1954.

9. Ibid., Clegg Notes, January 14, 1954.

10. Ibid., Clegg Notes, January 15, 1954.

11. Ibid., Clegg Notes, January 20, 1954.

12. USMOH, p. 113.

13. Ibid., p. 71.

14. Ibid., p. 113.

15. HHCUM, Chapter I, pp. 3–4.

16. Ibid.

17. FBIHHC Files, Memo from Hoover to Tolson, December 19, 1962.

18. Ibid., Telegram from F. D. Kirby to Francis Crosby, February 4, 1954.

19. Ibid., Memo from L. B. Nichols to Tolson, February 5, 1954.

20. Ibid.

21. Ibid., Letter from Clegg to Nichols, February 5, 1954.

22. USMOH, p. 70.

23. FBIHHC Files, Memo from L. B. "Wick" Nichols to Tolson, August 3, 1954.

24. Ibid., Memo from L. B. Nichols to Tolson, August 9, 1954.

25. Ibid., FBI Note, August 19, 1954.

26. USMOH, p. 133.

27. Charles W. Eagles, *The Price of Defiance: James Meredith and the Integration of Ole Miss*, University of North Carolina Press, 2009, p. 162.

28. The special agent in charge of the Memphis office described Clegg's responsibilities at Ole Miss: "He is the Director of Development for the University of Mississippi and in that capacity makes and maintains contacts with sources of revenue for the University. He makes special inquiries to determine what the possible sources of revenue are and looks up people of financial affluence in connection with raising funds for the University and promoting programs for the University. The programs are such things as setting up research projects and bringing to the campus conferences and similar activities relating to fields of activity of interest to business and professional life in the state" (FBIHHC Files, Memo from Memphis special agent in charge to Hoover, August 24, 1954).

29. Ibid., Memo from Memphis special agent in charge to Hoover, August 24, 1954

30. Ibid., Memo in Clegg's Files, August 24, 1954.

31. Ibid., Memo from Hoover, January 28, 1955.

32. Ibid., Note in Clegg's File, January 28, 1955.

33. Ibid., Letter from Hoover to Clegg, March 17, 1955.

34. Ibid., Clegg Telegram to Hoover, March 28, 1955.

35. USMOH, p. 114.

36. FBIHHC Files, Memo from H. G. Foster to Hoover, January 14, 1958.

37. Ibid., Letter from Hoover to Clegg, March 2, 1960.

38. USMOH, p. 78.

39. Supporters of Marvin cite the reorganization of the administration, the strengthening of the financial structure, the establishment of the School of Government and the College of General Studies, expansion and development of a "bona fide campus" through vast building programs, the beautification of the campus, and his ability to generate private donations as his

greatest achievements. During Marvin's administration, the student body doubled in size and the faculty tripled.

However, liberal faculty members experienced serious obstacles in receiving tenure and felt persecuted for their beliefs. During the first fifteen years of Marvin's administration, over one hundred faculty members appealed to the American Association of University Professors. Students recalled Marvin's suppression of the Liberal Club; student peace strikes; and suspension of the board of editors of the independent student newspaper, *The GW Hatchet*, because the paper criticized him.

Although segregation was still considered part of life in Washington in 1946, Marvin's administration would be remembered for one infamous incident at the University's Lisner Auditorium when the theater refused to admit African Americans to its first commercial production. Marvin attempted to expel a student who staged a protest outside the auditorium in opposition to Marvin's "white-only racial policy." In 1938, Marvin had prepared a memorandum explaining the fact that GWU did not admit "colored" students, stating that

> students of any race or color perform their best educational disciplines when they are happily situated in a congenial and homogeneous group, and the University, in its tradition and social environment has long preserved this policy. Consistent with this long standing observance, The George Washington University does not register colored students ("African-Americans at GWU: A Selected Chronology," in *The GW and Foggy Bottom Historical Encyclopedia*, at http://www.encyclopedia.gwu.edu).

GWU was the last school in Washington, DC, to retain a whites-only admission policy. Marvin's critics considered him to be a tacit supporter of segregation, a persecutor of liberal faculty members, and one who constantly disregarded student liberties ("Column: Rename the Marvin Center," by Andrew Novak, *The GW Hatchet*, February 3, 2005). Marvin's racial attitude was not inconsistent with the prevailing attitudes at Ole Miss and Mississippi at the time Clegg joined that administration.

40. USMOH, p. 74.

41. HHCUM, Chapter XII, p. 100.

42. "Huge Stars and Bars Pilfered From Rebels," *Miami News*, January 2, 1958.

43. Eagles, *Price of Defiance*, p. 148.

44. HHCUM, Chapter III, pp. 15–16.

45. James W. Silver, *Mississippi: The Closed Society*, Harcourt, Brace and World, 1963, p. 108.

46. USMOH, p. 76.

47. Ibid., p. 84.

48. Ibid., p. 80.

Chapter 11. Clennon King and Ole Miss "Liberals"

1. Silver, *Mississippi*, Harcourt, Brace and World, 1963.

2. USMOH, p. 78.

3. HHCUM, Chapter XVI, p. 117.

4. USMOH, p. 80.

5. Eagles, *Price of Defiance*, pp. 148, 161.

6. "States Legislate against 'Subversives': Mississippi Educators Worry About Legislative Probe," *Harvard Crimson*, June 20, 1950.

7. HHCUM, Chapter VI, pp. 24–28.

8. Ibid.

9. Ibid.

10. Ibid., Chapter VII, p. 30.

11. Eagles, *Price of Defiance*, p. 161

12. USMOH, p. 86.

13. Russell H. Barrett, *Integration at Ole Miss*, Quadrangle Books, p. 32.

14. Eagles, *Price of Defiance*, University of North Carolina Press, 2009, p. 121.

15. HHCUM, Chapter VI, pp. 24–28.

16. Silver, *Mississippi*, p. 109.

17. HHCUM, Chapter VI, pp. 24–28.

18. Charles W. Eagles, "The Closing of Mississippi Society: Will Campbell, the $64,000 Question, and Religious Emphasis Week at the University of Mississippi," *Journal of Southern History*, May 2001.

19. Eagles, *Price of Defiance*, p. 165.

20. USMOH, p. 122.

21. Ibid., p. 81.

22. David G. Sansing, *The University of Mississippi: A Sesquicentennial History*, University Press of Mississippi, 1999, p. 276.

23. Eagles, *Price of Defiance*, p. 86.

24. Barrett, *Integration at Ole Miss*, p. 33.

25. HHCUM, Chapter V, p. 21.

26. Ibid.

27. Eagles, *Price of Defiance*, pp. 91–93.

28. Sansing, *University of Mississippi*, p. 277.

29. Eagles, *Price of Defiance*, p. 94.

30. HHCUM, Chapter V, p. 21.

31. USMOH, p. 77.

32. HHCUM, Chapter VII, p. 30.

33. USMOH, p. 77.

34. *Providence*, by W. D. Campbell, Baylor University Press, 2002.

35. Eagles, *Price of Defiance*, pp. 164–171.

36. USMOH, p. 78.

37. Sansing, *University of Mississippi*, p. 278.

38. Jere R. Hoar, face-to-face conversation with the author, Fall 2011.

39. USMOH, p. 78.

40. HHCUM, Chapter VII, p. 30.

41. Ibid.

42. Ibid.

43. HHCUM, Chapter IV, p. 18.

44. "Anti-Red Group Formed: Mississippi Youths Organized – Ex-F.B.I. Men Help," *New York Times*, November 7, 1961.

45. HHCUM, Chapter XII, pp. 101–103.

46. FBIHHC Files, Letter from Clegg to Hoover, November 12, 1957.

47. Eagles, *Price of Defiance*, pp. 164–171.

Chapter 12. Meredith Applies to Ole Miss

1. "At Ole Miss: Echoes of a Civil War's Last Battle," in *Willie Morris: Shifting Interludes, Selected Essays* Ed. Jack Bales, University Press of Mississippi, 2002, p. 176; *Time*, October 4, 1982.

2. Eagles, *Price of Defiance*, p. 222.

3. *A Mission from God: A Memoir and Challenge for America*, by James Meredith with William Doyle, Atria Books, 2012, pp. 57–59.

4. Eagles, *Price of Defiance*, p. 224.

5. HHCUM, Chapter XVII, p. 125.

6. Sansing, *University of Mississippi*, p. 289.

7. HHCUM, Chapter XIX, p. 132.

8. Sansing, *University of Mississippi*, p. 290.

9. HHCUM, Chapter XVIII, p. 129.

10. Barrett, *Integration at Ole Miss*, p. 102. Eagles states that that the complaint was filed by forty-seven people, "including many with children at Ole Miss" (Eagles, *Price of Defiance*, p. 292).

11. HHCUM, Chapter XX, pp. 138–140.

12. HHCUM, Chapter XIX, p. 134.

13. HHCUM, Chapter XXXIII, p. 259.

14. USMOH, p. 88.

15. Ed Morgan, face-to-face conversations with the author, 1980s.

16. USMOH, p. 88.

17. USMOH, p. 89.

18. HHCUM, Chapter XXII, p. 151.

19. USMOH, p. 93.

20. USMOH, p. 117.

21. USMOH, p. 96.

22. USMOH, p. 95.

23. HHCUM, Chapter XXIII, pp. 154–155.

24. USMOH, p. 90.

25. HHCUM, Chapter XXIV, pp. 164–166.

26. Sansing, *University of Mississippi*, p. 300.

27. USMOH, p. 118.

28. HHCUM, Chapter XXIV, p. 182.

29. Barrett, *Integration at Ole Miss*, p. 102.

30. William Doyle, *An American Revolution: James Meredith and the Battle of Oxford, Mississippi, 1962*, Anchor Books, 2001, p. 277.

31. Barrett, *Integration at Ole Miss*, pp. 203–204; Eagles, *Price of Defiance*, pp. 387–388.

32. Barrett, *Integration at Ole Miss*, p. 110.

33. *Mississippi Liberal: A Biography of Frank E. Smith*, by D. J. Mitchell, University Press of Mississippi, 2001.

34. *Congressman from Mississippi*, by Frank E. Smith, Pantheon Books, 1964, p. 305.

35. Barrett, *Integration at Ole Miss*, p. 121.

36. HHCUM, Chapter XXV, p. 185.

37. USMOH, p. 95.

Chapter 13. The Riot and the Aftermath

1. Barrett, *Integration at Ole Miss*, pp. 136–137.

2. *Making Haste Slowly*, by D. G. Sansing, University Press of Mississippi, 1990, p. 192.

3. J. R. Hoar, Private conversation, November 21, 2013.

4. Sansing *University of Mississippi*, p. 301.

5. Barrett, *Integration at Ole Miss*, pp. 136–137.

6. HHCUM, Chapter XXVI, pp. 188–195.

7. Barrett, *Integration at Ole Miss*, p. 140.

8. HHCUM, Chapter XXVI, p. 188–195.

9. Sansing, *University of Mississippi*, p. 301.

10. HHCUM, Chapter XXVII, p. 200.

11. Eagles, *Price of Defiance*, p. 365.

12. Sansing, *University of Mississippi*, p. 303.

13. USMOH, p. 92.

14. HHCUM, Chapter XXX, pp. 237–239.

15. *Making Haste Slowly*, by D. G. Sansing, University Press of Mississippi, 1990, p. 195.

16. HHCUM, Chapter XXXI, p. 248.

17. Charles W. Eagles, "The Fight for Men's Minds: The Aftermath of the Ole Miss Riots of 1962," *Journal of Mississippi History*, Spring 2009, pp. 14–15.

18. Eagles, *Price of Defiance*, p. 426.

19. USMOH, p. 93.

20. Henry T. Gallagher Collection (MUM00558), Department of Archives and Special Collections, J. D. Williams Library, University of Mississippi, Oxford.

21. HHCUM, Chapter XXXII, p. 252.

22. Sansing, *University of Mississippi*, p. 303.

23. "Ole Miss Bars Negro Newsmen; Doesn't Discriminate," *Jet Magazine*, October 4, 1962, p. 14.

24. HHCUM, Chapter XXX, pp. 237–239.

25. HHCUM, Chapter XL, p. 307.

26. HHCUM, Chapter XLII, p. 323.

27. FBIHHC Files, Letter from J. J. Casper to J. P. Mohr, May 4, 1965.

28. FBIHHC Memo from J. F. Malone to J. P. Mohr, October 22, 1962.

29. HHCUM, Chapter XXXIX, p. 304.

30. USMOH, p. 86.

31. *Mississippi: The Closed Society*, by James W. Silver, Harcourt, Brace and World, 1963, p. 122.

32. Eagles, *Price of Defiance*, p. 365.

33. HHCUM, Chapter XXVII, p. 200.

34. Eagles, *Price of Defiance*, p. 351.

35. *Congressman from Mississippi*, by Frank E. Smith, Pantheon Books, New York, 1964, p. 302.

36. *Mississippi Liberal: A Biography of Frank E. Smith*, by D. J. Mitchell, University Press of Mississippi, 2001, chapter 11.

37. USMOH, p. 117.

38. *Making Haste Slowly*, by D. G. Sansing, University Press of Mississippi, 1990, p. 195.

39. *Mississippi: The Closed Society*, by James W. Silver, Harcourt, Brace and World, 1963, p. 172.

40. Barrett, *Integration at Ole Miss*, p. 187.

41. Ibid., p. 179.

42. Ibid., p. 174.

43. FBIHHC Memo from J. F. Malone to J. P. Mohr, October 22, 1962.

44. USMOH, p. 93

45. Private conversation with James Meredith, November 9, 2013.

46. *Rebel Coach: My Football Family*, by John Vaught, Memphis State University Press, 1971, p. 114.

47. Sansing, *University of Mississippi*, p. 352.

Chapter 14. Ole Miss Accomplishments and Retirement

1. HHCUM, Chapter VII, p. 29.

2. Eagles, *Price of Defiance*, p. 479.

3. "High Honors for Hugh Clegg," *The Grapevine*, June 1969, p. 14.

4. USMOH, p. 121. White served as governor from 1936 to 1940 and again from 1952 to 1956.

5. HHCUM, Chapter XIII, p. 105.

6. "Band on the Run Marks its 50th Reunion: The Cal Band of '58 Was All Over the Map: From Berkeley to Brussels and Back, With a Quick Detour to the Russian Pavilion," by Barry Bergman, UC Berkeley News, October 2, 2008, at http://berkeley.edu/news/berkeleyan/2008/10/02_band.shtml.

7. USMOH, p. 83.

8. E-mail from Dr. William DeJournett, Associate Professor of Music, University of Mississippi, May 31, 2012.

9. USMOH, p. 84.

10. FBIHHC Files, Letter from Hoover to Hugh Clegg, April 13, 1957, and Memo from SAC Memphis to Hoover, April 18, 1957.

11. Ibid., Memo from Agent Tamm to Clyde Tolson, April 15, 1957.

12. Ibid., Memo in Director Hoover's file, April 15, 1957; FBIHHC Telegram Hoover to Clegg, April 13, 1957.

13. Ibid., Memo from the special agent in charge of Memphis to Hoover, April 14, 1957.

14. Ibid., Letter from Ruby Kathryn Clegg to Director Hoover, April 20, 1957.

15. Ibid., Letter from Hoover to Clegg, September 4, 1957.

16. FBIHHC Files, Letter from Clegg to Senator Dirksen, July 10, 1957.

17. USMOH, p. 97.

18. FBIHHC Files, Memo from C. D. DeLoach to Clyde Tolson, May 19, 1959.

19. Howard Smead, *Blood Justice: The Lynching of Mack Charles Parker*, Oxford University Press, 1986.

20. Examples of newspaper interviews: "Mississippi 'Crime Buster' Now Finds Time for Talk," *Commercial Appeal*, October 3, 1960; "Clegg Named as Honorary U.M. Alumni," *Jackson Daily News*, December 10, 1962.

21. FBIHHC Files, Telegram from Hoover to Clegg, June 20, 1968.

22. Citation from Chancellor Porter L. Fortune, University of Mississippi Commencement Exercises, University of Mississippi archives, University, MS, May 26, 1968.

23. "On the Hill," *Clarion Ledger*, August 27, 1968.

24. "Hugh Clegg to Be Honored," *Clarion Ledger*, February 13, 1969.

25. FBIHHC Files, Memo from Jenkins to Callahan, November 9, 1973.

26. Ibid., Letter from Clegg to Director Kelley, November 19, 1973.

27. USMOH, p. 134.

28. Craig Roberton, "Former G-Man Recalls Crime-Busting Experiences," *Delta Democrat Times*, November 11, 1976.

29. Ness was an investigator for the US Treasury Department and the Bureau of Prohibition and not, as many people thought, for the FBI.

30. "High Honors for Hugh Clegg," *The Grapevine*, June 1969, p. 14.

31. HHCUM, Chapter XLIV.

32. Sansing, *University of Mississippi*, p. 352.

33. Bob Schieffer, *Face the Nation*, CBS News, September 28, 2008.

Epilogue

1. Demspey Blanton, face-to-face conversation with the author, July 29, 2013.

2. Purvis and Tresniowski, *The Vendetta*, pp. 93–94.

3. Ibid., *The Vendetta*, p. 43.

4. Ibid., pp. 268-269.

5. USMOH, p. 31.

6. FBIHHC Letter from George E. Harding to Director Hoover, February 11, 1954.

7. Citation from Chancellor Porter L. Fortune, University of Mississippi Commencement Exercises, May 26, 1968.

8. USMOH, p. 101.

9. Ibid., p. 132.

Index

interviewed by Hugh, 203; and Robert Kennedy, 185–86, 194

Barrett, Russell, 176; faculty resolution, 191

Barrow, Clyde, 68

Bates, Lyle, 173

Bates, Sanford, 56

Baughman, Frank, 33, 34

Baum, Carter W., 92, 97–99, 101

Bedeaux, Charles, 245n8

Bennett Academy, 15

Bethlehem Newport News, 37

Betillo, David, 66

Bilbo, Theodore, 9, 13, 19, 20, 227

Bilbo Bath, 19

Biograph Theater, 107

Birdsong, T. B., 195

Black, Hugo, 179

Blair, Harry Wallace, and Homer Cummings junket, 54, 59

Blair, Emily Newell, and Homer Cummings junket, 54, 55

Blanton, Dempsey, x

Bogart, Humphrey, 68

Bogert, Marston T., 48

Boisneau, Eugene, 97, 98, 101, 106, 247n15

Bolt, Frank, 57

Borah, William, 23, 37

Boyd, J. D., 167

Brady, Bob, 80

Brantley, Dwight, 87

Bremer, Adolph, 76

Bremer, Edward, Jr., 53; kidnapping of, 75

Brennan, John E., 95

Brennan, Richard E., and Fuchs case, 132

Brower, Sidna, 190, 201

Brown, Elgar, 83

Brown, John R., 178

Brown vs. Board of Education of Topeka, 160, 170, 175

Brownell, Herbert, Jr., 148

Brussels World Fair (1958), 211–13

Bryant, W. Alton, 171–73

Buchalter, Louis "Lepke," 64–65

Buchanan, W. L. "Buck," 87

Bunche, Ralph, 18

Bureau of Identification, 60

Burns, William J., 25, 133; replaced as Director of the Bureau, 24

Burrough, Bryan, ix, x

Busby, Jeff, 26

Caffrey, Ray, 78–80

Cagney, James, 56, 68, 71, 243n17

Calhoun, Leonard, 17

Cameron, Ben F., 179, 183

Cameron, John E., 166

Camp Ritchie, 139

Campbell, Boyd, 13, 14, 16, 139

Campbell, William Davis, 164–66, 171

Capone, Al, 57, 68–69, 90

Carley, Jack, 147

Carroll, Tommy, 96, 247

Carter, Hodding, 157, 171

Carter, S. M., 173

Carusi, Hugo, 54

Georgia Pacific Railroad Company, 6

German Americans, 221

Gillespie, Bob, 107

Gillis, Helen, 82–84, 247n14

Gillis, Lester M., 82. *See also* Nelson, "Baby Face"

Glacier National Park, 54, 59

Glass, Sen. Carter, 23

"G-Men," 71

Gold, Harry, 128–31

Gold Clause Cases, 55

Golden Link Cemetery, 223, 237n4

Golding, E. Boyd, 218

Goldsmith, Oliver, 249n6

Goldwater, Barry, 174

Gorhambury, Lord, 117

Graham, Billy, 158

Gray, L. Patrick, 31, 220

Green, Beth, 93. *See also* Skinner, Bessie (Beth)

Green, Eddie, 92–93

Greenglass, David, 131

Greenwood Citizens' Council, 206

Griffin, William S. "Bill," 63, 173

Grooms, W. J., 78–79

Guihard, Paul, 196

Gunter, Walter Ray, 196

Haberfield, Harold D., 244n8

Hall, O. G., 95

Hall, Stanton A., 157

Hamilton, John "Red," 247n14

Hamm, William, 53; kidnapping of, 72, 76

Hanni, Werner, 95–96, 99, 104–6

Hardin, H. M., 7

Harding, George E., 142

Harding, Warren, 24, 133

Hardy, S. W., 95

Hargis, Andrew B., 211

Harper, A. Y., 17

Harrell, George Lott, 16, 17

Hartford Courant, 48

Harvey, Paul, 174

Harvey's Restaurant, 137

Harwell Atomic Energy Research Establishment, 126

Harzenstein, Norris, 132

Hauptman, Bruno, 73–75

Hawkins, Thomas J., 35

Haywood, Charles, 196

Hearst, William Randolph, 37

Heflin, Tom "Cotton Tom," 242n8

Heidelberg Hotel, 173

Heinemann, Kristel, 130

Hendricks, George, 201

Hermanson, Frank, 78–79

Heth, Robert M., 26

Hilbun, Ben, 155

Hince, Lawrence, 116–18, 139

Hines, Tom, 168, 169

Hoar, Jere R., 193

Hoffman, Harold, 74

Hoffman, John, 97–98

Hofheinz, Roy, 151–52

Hollis, Herman "Ed," 82, 84–85

Holmes, Oliver Wendell, 124

Hood, Will B., 35

Hoogenakker, John, 247n9

Hooker, Edwin Wilburn, 170–73

Hooker, Edwin William, Sr., 211

Hoover, Herbert, 42; and US National Commission on Law Observance and Enforcement, 49

Hoover, J. Edgar, x, xi, 3, 4, 22, 24–28, 31–35, 41–47, 88, 136, 137, 142, 226; American Censor, 119; appointed director, 24; assistant director BOI, 133; capture of Karpis, 86–88; on Hugh's retirement, 147; Cleggs' wedding gift, 109; communism, 123; creates national defense investigation unit, 116–17; death, 142; dress code for women, 239n29; feud with Sen. McKellar, 85–86; first meeting with Hugh, 24; Little Bohemia Lodge raid investigation, 100–104; micromanaging, 137–40; named interim director, 133; raises qualifications, 134; relationship with McCarthy, 125; relationship with Tolson, 136–37; relationship with Walsh, 124; Retirement Division, US Civil Service Commission, 153

Hotchkiss, Emma R., 31

Houston, Lenore, 31, 221

Houston Post, 152

Hugh H. Clegg Field, 211

Hunter, Fred, 87

Hurley, G. F., 95

Hurt, Clarence O., 87

Independent Afro-American Party, 169

"Indian Charlie," 50

Indiana Pendleton Reformatory, 91

Indiana State Prison, 48

"Inside the FBI," xiv, 221

Institute of Arts and Sciences, 48

Institutions of Higher Learning (IHL) Board, 110, 162–63, 165, 167, 171–72, 174, 177–78, 180, 183, 195–96, 232

International Association of Chiefs of Police, 43–44

Italian Americans, 221

J. D. Williams Library, xiv

J. Edgar Hoover Building, 142

"J. Edna and Mother Tolson," 137

Jackson, Robert H., 63; Nuremberg trials, 251n3

Jackson Citizens' Council, 163

Jackson Daily News, 18, 149, 155

Japanese Americans, 221

Japanese balloon bombs, 120

Jencks, Clinton, 216

Jencks Act, 215

Jencks v. United States, 216

Jensen, Robert G., 132

Jet magazine, 200

Jobe, E. R., 167

Johnson, Hiram, 23

Johnson, Paul, 183, 186, 216; interviewed by Hugh, 204

Johnston, Warden James A., 57

Jones, Laurence, 217